CW00670740

The Football and Rugby

Playing Fields of Wales

Er cof annwyl am fy ewythr David Walters (1928-2003)
San Clêr a Phen-y-bont ar Ogwr
a'm cyflwynodd i'r *Swans* yn Rhagfyr 1958.

In memory of a dear uncle, David Walters (1928-2003),
St Clear's and Bridgend,
who took me to my first game at the Vetch Field in December 1958.

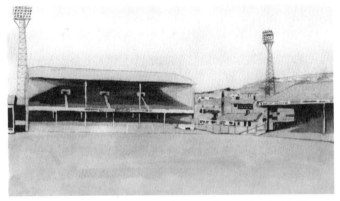

Vetch Field, Swansea in 1970. From the original watercolour by Ted Foxton, Stoke-on-Trent. Reproduced by kind permission of the artist.

The Football and Rugby

Playing Fields of Wales

RICHARD E HUWS

y Lolfa

First impression: 2009

© Richard E Huws & Y Lolfa Cyf., 2009

This book is subject to copyright and may not be reproduced
by any means except for review purposes without the prior
written consent of the publishers.

Photographs courtesy of the author unless noted otherwise.

Cover design: Y Lolfa

ISBN: 9781847711458

Printed on acid-free and partly recycled paper
and published and bound in Wales by
Y Lolfa Cyf., Talybont, Ceredigion SY24 5HE
e-mail ylolfa@ylolfa.com
website www.ylolfa.com
tel 01970 832 304
fax 832 782

INTRODUCTION

I have had a life-long passion for sport, and my work at the National Library of Wales, Aberystwyth for almost forty years helped enormously to improve my knowledge of Welsh geography, local history and place-names as these were essential requirements in order to deal effectively with the wide-ranging requests that the library receives on a daily basis from its readers and remote enquirers. In many senses this book combines and reflects these two key influences.

My love of football took me on 17 July 1996, a fine summer's night, to an enthralling game at Latham Park, Newtown between the local team and FC Skonto of Riga, Latvia. This was the first leg of a UEFA Cup preliminary round, and the impressive Latvians won the match convincingly by the comfortable margin of four goals to one. However, the occasion was memorable for all those fortunate enough to be present, and I was left with a lasting impression of the positive benefits that European football was bringing to the infant League of Wales. I was also impressed with the facilities at the ground, and began to wonder why this picturesque and compact stadium was called Latham Park. My subsequent research revealed that the ground had been named after George Latham (1881-1939), a famous local footballer, who went on to represent his country and to coach Cardiff City to their 1927 Cup Final triumph. My visit to Newtown sparked a decade of research into the history of playing-field names, which has now culminated in this volume.

I wish to acknowledge my huge debt to many local historians who have chronicled the history of individual local rugby and football clubs in great detail. Many of these published works include important information on field names, and these sources are acknowledged in the appended bibliography. The growing proliferation of individual club websites, many of which replicate and add to these printed sources, also proved a rich source of information. I have not listed these sites individually, but if extensive use of their content has been made, this has been acknowledged in the narrative. I also found many general websites invaluable in providing useful background information. Of particular importance were the websites of the Welsh Football Data Archive, the Welsh Rugby Union, the Football Association of Wales, the Principality Welsh Premiership, the website and hard copies of the magazine *Welsh Football* (with a special mention to the editor Dave Collins, for his invaluable and humorous groundblog features), and in a similar vein 'Seagull's' amusing and informative *50 Yards Wide: Groundhopping in Wales* blog. I also found the many excellent websites of the various feeder leagues within the Welsh football pyramid a vital source of relevant information. The pyramid is reproduced at the end of this introduction. In addition, the WRU national league structure has been charted for ease of reference.

I have endeavoured to record the playing fields used by all current senior football and rugby teams in Wales. Fields used by some defunct teams have also been included if they can be clearly identified. I have also attempted to record some special events which have been held on certain fields. These range from agricultural shows to national eisteddfodau, and to other sporting events and unique occasions such as papal visits. During the course of my research, I have received a great deal of assistance with specific enquiries from a large number of individuals and organisations, many of whom responded to my e-mail requests, letters and telephone calls, for which I am very grateful. I wish to thank all these people for their responses, and especially the following: Mel ab Ifor Thomas, Blaenau Ffestiniog; Steffan ab Owain, Gwynedd Archives; David Atwell, Newport; Rob Bailey, Graig-y-Rhacca; Barmouth Library; Claire Beard, Arturus Architects, Bristol; Bryan Bees, Llwynypia; Roy Bergiers, Carmarthen; Christian Branch, Anglesey; Joan Cole, Milford Haven Library; Sue Contestabile, Llandrindod Wells; Neil Cooper, Swansea Library; Terry Crump, Cwm, Ebbw Vale; Andrew Dulley, West Glamorgan Archive Service; Dafydd Iwan, Caeathro; Einion Dafydd, Bangor University; Alun Davies, Tregaron; Ann Davies, Aberystwyth; Clare Davies, Pontardawe Library; Clifford Davies, Bryn-crug; Dilwyn Davies, Pen-bont Rhydybeddau; Edwina Davies, Pen-bont Rhydybeddau; Elwyn Davies, Narberth; John F Davies, Carmarthen; Phil Davies, Neath; Rhian Davies, Montgomery; Robin Davies, Cardiff and District Football League; Scott Davies, Bryn-coch, Neath; Simon Davies, Wattstown; Stuart Davies, Briton Ferry; William Davies, South Wales Senior League; Katrina Demery, Port Talbot Library; Michael Donovan, Merthyr Tydfil; Ann Dorsett and Dara Jasumani, Carmarthenshire County Museum; Dick Downes, Newport and District League; Alexandra Dukes, Caerphilly

Libraries; Dylan Ebeneser, Cardiff; J D Edwards, Trebanos; Jim Edwards, Mathern; Siân Eiran, Canolfan Cae'r Gors, Rhosgadfan; Dylan Elis, Minffordd; Helen Ellis, Penrhyndeudraeth; James Ellis, J-Ross Developments, Oswestry; Rolant Ellis, Aberystwyth and District League; Dafydd Evans, Penisa'r-waun; Dafydd R Evans, Llangadfan; Glyn and Gwanwyn Evans, Sennybridge; Jacqueline Evans, Swansea Library; Jayne Evans, Hay-on-Wye Library; Kath Ewins, Llantwit Major; Patricia Foot, Newport (Pembs.) Library; Frances Foster and Anna Skarzynska, Royal Commission on the Ancient and Historical Monuments of Wales, Aberystwyth; Ted Foxton, Stoke-on-Trent; Sheila Francis, Loughor; Angharad Fychan, Aberystwyth; Lukas Gamble, Kilgetty; Barry Gardner, Newtown FC; Alan George, Merthyr Tydfil; Mike Gibbons, Taff's Well; Dawn Gill, Powys Archives Service; S Green, Neath; Julia Greenway, Abergavenny Library; Beryl Griffiths, Llanuwchllyn; Peter Hughes Griffiths, Carmarthen; Tony Griffiths, Welsh Football League; Robert Guy, Arturus Architects, Bristol; Hywel Gwynfryn, Cardiff; Steve Haines, Cardiff; Les Harber, Cwmtillery; Paul Harries, Newport (Pembs.) Town Council; Brian Hawkins, Milford Haven; Rosemary Hayes, Saundersfoot; Natalie Haynes, Caerphilly Council; Peter Harding, Carmarthen; June Harries, Walton East; Mal Hicks, Aberystwyth; Gavin Hooson, Powys County Council; Gill Hopley, Newquay; Richard Hopkins, Aberystwyth; Carol Hosking, Rhondda and District Football League; Lawrence Hourahane, Tenby; Simon Howarth, Gilwern; Marian Beech Hughes, Bow Street; Bleddyn Huws, Tal-y-bont; O P Huws, Llanllyfni; Jenni Hyatt, Aberystwyth; Carolyn Jacob, Merthyr Libraries; Howell Eynon James, Cardiff;

Richie Jenkins, Penrhyn-coch; Valerie Jenkins, Caldicot Library; Adie Jones, Clydach; Allun Jones, Treherbert RFC; Ann Jones, Monmouthshire Libraries; Dave Jones, *Holyhead & Anglesey Mail*; David J K Jones, Cardiff; Diana Jones, Llandre; Dennis Jones, Llandysul; Elrydd Jones, Meifod; Heulwen Jones, CPD Llanllyfni FC; John Jones, Capel Seion; Lewis Jones, Trevethin; Mark Jones, Swansea; Marilyn Jones, Swansea Libraries; Paul Jones, Maesglas FC; Penri Jones, Parc, Y Bala; Rachel Jones, Chepstow Town Council; Wyn Jones, INCO, Clydach; Nick Kelland, Treherbert Library; Kington Tourist Information Centre; David King, Port Talbot Football League; Michael Lambert, Garw Athletic FC; Simon Lane, Newport; Ron Lawrence, Pontypridd; Sue Levers, Rhos-goch; Gillian Lawson, Lisvane; Tomos Lewis, Cardiff; Wyn Lewis, Bow Street FC; Alun Llewelyn, Ystalyfera; Andrew McDonald, Monmouth Library; P Mansfield, Trefonen; Iris Mathias, Eglwyswrw; Sid Meredith, Newbridge-on-Wye; Jack Middleton, Aberystwyth; John Millard, Gorseinon Town Council; John G Morris, Crickhowell; Sue Morrison, Builth Library; Mountain Ash Library, Rhondda Cynon Taf; Jackie Myers, Godre'rgraig, Neath; Gareth Oldham, Powys County Council; Garry Owen, Yr Hendy; Hywel Wyn Owen, Bangor; Kevin Wyn Owen, Llanrug; Jonathan Parker, Bont-goch; Geraint Parry, Wrexham FC; Geraint O Parry, Llangoed; Krish Pathak, Coelbren; Penrhiw-ceibr Library; Penrhyndeudraeth Library; Patricia Perkins, Gorseinon Library; Harry Petche, Bow Street; Port Talbot Library; John C Price, Newquay; Gary Pritchard, BBC Bangor; Alan Randall, Carmarthen; Catherine Richards, Powys County Archives; D Gwyn Richards, Pont-rhyd-y-groes; Ioan Richards, Ynys-ddu; Emlyn Rees, Bow Street; Laurence

Rees, North Gwent Football League; Donna Sherret, Llanllyfni; Ray Smiles, Garw Athletic FC; Phil Smith, Llanrwst; Marcia Spooner, Rhos, Neath; Eluned Stephen, Menai Bridge Library; Margaret Stimson, Chepstow Library; Tal-y-sarn Celts FC; Mark Tanner, Aberystwyth Town FC; Alun Thomas, Aberdare; Elgan Thomas, Penmachno; Huw Thomas, Pontarddulais; Mary Thomas, New Moat; Matthew Thomas, Rhondda Cynon Taf Libraries; Meirion Thomas, Llangadog; Morlais Thomas, Gorseinon; Tito Girolami, Cardiff Combination Football League; Martin Tong, Hay St Mary's FC; George and Jane Tremlett, Laugharne; W D Walters, Tonna; Anne Webb, Tintern; Richard White, Newport; Bryngwyn Williams, Swansea Reference Library; Dafydd Whiteside Thomas, Gwynedd Archives; Paul Wigley, Hirwaun Library; Lorraine Williams, Llanfyllin Library; Jonathan Wilsher, Swansea City FC; Derek Wolfe, Barry Town Council; Anthony Woolford, *South Wales Echo*; Paul Worts, Powys County Council and Ray Young, Lisvane.

I also wish to record my special thanks to Andrew Green and the staff of the National Library of Wales for their support, patience and consistently helpful and efficient service. Iwan ap Dafydd, Jayne Day, Rhian Davies, Rhydian Davies and Rob Rhys and colleagues in the North Reading Room have helped me enormously, and I also owe a great debt to three good friends in Emyr Evans, Robert Mathias and Gwynant Phillips for their consistent support, advice and interest. I would also like to thank the following present and retired staff members who provided me with specific pieces of information on particular fields, or who made enquiries on my behalf, which bore fruition: Sara Branch, Brian Dafis, Alun Davies, Geraint Davies, Hawys Davies, Heini

Davies, Karen Davies, Linda Davies, Rhys Davies, Richard W Davies, Carol Edwards, David Edwards, Gwyndaf Evans, Manon Foster-Evans, Haydn Foulkes, David Greaney, Hugh Griffiths, Rhidian Griffiths, Ceris Gruffudd, Sarah Humphreys, Gwyn Jenkins, Aled Jones, Angharad-Medi Jones, Arwel Jones, Clive Jones, Diana Jones, Eryl Jones, Gwynfor Jones, Iwan M Jones, Diana Jones, Jean Jones, Lona Jones, Morfudd Nia Jones, Rhys Bebb Jones, Bethan Lewis, Owen Llewelyn, Martin Locock, Lona Mason, Irfon Meredith, Wyn Morgans, Dilwyn Phillips, Menna Phillips, Rob Phillips, Anwen Pierce, Gerwyn Powell, Gethin Roberts, Mark Strong, Ted Sandford, James Thomas, Siân Thomas, Meryl B Tomkinson, Dafydd Tudur, Huw Walters, Gethin Williams and Wil Williams.

I have been surprised to discover that the history of sporting organisations has sometimes failed to receive the attention it deserves in general local histories. I very much hope that this work will inspire local historians to delve deeper into the history of sport in their area and to record in greater detail this somewhat neglected aspect of community activity. I feel that this is especially important as an alarming number of traditional playing fields are falling victim to commercial, housing or transport developments.

I have relied to a large extent on the *Dictionary of the Place-Names of Wales*, by Hywel Owen and Richard Morgan (2007), as the authority on orthography, and I am grateful to Professor Owen for the interest he has shown in my research. I have also chosen to follow a similar A-Z arrangement, but an index of place-names arranged within local authorities has also been appended, which I hope will prove helpful.

I am grateful to my wife Eirlys for her many useful comments and corrections, and to Gwion for his help with the photographs. However, I am sure that many errors, omissions and inconsistencies remain, for which I must take full responsibility. Every effort has been made to keep the information relating to league and division membership as current as possible. However, in some instances, especially in the more junior association football leagues, the status quoted may reflect the position of clubs at the end of the 2008-09 season, rather than at the beginning of the 2009-10 campaign.

I am very grateful to Y Lolfa, Talybont for undertaking the publication of this work and for their close co-operation throughout, especially Lefi, Garmon, Stuart and Alan.

Richard E Huws

The Welsh Football League Pyramid

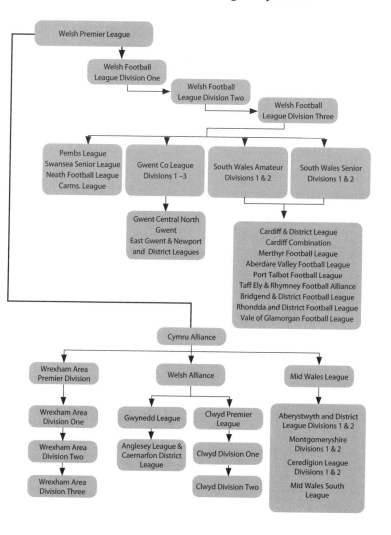

The Welsh Rugby Union National Leagues

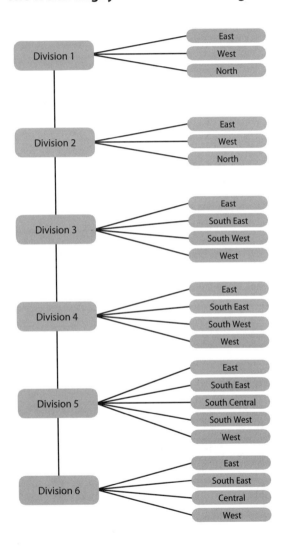

Division 1
- East
- West
- North

Division 2
- East
- West
- North

Division 3
- East
- South East
- South West
- West

Division 4
- East
- South East
- South West
- West

Division 5
- East
- South East
- South Central
- South West
- West

Division 6
- East
- South East
- Central
- West

ABBEY LIFE FC

see RHUDDLAN (Flintshire)

ABER VALLEY YMCA FC

see ABERTRIDWR (Caerphilly)

ABERAERON (Ceredigion) SN4562

Cae Sgwâr is the home of Aberaeron FC who play in the Ceredigion League, Division 1. The field, which had acquired its name as early as 1836, is named after Alban Square, which in turn is named after the Revd Alban Thomas Jones Gwynne (1749-1819) who planned this new town at the mouth of the river Aeron. Due to Aberaeron's central location in Ceredigion, Cae Sgwâr has been regularly used for local cup finals which are often attended by large numbers of spectators. The use of Square Field as an English alternative to Cae Sgwâr has been evident for a least sixty years.

Clwb Rygbi Aberaeron of the WRU National Division 5 West play their games at Parc Drefach north of the town, on a field named after the neighbouring farm. Parc Drefach also hosts the popular annual Aberaeron Rugby Sevens Festival held in August.

ABERAMAN (Rhondda Cynon Taf) SO0100

ENTO Aberaman Athletic FC of the Welsh League, Division 1 play at Aberaman Park, where it is claimed that over 10,000 once attended the ground for a game held during the Second World War. In 2004 ENTO, the Cardiff-based vocational education organisation, signed a sponsorship deal with the club. Aberaman FC was formed in 1892 and was a founder member of the Welsh League in 1902-03. Michael van Baaren, in a historical note on the club's website, also cites the Blaengwawr Field and Michael's Field as other early grounds used by the club. ENTO, as league champions, had hoped to take their place in the Welsh Premiership in 2009-10 but failed to meet the deadline for improvements to their ground required by the league. ENTO's four-year sponsorship deal with the club has also been terminated. Aberaman have applied to change their name to AFC Aberdare.

Aberaman Park was also the home of Aberaman RFC until 1972. The club subsequently changed its name to Aberdare RFC.

Aberaman Legion of the Aberdare Valley Football League, Premier Division play on Mike's Field/Michael's Field.

Abercwmboi RFC play in the WRU National Division 4 South East at the Welfare Ground, Cardiff Road, Aberaman.

ABER-ARTH (Ceredigion) SN4763

Aber-arth enjoyed a brief period of three seasons in the Aberystwyth and District League from 1948-51. Most of their home games were played in the neighbouring village of Llan-non. However, some friendly matches were played on the Garth Villa Fields in Aber-arth, which were subsequently developed for council housing. Professor Hywel Teifi Edwards played in goal for the club.

ABERAVON (Neath Port Talbot) SS7590

The Talbot Athletic Ground, Manor Street, Port Talbot, home of Aberavon RFC, who play in the WRU National League Premier Division, is the town's most famous sporting location. Rugby was first played in the Aberavon area as early as 1876, and the popularity of the game is chiefly attributable to the growth of the tin-plate industry. The first game was apparently played on Lang's Field (the Langs were a Gloucestershire family who came to work in the local copper works), off New Street, against neighbouring Neath, and other early games were played at Mansel Field, adjacent to the works owned by the powerful Mansel family of Penrice and Margam Castle. At the beginning of the twentieth century Mansel Field was incorporated into the emerging Port Talbot steelworks, and rugby was subsequently played at various other venues such as Daycock's Field, named after a family from Cwmafon who worked at the tin works and whose descendants still live in the town. The field was later absorbed into the steelworks.

In 1907 Aberavon RFC moved to the Central Athletic Ground, and in 1913 Miss Emily Charlotte Talbot (1840-1918) of Margam Castle gave exclusive rights to the club to use the pitch, granting them a lease for thirty-nine years. In 1914, following the outbreak of the First World War, the committee of Aberavon RFC decided that rugby football should cease until the end of the hostilities. During the war years the ground was sectioned into allotments to help the war effort. The Central Athletic Ground was renamed the Talbot Athletic Ground, and was officially opened on 3 December 1921. Aberavon RFC enjoyed considerable success in the 1970s with Welsh internationals Allan Martin and the late John D Bevan (1948-86) among their most prominent players.

On 8 August 1995 the Talbot Athletic Ground hosted a UEFA Cup tie between Afan Lido and RAF Riga of Latvia in front of 2,117 spectators. The home side narrowly lost 1-2, before they were eliminated from the competition after drawing the away leg at the Latvian National Stadium a fortnight later.

Sitwell Way, situated on the Sandfields Estate, Port Talbot, is the home of Aberavon Green Stars RFC, founded in 1887 to serve the growing Irish community. They play in the WRU National Division 4 South West. The street is named after the eminent poet and critic Dame Edith Sitwell (1887-1964).

Aberavon Harlequins, founded in 1891, of the WRU National Division 3 South West, play at Harlequin Road – also in the Sandfields area of Port Talbot. They secured the league championship in 2008-09 and were promoted to Division 2 West.

Aberavon Naval RFC play in the WRU National Division 6 West at the Western Avenue Playing Fields, Sandfields, Port Talbot.

It is believed that the Miller family from Grangetown, Scotland introduced association football to Port Talbot in 1895 and formed Port Talbot FC probably in 1901. Port Talbot Town FC, descended indirectly from this club, celebrated their centenary in 2001 and currently play at the Victoria Road Ground, in the Principality Welsh Premiership. The first match at the ground, acquired after the Second World War, was against

Pontardawe on 29 October 1949. Since that date it has developed into one of the better Premiership grounds, with good facilities and a capacity set at 3,000. Under a sponsorship deal with an international firm of estate agents, the stadium was for many years known as the Re/Max Stadium, but for 2008-09 a change in sponsorship to GenQuip, a local firm supplying industrial welfare units, has involved another name change for the stadium. Port Talbot Town FC's earlier games were played on Daycock's Field and on the Talbot Athletic Ground.

Marston's Stadium is the home of Afan Lido FC, a club founded in 1967 that became an influential force in Welsh football. Lido were founder members of the League of Wales in 1992 and, as already noted, qualified for a UEFA Cup place in 1995. They were relegated from the Welsh Premiership in 2005 and now play in the Welsh League, Division 1. Their ground, situated in Princess Margaret's Way in the Sandfields district of Port Talbot, has been named Marston's Stadium as part of a three-year sponsorship deal with the Wolverhampton and Dudley Brewery signed in January 2005. It has a capacity of 5,000. It was formerly sponsored by a tracksuit company and known as the Runtech Stadium.

see also PORT TALBOT

ABERBARGOED (Caerphilly) SO1500

Aberbargoed Buds, who started their football life in the West Monmouthshire League and the Gwent Football League, and who now field a team in the Welsh League, Division 3, are based at the Recreation Ground, Bedwellty Road, Aberbargoed. The club was founded in the 1950s after the demise of Aberbargoed Town, who also played in the Welsh League before folding in 1950.

ABERCANNAID (Merthyr Tydfil) SO0503

Abercannaid FC of the Merthyr Tydfil Football League, Premier Division play at the Park.

Gwynne's Field and Glyndyrus Field were both venues once used by Merthyr RFC.

ABER-CARN (Caerphilly) ST2195

Aber-carn Rugby Club was founded in 1895, and since 1919 the team have played and enjoyed good facilities at the Welfare Ground. They compete in the WRU National Division 5 East and were declared champions in 2008-09.

Aber-carn United, formed in 1997 from Aber-carn Town and Aber-carn Rangers of the Gwent County League, Division 1, also play at the Welfare Ground.

ABERCRAVE (Powys) SN8112

Abercrave RFC, a club formed in the 1890s, play at Cae Plas-y-ddôl in the WRU National Division 4 South West and were crowned champions of Division 5 in 2008-09. The club's second team now play on the Old Gilbertson Church Field where cricket was played until 1982. The Gilbertson family of Pontardawe were significant coal owners who also had financial interests in the village of Abercrave.

ABERCREGAN REFRESH FC

see CYMMER (Neath Port Talbot)

ABERCWMBOI (Rhondda Cynon Taf) ST0299

FC Abercwmboi of the South Wales Amateur Football League, Division 2 play at the Recreation Ground, Abercwmboi.

ABERCWMBOI RFC

see ABERAMAN (Rhondda Cynon Taf)

ABERCYNON ATHLETIC FC

see CARNETOWN (Rhondda Cynon Taf)

ABERCYNON RFC

see MOUNTAIN ASH (Rhondda Cynon Taf)

ABERDARE (Rhondda Cynon Taf) SO0002

Aberdare could once boast a team in the English Football League. Aberdare Athletic was elected to the Football League, Division 3 South in 1921-22, and remained in the league for a total of six seasons. An unsuccessful application for re-election at the end of the 1927 season heralded the end of league football in the Cynon Valley.

The eminent football historian Dave Twydell has documented the history of this club in some detail. He notes that football was first played in Aberdare in 1893, and a local club, Aberdare Town, entered the South Wales League in 1898, graduating to the Southern League by 1909. The club could certainly boast one of the best grounds in the league at its Ynys Stadium, but its stay at this level was short-lived, and soon after the outbreak of war in 1914 the club folded. Once hostilities ceased, football again returned to Aberdare with the formation of a new club, Aberdare Amateurs, who won the Welsh League championship in 1919-20, their one and only season of existence. This success re-kindled an interest in football, and a strong local committee, formed with the support of Aberdare Amateurs, embarked on creating a professional club in Aberdare with the promise of first-class facilities at Ynys Stadium. The new club, called Aberdare Athletic, played their first game on 28 August 1920 in the Welsh League, and their impressive set-up ensured that they were elected to the Football League during the following season, playing their first match against Portsmouth at Ynys Stadium in front of an estimated crowd of 10,000. The club enjoyed a fair amount of success during its first three seasons and in January 1923 the glamorous Preston North End visited Ynys Stadium in the FA Cup, recording a 1-3 victory in front of a crowd exceeding 16,000 spectators. However, this success was relatively short-lived and the next few seasons saw reduced gates and poorer results.

After finishing bottom in 1927, Aberdare were voted out of the Football League, losing out narrowly to Torquay United, and by now the heavily mortgaged Ynys Stadium faced an uncertain future. A re-formed Aberdare played some matches at Ynys Stadium in 1934-35 before acquiring a new ground at Plasdraw Park.

Today the site of Ynys Stadium retains its association with sport. The local leisure centre, named after Sir Michael Sobbell (1892-1993), the industrialist, television manufacturer and benefactor, has been built on part of the original ground, while another section incorporates an all-weather pitch. Several teams who compete in the Aberdare Valley Football League play their home matches at the Ynys Fields. These include Abernant Rovers 97 FC (discontinued 2008), Blaengwawr Inn FC, Gadlys Rovers FC, Lamb Inn FC and Mackworth FC, who play in the league's Premier Division, and Dinas Rock FC and Plough Inn FC, who play in the Aberdare Valley League, Division 1.

Rugby has probably been played in the Cynon Valley since the 1870s, and Philip M Walters has cited the Eisteddfod Field in Cwm-bach Road as one of the earliest venues. Aberdare Rugby Club, of the Welsh National Division 3 South East, trace their origins to the Aberaman RFC founded in 1882, which was re-named Aberdare RFC in 1995. They play their home games on the Ynys Fields, adjacent to the leisure centre. Early games were played on a field on the left-hand side of Farm Road and on the Ynys Field. Aberaman RFC played at Aberaman Park until 1972.

The short-lived Aberdare rugby league club who operated between 1908-09 also played on the Ynys Fields.

ABERDULAIS (Neath Port Talbot) SS7759

Ynysygerwn FC play in the Neath Football League Premier Division at the Aberdulais Cricket Club.

ABERDYFI (Gwynedd) SN6196

Aberdyfi's high point in football was achieved in 1937 when they defeated Aberystwyth Town in the final of the Welsh Amateur Cup at Newlands Park, Machynlleth. The village was without a football team for many years until the present team, who play in the Aberystwyth and District League, Division 1, was formed in 1996. They play at Penrhos Playing Field, once a rubbish tip, which was much improved in 2003 after funding was obtained to re-lay and level the pitch. The ground is located behind Aberdyfi Railway station.

ABERFAN (Merthyr Tydfil) SO0700

Aberfan SDC of the Merthyr Tydfil Football League, Premier Division, and Georgetown BGC FC of the Merthyr Tydfil Football League, Division 1, both play at the Grove Field, Aberfan. Gordon Lennox [sic] FC of the Merthyr Tydfil Football League, Premier Division, also play at the Grove Field. The team is based at the Gordon Lenox Constitutional Club, Aberfan, and takes its name from Gordon Lenox of Ynysangharad House, Pontypridd. Lenox not only owned land along the Taff River on which the club stands, he also provided land and money to form a cricket club at Pontypridd, converting farm land for recreational use which developed into Ynysangharad Memorial Park, opened in 1923. He was the proprietor of the Brown Lenox Chain and Anchor Works at Pontypridd, which survived until 2000. They supplied the Royal Navy with anchors and also produced cables for suspension bridges built by Thomas Telford (1757-1834) and Isambard Kingdom Brunel (1806-59).

Ynysowen RFC, of the WRU National Division 6 Central, also play at Grove Field.

ABERGAVENNY (Monmouthshire) SO2914

Pen-y-pound Stadium, which adjoins Abergavenny Cricket Club, is home to Abergavenny Thursdays FC. Dr Andrew Hignell has described it as one of the most picturesque grounds on the first-class cricket circuit. He adds that the Abergavenny club, formed in 1834, is one of the oldest in Wales and that, after playing at a variety of grounds, the club approached the Marquess of Abergavenny in 1896 for the lease of a four-and-a-half-acre field off Avenue Road, called Pen-y-pound. The name is associated with a mill pond, and is traceable to several early eighteenth-century documents deposited at the National Library of Wales by the Marquess of Abergavenny and the Baker-Gabb family of Abergavenny.

Football was played in Abergavenny as early as the 1890s, and the name Abergavenny Thursdays had certainly evolved by 1908. Early games were played at Bailey Park, before the Thursdays finally settled at Pen-y-pound during the 1930s. Abergavenny Thursdays were certainly one of the most feared teams in the post-war Welsh League, winning the championship on no less than four occasions and finishing runners-up on three occasions. The club was among the inaugural members of the League of Wales in 1992, but few clubs in Wales have fallen so significantly from grace since their relegation from the top flight after only one season. Today, they compete in the Gwent County League, Division 3.

Bailey Park, the present home of Abergavenny RFC, who play in the WRU National Division 3 East, hosted Abergavenny Thursdays FC during its early days (as noted above). Rugby has been played in Abergavenny since 1867, and early games were played at Castle Meadows and Ysguborwen Fields. In later seasons the club moved to Bailey Park, a field named in honour of Crawshay Bailey II (1821-87), a wealthy local iron and coal entrepreneur of Maindiff Court, Abergavenny, who married Elizabeth, the only daughter of Jean Baptiste, Count Metaxa. The court later became a hospital and, from 1942 to 1945, Rudolf Hess (1894-1987), Hitler's deputy, was held there as a prisoner following his capture after his flight to Britain in 1941. Maindiff Court continues to operate as a hospital, run by the Gwent Healthcare NHS Trust.

ABERGELE (Conwy) SH9477

Abergele Rovers, of the Clwyd League Premier Division, play at Parc Pentre Mawr. Pentre Mawr was a local estate of some importance dating from the sixteenth century and is associated with the Williams, Jones and Jones-Bateman families. It is also the home of Abergele Rugby Club, a Welsh District League side.

ABERGWILI (Carmarthenshire) SN4321

Abergwili FC play in the Carmarthenshire League, Division 2 on a field adjacent to the A40, which is particularly susceptible to flooding. Photographs of the field often portray floodwater reaching cross-bar level!

In 1962, Carmarthen Quins RFC purchased an eight-acre field at Parc-y-deri, on the Castell Pigyn Road, Abergwili, which it still owns, using it for reserve and youth fixtures.

ABERKENFIG (Bridgend) SS8983

Tondu RFC, founded in 1880, of the WRU National Division 3 South West, play at Pandy Park, Aberkenfig.

Tondu Robins FC, formerly of the Welsh League, and now of the Bridgend and District League, Division 1, also play on an adjacent pitch at Pandy Park. *Pandy* is Welsh for fulling mill, and these fields are located in an area once occupied by a mill which has since been demolished.

ABERMAGWR (Ceredigion) SN6673

Traws-goed FC of the Aberystwyth and District League, Division 2 play at Cae Siop, Abermagwr. The field and changing facilities are located behind the former village shop. Traws-goed re-formed in 1988, but an earlier team enjoyed a brief period of success in Division 2 of the league from 1948-53 when they played on a field on Berllanber Farm, through the generosity of the farmer, Mr Bound.

ABERMULE (Powys) SO1694

Abermule FC play in the Montgomeryshire Amateur League, Division 1 at the Abermule Community Centre Field.

ABERNANT ROVERS 97 FC

see ABERDARE (Rhondda Cynon Taf)

ABER-PORTH (Ceredigion) SN2651

Aber-porth FC of the Ceredigion League, Division 1 play at the Civil Service Ground, Parcllyn, Aber-porth. RAE Aber-porth first entered the Cardiganshire League in 1948, and some of their early games were played at Rhydalen Farm, Cross Inn, Newquay. The team was affectionately known as the 'Rockets'.

ABERTILLERY (Blaenau Gwent) SO2014

Abertillery Park has been described as one of the most picturesque grounds in world rugby. Rugby has been played in the town since 1883, and the famous green and white hoops of Abertillery have hosted New Zealand, Australia and South Africa. In 1908, Abertillery secured a famous 6-6 draw against Australia, whilst in 1931 over 30,000 squeezed into the park to witness a narrow 10-9 win for the South African Springboks over a combined Abertillery and Cross Keys team. The club now play under the name Abertillery-Blaenau Gwent, having merged with reputedly the oldest club in Wales. The club's excellent website cites several grounds at which Blaenau Gwent played during their early years. These include the Gas Works Field, and the Old Barn Field from 1895. In 1900 the club was again on the move to a field in the Rose Heyworth area, named after the wife of Lawrence Heyworth, a lieutenant colonel in the army. He was the first managing director of the South Wales Colliery Company, which raised its first coal in 1874. The team currently play in the WRU National Division 4 East.

Abertillery Park, home of Abertillery-Blaenau Gwent RFC. Reproduced by kind permission of the photographer: Les Harber, Cwmtillery.

ABERTILLERY BLUEBIRDS FC

see SIX BELLS (Blaenau Gwent)

ABERTILLERY EXCELSIORS FC

see CWMTILLERY (Blaenau Gwent)

ABERTRIDWR (Caerphilly) ST1236

Aber Valley YMCA FC of the South Wales Amateur Football League, Division 1 play at Abertridwr Park.

ABERTRIDWR (Powys) SJ0319

Llanwddyn FC play in the Montgomeryshire Amateur League, Division 2. The ground, Wddyn Park, is located in the neighbouring settlement of Abertridwr.

ABERTYSSWG (Caerphilly) SO1305

Abertysswg Falcons play in the WRU National Division 6 East on the Green.

ABERYSTWYTH (Ceredigion) SN5881

Coedlan-y-Parc/Park Avenue is the home of Aberystwyth Town AFC, founded in 1884, one of the leading non-league clubs in Wales and founder members of the Welsh Premiership League in 1992. Originally the Smithfield Athletic Ground, it was re-named Park Avenue in October 1934. It has staged many memorable matches including an under-16 international match in May 1963 when a local reporter was rather impressed with the skills of a slightly built schoolboy named George Best, stating that he 'looked like a star in the making'! The ground is considered one of the best non-league stadiums in Wales, and now has seating on three sides. The pitch was re-laid in 2008, making it unlikely that the club will move to an out-of-town location in the foreseeable future as has been widely predicted for many years.

Cae'r Ficerdy/Vicarage Field is adjacent to the former vicarage of St Padarn's Church, Llanbadarn Fawr, which is now St Padarn's Roman Catholic primary school. In 1922 the vicarage was sold to the Catholic Church to provide improved accommodation for the school. The field was purchased and given to the University College of Wales, Aberystwyth in 1906 by Baron David Davies (1880-1944), Plas Dinam, Llandinam, Powys. It is still owned by Aberystwyth University, and is used for football, cricket and rugby. Glamorgan County Cricket Club staged two one-day matches at the ground in 1977 and

Park Avenue, Aberystwyth, home of Aberystwyth Town FC. Elevated photograph reproduced by courtesy of www.imagemast.co.uk. By kind permission of Aberystwyth Town FC.

1989. The Vicarage Field also hosted the very first Royal Welsh Agricultural Show in 1904 and the National Eisteddfod of Wales in 1916. UW Aberystwyth FC of the Mid Wales League and the university's Senior Commoners Cricket team currently share these facilities. The large and impressive grandstand which once dominated the field was demolished in August 2007. A smaller replacement stand, located on the Llanbadarn Road side of the football pitch, was officially opened in April 2009 by Anne and Trefor Thomas in memory of their son Gareth Llywelyn, a politics and law graduate, who died suddenly in February 2007 from an inherited cardiac condition. The new stand has been named the Gareth Llywelyn Thomas Memorial Stand.

Min-y-ddôl is the home of Penparcau FC who, since 2008, have competed in the Mid Wales League. The Neuadd Goffa Field, with its infamous slope, formerly used by Penparcau and other district league teams such as Neuadd Goffa and the GPO (General Post Office), has largely been sacrificed to create a new approach road to Aberystwyth. Aqua Terra, a field also in the Penparcau area of Aberystwyth which was once the home of defunct Trefechan FC, is now a camping ground.

Aberystwyth RFC, formed in 1947 and promoted from the WRU National Division 3 West in 2009, play at Plas-crug, on land that was reclaimed from its use as the borough council's refuse tip, known locally as Domen Dre. When the club was first formed, games during the first two seasons were played on the Padarn Dairy Fields, adjacent to the Aberystwyth gasworks. The playing field at Plas-crug was officially opened in February 1949 with a match between a Cardiganshire XV and a Pembrokeshire XV.

District league football was also played on fields at Plas-crug, and today the old Padarn Dairy Fields that now adjoin Ysgol Penweddig are a hive of activity on Saturday mornings, when cheering parents descend on the area to support their children in the vibrant Aberystwyth and District Junior Football League. This now boasts no less than 57 teams and over 750 registered players.

AC CENTRAL FC

see PONTCANNA (Cardiff)

ACRE-FAIR (Wrexham) SJ2743

The playing field of Acre-fair Youth, who play in the Welsh National League (Wrexham Area), Premier Division, is known as the Bont, owing to its location under the world famous and spectacular Pontcysyllte Viaduct built by Thomas Telford (1757-1834).

ADAMSTOWN FC / ADAMSTOWN ATHLETIC FC

see SPLOTT (Cardiff)

ADMIRAL FC

see BARRY (Vale of Glamorgan)

AFAN LIDO FC

see ABERAVON (Neath Port Talbot)

AFC ...

see under name of club: e.g. CAEWERN: AFC

AIRBUS UK BROUGHTON FC

see BROUGHTON (Flintshire)

ALBION ROVERS FC

see NEWPORT

ALLTWALIS (Carmarthenshire) SN4431

The field adjoining Alltwalis School provided a home for Peniel FC during their abortive venture into the Cardiganshire League in 1958-59. A former player, Peter Harding, recalls that the village smithy was used as the changing room and two tin baths were provided for a post-match wash.

see also PENIEL (Carmarthenshire)

ALLT-WEN (Neath Port Talbot) SN7203

Allt-wen RFC play in the WRU National Division 5 South West at Allt-wen Hill, Allt-wen, Pontardawe.

ALLTYBLACA (Ceredigion) SN5245

Llanybydder FC play in the Ceredigion League, Division 2 at Llwynyreos Farm, Heol Llanfechan, on the Ceredigion side of the river Teifi in the neighbouring village of Alltyblaca. It is believed that the club played on a field at Dôlwlff, Llanwennog during the 1959-60 season.

AMLWCH (Anglesey) SH4493

Amlwch Town, founded in 1897, of the Welsh Alliance League, play at Lôn Bach. The club enjoyed a brief period in the Cymru Alliance League from 2002 until 2004.

AMMAN UNITED RFC

see GLANAMAN (Carmarthenshire)

AMMANFORD (Carmarthenshire) SN6212

Ammanford RFC of the WRU National Division 2 West play at the Recreation Ground. The club has a rich sporting tradition. Formed in 1887, its first game was staged at the Ynys Field, adjoining the river Aman, on the site of the now defunct Baltic Saw Mills. During the 1904-05 religious revival, the use of the playing field was temporarily withdrawn, and the club discontinued its membership of the Welsh Rugby Union until it was re-established in 1907. The club celebrated its centenary in 1987 with home games against three of its illustrious neighbours: Llanelli, Neath and Swansea.

Rice Road, Betws was the home of Ammanford FC, a team formed in 1991 from the merger of Ammanford Town and Ammanford United, who play in the Welsh League, Division 2. The team was originally founded as Betws FC at the end of the Second World War, changing its name to Ammanford in 1960. Association football was played at Betws in the 1920s by Ammanford Thursdays, who played their matches on Caemawr, on which a council housing estate was built in 1947. In the 1930s the Ammanford Corries, who were members of the Gwalia and Llanelli leagues, played at Betws Park.

The name Rice, an anglicisation of the family name Rhys, is associated with the Dynevor family, once owners of most of the land in the area. Although the ground is known as Rice Road, it is actually in Rice Street! This famous Welsh League ground, purchased in 1947, has a capacity of 2,000 and claims a record attendance of 4,000, but is now in a rather neglected state. The main stand was destroyed by fire in February 2003, and the club has since been based at the Recreation Ground, Ammanford.

The Recreation Ground, which has several rugby and football pitches, is also home to KRUF FC who play in the Carmarthenshire League, Division 3.

ANCHOR FC
see TROEDYRHIW (Merthyr Tydfil)

ANGLE (Pembrokeshire) SM8602
Angle FC play in the Pembrokeshire League, Division 2 at Angle Lane.

ASTON PARK RANGERS FC
see SHOTTON (Flintshire)

AVENUE HOTSPURS FC
see ELY (Cardiff)

AZTEC SPORTS FC
see RHYL (Denbighshire)

BAGLAN (Neath Port Talbot) SS7592
Evans Bevan Fields, the home of Baglan Red Dragons FC of the South Wales Amateur Football League, Division 1, is named after one of the most important industrial families of South Wales which held extensive mining and brewing interests, particularly in the Vale of Neath.

BAGLAN FC

see TYNEWYDD (Rhondda Cynon Taf)

BAGLAN RFC

see BRITON FERRY (Neath Port Talbot)

BAILI GLAS FC

see MERTHYR TYDFIL

BALA (Gwynedd) SH9236

Maes Tegid, Castle Street, takes its name from Llyn Tegid (Bala Lake). It is the home of Bala FC, formed in 1921 and champions of the Cymru Alliance League in 2009. Football has been played at Bala since the end of the nineteenth century, while Maes Tegid has been a football ground since the early 1950s. The team, however, played at various venues prior to that date including Castle Park (adjoining Maes Tegid) where they drew against Shrewsbury Town (then of the English Midland League) in the Welsh Senior Cup in 1946, and in the nineteenth century on the foreshore of Llyn Tegid. The identity of Tegid is unknown, but the name is known to date from at least the twelfth century. The ground is neat and includes two covered areas, and the club has now successfully realised its ambitions to play in the Welsh Premiership.

Bala Rugby Club, established in 1980, play in the WRU National Division 2 North at Tegid Street, on the outskirts of the town.

BANCFFOSFELEN FC

see PONTYBEREM (Carmarthenshire)

BANC-Y-DARREN (Ceredigion) SN6782

Trefeurig and District United FC played for five seasons in the Aberystwyth and District League from 1948-53. Home games were played on a field at Darren Bank Farm, and the team changed in one of its barns. The team lost all fourteen league games in its final season.

BANGOR (Gwynedd) SH5771

Bangor City FC, founded in 1876, played their early games at Maes-y-dref in the Hirael district of Bangor, a field which has long given way to housing developments. Farrar Road, the present home of Bangor City FC, is one of the better known football grounds in Wales. The name Farrar is attributable to William Farrar Roberts of Llwyn Eithin, Bangor, who provided the land on which the street named Farrar Road was built in 1896. It has witnessed many historic encounters, none more significant than the European Cup Winners' Cup tie in 1962, when the home side defeated Italian giants Napoli 2-0 in front of 12,000 spectators.

Bangor City plan to move to a new stadium on the Nantporth Farm fields, Holyhead Road. At the time of writing the move has yet to be finalised.

Rugby has been played in Bangor since the 1870s. The town's club was well established by the mid twentieth century, playing at the Wern Fields, Caernarfon Road, on the site of a former rubbish tip from 1963 until 1995, when they sold out to Tesco and moved to a new ground at Cae Milltir, Llandygái. Bangor RFC now play in the WRU National Division 2 North. Early games were played at several venues including Maes-y-dref, the university fields at Ffriddoedd, Bangor City's Farrar Road, Penrhyn Park and Tŷ Newydd, the field used by Highgrove School.

Bangor University play in the Gwynedd League at Maesglas, Ffordd Ffriddoedd.

BANWEN (Neath Port Talbot) SN8509

Banwen Rugby Club, formed in 1947, play at Banwen Park in the WRU National Division 5 South Central.

BARGOD RANGERS FC

see DREFACH FELINDRE (Carmarthenshire)

BARGOED (Caerphilly) ST1499

Bargoed RFC, founded in 1882, play at Bargoed Park. Caerphilly Council's website records that it is the largest urban park in the county borough at over 19 hectares, and that the wrought iron memorial gates on Upper Wood Street were erected in 1952 to commemorate the Festival of Britain. The earliest records for Bargoed Park date from 1905 and refer to an area of land leased by Gelli-gaer Parish Council from the Hanbury family for £25 per year. In 1929, the parish council were able to purchase the land for £500 from the then owners, the Pontypool Estate. Bargoed RFC currently play in the WRU National Division 1 East.

AFC Bargoed Redz of the South Wales Amateur Football League, Division 1 also play at Bargoed Park.

BARMOUTH (Gwynedd) SH6115

Barmouth and Dyffryn United FC play in the Welsh Alliance League at Wern Mynach.

BARRY (Vale of Glamorgan) ST1168

Jenner Park is the home of Barry Town FC. Barry's chequered history dates back to 1892 with the formation of a club entitled Barry and Cadoxton District. During its early years, the club played on five different grounds and was variously known as Barry Unionist Athletic, Barry United Athletic and Barry District. In 1913, however, the club re-formed as Barry AFC, secured a lease on land owned by the Jenner family of Wenvoe Castle and joined the Southern League. The club has always been one of the strongest sides in Wales, but enjoyed little success until it opted to join the Welsh pyramid system. It dominated Welsh football during the 1990s and won no less than seven league titles with a fully professional team. It represented Wales in the European Cup Winners' Cup, UEFA Cup and Champions League playing prestigious opposition at Jenner Park including Dynamo Kiev, Aberdeen and FC Porto. Although the club managed to win five European ties from 1994-2004, its overall European performance was disappointing. After suffering financial difficulties, it went into administration and was relegated to the Welsh League. The club was also temporarily barred from Jenner Park, and played briefly at the White Tips Stadium, Treforest from January 2005 until

May 2006. Barry Town secured promotion to Welsh League, Division 1 in May 2008, and face the future with confidence and a determination to re-gain their Welsh Premiership status.

Barry Villa FC, established in 2003, of the Vale of Glamorgan Football League, Premier Division, and Island Marine FC of Division 2 play at Maslin Park, Barry Island. The park was named in honour of Alderman John Thomas Maslin (1873-1940), a native of Portsmouth who became a prominent Conservative figure in the life of his adopted town. He served as chairman of Barry Urban District Council in 1928 and was instrumental in re-developing and draining a marshy piece of land known as Leech Pool, provided by the earl of Plymouth for the community use of the residents of Barry Island.

Barry Sports Centre has extensive playing fields on the northern side of the town in the suburb of Colcot. Many teams that compete in the Vale of Glamorgan League use these facilities including Cadoxton Imps and Master Mariners FC (Premier Division); Barry Dockers, Colcot FC, Holton Road FC, Knap FC and Wenvoe Exiles (Division 1); and AFC Galaxy, Barry Dynamos, Park Vets FC, Tynewydd FC and Windsor FC (Division 2). Former teams Old College Inn (OCI) FC and Pit Stop FC also played at this venue.

Admiral FC (now defunct) and AFC Galaxy, of the Vale of Glamorgan League, Premier Division, played some games at the Buttrills Playing Fields.

Barry Bluebirds of the Vale of Glamorgan Football League, Premier Division, play at the Severn Avenue Playing Fields.

SP Construction FC of the Vale of Glamorgan Football

League, Premier Division, AFC Tadross (based at the Tadross Hotel) and Cadoxton Athletic and Wenvoe Exiles of Division 1, play many of their home fixtures at Pencoedtre Park. A former team, Borough Arms FC (based at the public house of that name), was also based at Pencoedtre.

Barry RFC play in the WRU National Division 5 South East at the Reservoir Field along Merthyr Dyfan Road.

Rugby league was also played at the Trinity Street ground, Barry during 1908-09.

BASSALEG (Newport) ST2787

Whiteheads FC play in the Gwent County League, Division 3 at Whitehead's Sport Ground, Bassaleg.

Whiteheads RFC play in the WRU National Division 6 East using the same facilities. The club traces its origins to the Whitehead Steel Company, which purchased the ground at Bassaleg in 1937 for the use of its work force. Prior to that date the team had played at Maesglas. After nationalisation of the steel industry in 1967, Whitehead Steel Company became a part of British Steel.

BEAR FC

see NEATH ABBEY (Neath Port Talbot)

BEAUFORT RFC

see CARMELTOWN (Blaenau Gwent)

BEAUMARIS (Anglesey) SH6076

Beaumaris Town FC play in the Gwynedd League at the Green. During the 1960s they played at Henllys Lane, near Henllys Hotel.

BEDDAU (Rhondda Cynon Taf) ST0685

Beddau RFC, a successful village team based on the outskirts of Pontypridd, play at Mount Pleasant Park, which first opened in 1938. Although rugby has been played in the area since the nineteenth century, the present club dates from 1951. They currently play in the WRU National League, Division 1 East.

Cwm Welfare FC of the South Wales Senior League, Division 1 also play at Mount Pleasant Park.

BEDLINOG (Merthyr Tydfil) SO0901

Bedlinog Rugby Club, nicknamed the 'Foxes', because of the nearby river Llwynog (fox), was formed in 1971. They play at the Recreation Ground and were champions of Division 4 South East in 2006-07. Having secured three promotions in successive seasons, they will play in the WRU National Division 1 East in 2009-10.

Bedlinog FC, formed in 1979, of the Merthyr Tydfil Football League, Division 1 play at Coed-yr-hendre.

BEDWAS (Caerphilly) ST1789

Bedwas Rugby Club dates from 1889 and its present ground, the Bridge Field, was acquired in 1947. The club play in the WRU National Premier Division.

BENLLECH (Anglesey) SH5182

Benllech Rugby Club play in the Gwynedd League. Their pitch is located at the Pacemaker Sports and Country Club, Bwlch Lane, Tyn-y-Gongl, Benllech.

BERRIEW (Powys) SJ1810

Berriew play in the Mid Wales League at Talbot Field. Sir Stanley Matthews (1915-2000) played at Berriew in a testimonial match in 1968, when he was 53 years old. Berriew FC will compete in the Cymru Alliance League from 2009-10.

BETHEL (Gwynedd) SH5265

In 2002 Bethel FC purchased a new field, Cae Coed Bolyn, with the financial support of Gwynedd County Council. They had previously played on the school pitch at Ysgol Brynrefail, Llanrug. The club play in the Gwynedd League.

BETHESDA (Gwynedd) SH6266

Parc Meurig/Meurig Park, home of Bethesda Athletic, 2008-09 champions of the Welsh Alliance League, is situated in the middle of a park where the country house Bryn Meurig still stands. At one time the house had a lake on its ground entitled Llyn Meurig. Meurig, a historical figure dating from the Roman period, is also commemorated in other local place-names such as Bodfeurig and Glan Meurig. Bethesda Athletic will compete in the Cymru Alliance League from 2009-10.

Clwb Rygbi Bethesda play at Dôl Ddafydd, Station Road, Bethesda. Established in 1974, the club became a full member of the Welsh Rugby Union in 1998 and now play in the WRU National League, Division 2 North. Local tradition notes that Dôl Ddafydd (Dafydd's Field) is named after Dafydd ap Llywelyn (*d.*1246), brother of Llywelyn Fawr (1173-1240) who apparently used this field as a practice ground for his soldiers in preparation for his war of independence. The field and all neighbouring lands were originally part of the Penrhyn Estate. The rugby pitch was purchased by the club with assistance from the local authority and the Welsh Office, and was officially opened by Sir Wyn Roberts, the Minister of State, in October 1984. A housing estate bordering on Dôl Ddafydd has been named Llain y Pebyll, suggesting that the land was once used as a camp to house soldiers. Cardiff RFC visited Dôl Ddafydd in December 2008, recording an emphatic 55-17 win in the Swalec Cup in front of a large crowd.

BETTWS (Bridgend) SS9086

Bettws FC, founded in 1995, of the Welsh League, Division 1, play at North Site, Bettws Road, Bettws, Bridgend.

BETTWS (Newport) SO2919

Bettws RFC of the WRU National Division 5 East play at the Tŷ-Coed Playing Fields, Leach Road, Bettws, Newport.

Newport Civil Service Club FC of the Gwent County League, Division 1 play at the Newport Civil Service Ground, Shannon Road, Bettws.

Bettws Social Club FC play in the Newport and District Football League, Division 3 at Bettws Lane.

BETWS (Carmarthenshire) SN6311

Betws RFC of the WRU National Division 4 West play at Maes-y-Felin, Mill Street, Betws, Ammanford.

BETWS FC

see AMMANFORD (Carmarthenshire)

BETWS-YN-RHOS (Conwy) SH8974

Betws-yn-Rhos FC play in the Clwyd League, Division 1 at the Betws-yn-Rhos Playing Field. The team was previously known as Mochdre Sports Reserves.

BIRCHGROVE (Swansea) SS7098

Birchgrove RFC play in the WRU National Division 4 South West at Parc Bedw, Heol Dulais, Birchgrove, Swansea. *Bedw* is Welsh for birch, and the village takes its name from the farm Birchgrove, also recorded as Tir y Bedw.

BIRCHGROVE COLTS FC

see TRALLWN (Swansea)

BISHOPS CASTLE (Shropshire) SO3288

Bishops Castle Town FC, established in 1900, play in the Montgomeryshire Amateur League, Division 1 at the Community College, Bishops Castle.

BISHOPSTON (Swansea) SS5789

South Gower RFC play in the WRU National Division 6 West at Pwll Du Lane, Bishopston.

BLACKWOOD (Caerphilly) ST1797

Blackwood RFC, which was formed in 1889 and gained membership of the Welsh Rugby Union in 1918, play in the WRU National Division 1 East and were champions of the division in 2009. However, their home ground, Glan-yr-Afon Park, did not meet the criteria for Welsh premiership rugby. In the 1960s the club purchased an old police station and converted it for use as a clubhouse, and in 1997 a new 800-seater stand was constructed with the capital coming from match sponsorship and donations. Two additional fields, Woodfield Side and Libanus, are also used by the club's reserve side, Blackwood Stars, who play in the WRU National Division 5 South East.

Fleur De Lys Welfare FC of the North Gwent League, Premier Division play at St David's Field, Blackwood.

Fleur De Lys FC of the North Gwent League, Division 1 play at the Ynys Welfare Ground, Blackwood.

BLAENAU FFESTINIOG (Gwynedd) SH7045

Blaenau Ffestiniog has an immensely proud and rich footballing tradition that has been thoroughly researched by Mel ab Ifor Thomas. The town has produced at least ten footballers who have played at the highest level, including Dr R H Mills-Roberts (1862-1935), who played in two consecutive FA Cup finals in 1888 and 1889 for Preston North End and, more recently, David

Felgate, who played as goalkeeper in over 600 league matches, chiefly for Lincoln City and Bolton Wanderers, before retiring in 1996.

Football was probably first played in the town in 1885, with Blaenau FC being formed in 1889. Early games were played at Holland Park, a rather wet field named after a slate mine, which is now buried under a *domen fawr* (slag heap). It was certainly common practice for the coal and slate mine owners to dump their extracted waste on playing fields to meet the insatiable demand for their products. In most instances, they were entitled to do so as they owned the land, and economics, of course, also dictated that work should take precedence over play. In 1898, the club moved to the Manod Recreation Ground, later the site of the Manod Granite Quarry and now the lorry yard of Hughes Specialised Transport Ltd. It moved again in 1907, to Newborough Park in the centre of the town, where the club played continuously until 1930. (Newborough Park is now the site of Somerfield supermarket.) After a very brief stay at Oakley Park, the club rented a field at Glanypwll in 1929, called Haygarth Park. In 1952 the club had to relinquish this site, at the request of the Ffestiniog Urban District Council, to provide land for the building of a factory currently occupied by Metcalf Catering Equipment Ltd. After a brief period at Y Ddôl, Tanygrisiau (where Tanygrisiau FC played in the Cambrian Coast League for three decades), the council provided a new home at a former refuse tip at Congl-y-Wal, Manod which was named Cae Clyd in 1956. Blaenau FC folded after a century of activity during which they won surprisingly few league and cup competitions. A new club, Blaenau Ffestiniog Amateurs, formed in 1980, now play at Cae Clyd, and were runaway champions of the Gwynedd League in 2008-09. They will compete in the Welsh Alliance League from 2009-10.

BLAENAVON (Torfaen) SO2509

Blaenavon RFC of the WRU National Division 5 East play at the Recreation Ground, Coed Cae Road, Blaenavon.

Blaenavon Blues FC of the Gwent County League, Division 1 play at the Co-op Field (Recreation Ground), Blaenavon. The club, formed in 1946, played in the Welsh League until 1991. Their reserve and junior teams also use the neighbouring Memorial Field, the former home of disbanded Blaenavon Harlequins RFC, and the Rifle Green Pitch on the Abergavenny Road.

Terry Williams has recorded in detail the history of Forgeside RFC, a junior club which has operated in the town since 1880, although not continuously. The club play at Blaenavon Recreation Ground. Forgeside is a district on the west side of Blaenavon. The club now plays in the WRU Division 6 East.

BLAENGARW (Bridgend) SS9092

Blaengarw RFC of the WRU National Division 5 South Central play at the Recreation Ground.

BLAENGWAWR INN FC

see ABERDARE (Rhondda Cynon Taf)

BLAEN-GWRACH (Neath Port Talbot) SN8605

Cwm-gwrach RFC play in the WRU National Division 5 South Central. Rugby has been played at Cwm-gwrach since the early twentieth century, and prior to 1929 eight different pitches were used in the locality including Maesgwyn, which was lost when the railway was extended to Aberpergwm. The School Field was used from 1929 until the local Welfare Committee went about creating a fine new ground after volunteers moved over 25,000 tons of earth and rock. The new Welfare Ground at Blaen-gwrach was officially opened in 1935. However, by 1958 the club was temporarily denied the use of the field as a new colliery was opened which apparently went 'straight through the pitch'. The status quo was restored by 1982 and the Welfare Ground was officially re-opened on 27 April of that year with a commemorative game against a star-studded side led by David Richards of Swansea, Wales and the British Lions.

BLAENGWYNFI (Neath Port Talbot) SS8996

Gwynfi United FC, formed in 1971, play in the Port Talbot Football League, Premier Division at the Welfare Ground. The ground and the area are often referred to as the Cape, as the area was once apparently marketed as being similar to the Cape of Good Hope! The team were formerly known as Gwynfi Welfare and were a significant force in Welsh league football during the 1950s. Derek Tapscott (1932-2008), the former Wales, Cardiff and Arsenal star, makes a humorous reference to the field in his autobiography when he played there in a Welsh league fixture for Barry Town: 'The football pitch was the only flat ground in the place. I had a couple of shots which went wide of the goals and it took about ten minutes for someone to run down the hill to retrieve the ball each time.'

BLAENRHONDDA (Rhondda Cynon Taf) SS9299

Blaenrhondda FC, founded in 1934, once a major force in Welsh football, now play in the South Wales Amateur Football League, Division 2, having lost their Welsh League, Division 3 status at the end of 2008. Cwm Ni FC (formerly Wyndham FC) of the same league also share the same ground at Blaenrhondda Park, a picturesque venue located in Brook Street, Blaenrhondda which boasts impressive terracing, clearly visible from the Rhigos mountain road on the descent into the Rhondda Valley.

Blaenrhondda Park, home of Blaenrhondda FC and Cwm Ni FC, viewed from the Rhigos mountain road. Photograph: the author.

BLAENYMAES FC

see PENLAN (Swansea)

BLAINA (Blaenau Gwent) SO1908

Blaina RFC, formed in 1875, of the WRU National Division 3 East play at Central Park, Blaina.

Blaina United of the North Gwent Football League, Division 1 play at Duffryn Park. Blaina West Side, formerly of the Welsh League, also played at Duffryn Park.

Local football is also played on a field known as Fan Tips.

BLUE STARS FC

see PORT TALBOT (Neath Port Talbot)

BLUEBIRDS FC

see MERTHYR TYDFIL

BODEDERN (Anglesey) SH3380

Bodedern FC played in the Cymru Alliance League during the 2006–07 season, but resigned in October 2007 due to a shortage of players. The club now play in the Gwynedd League at Cae'r Ysgol, Ysgol Uwchradd Bodedern. During the 1980s it played at Tŷ Christian Field.

BODORGAN (Anglesey) SH3867

Glantraeth FC, founded in 1984, play in the Cymru Alliance League at Cae Trefdraeth, Bodorgan. In a surprise statement issued in August 2009, the club announced it was withdrawing from the Cymru Alliance League. It will now take stock of its situation for a year, and fully intends to resume competing at a lower level in 2010.

BONCATH FC

see TEGRYN (Pembrokeshire)

BONT (Pontrhydfendigaid) FC

see PONTRHYDFENDIGAID (Ceredigion)

BONTNEWYDD (Gwynedd) SH4859

Bontnewydd FC play in the Gwynedd League at Cae Stanley. The field name is recorded in the Glynllifon archives as early as 1781. 'Stanley' may be Sir Piers Stanley, sheriff of Merioneth from 1485-1509 whose daughter married into the Wynn family of Glynllifon. Other field names in Bontnewydd such as Cae Samuel and Cae Spencer are connected with the Newborough family.

Mountain Rangers of the Caernarfon and District League once played on a field behind the Newborough Arms. The exterior of this public house was used in filming *C'Mon Midffild*, the Welsh-language television comedy.

BÔN-Y-MAEN (Swansea) SS6895

Bôn-y-maen RFC, a club located on the outskirts of Swansea, play at Parc Mawr, Cefn Hengoed Road, Bôn-y-maen. The club was denied promotion to the top flight of Welsh rugby after winning the WRU National Division 1 West championship in 2007 because the ground was deemed unsuitable.

Bôn-y-maen Colts FC of the Swansea Senior Football League, Division 1 play at Bôn-y-maen Park.

BOROUGH ARMS FC

see NEATH ABBEY (Neath Port Talbot)

BOROUGH UNITED FC

see LLANDUDNO JUNCTION (Conwy)

BORRAS PARK ALBION FC

see WREXHAM

BORTH (Ceredigion) SN6089

Borth United were founder members of the Aberystwyth and District League in 1934. The team that folded in 2000 played at the Uppingham Playing Fields. The name is connected with the temporary relocation of Uppingham School, Rutland to Borth in 1876-77 following an outbreak of typhoid fever. There is also an Uppingham Path, paid for by the Revd Dr Edward Thring (1821-87), headmaster of the school, which crosses the peat bog and links Borth with the villages of Tre-Taliesin and Tal-y-bont.

*Uppingham Playing Fields, Borth, home of Borth United FC. Elevated
photograph reproduced by courtesy of www.imagemast.co.uk*

Borth United FC re-formed in May 2009 and will compete in
the Aberystwyth and District League, Division 2 from the 2009-
10 season.

BOW STREET (Ceredigion) SN6284

Bow Street FC, who play at Cae Piod (Field of the Magpies),
were founder members of the Aberystwyth and District League
in 1934, and have always been known as the Magpies owing
to their black and white striped shirts. However, records show
that football has been played in the village since at least 1918.
Throughout their intermittent membership of the league, Bow
Street have found a home at various fields in the neighbourhood
including two fields at Cae Bryncastell, below the railway line at
the southern end of the village, and Cae Sir Pryse, located behind

Bow Street Post Office, owned by the neighbouring Pryse family of Plas Gogerddan. (This field was also used for cricket and rugby matches by Uppingham School, Rutland during their enforced stay at Borth in 1876-77 to recuperate from an outbreak of typhoid fever.) During the mid 1950s the 'defiant goalkeeeping' of local boy Dafydd Elystan Morgan, later MP for Cardiganshire and now a Labour peer, was frequently mentioned in the local press.

When Bow Street FC re-formed in 1977 after an absence of over twenty years, they played on a field at Pwllglas in neighbouring Dole, kindly loaned by a local farmer. In October 1979, Ceredigion District Council purchased 26 acres of land at public auction for housing in Bow Street village and, due to public pressure, designated five acres for recreational use. The field, situated opposite the local primary school, eventually became known as Cae Piod and was first used for a competitive match on 8 November 1980 when Bow Street entertained local derby rivals Borth United in a goalless draw. The club also played for one season on a field adjoining Cae Piod. Bow Street FC can now boast excellent facilities developed by an energetic local committee. After many years of success in the Aberystwyth and District League, the club submitted a successful application for promotion to the Mid Wales League in 2007.

BP LLANDARCY RFC

see LLANDARCY (Neath Port Talbot)

BRACKLA FC

see COYCHURCH (Bridgend)

BRADLEY (Wrexham) SJ3165

Garden Village Youth of the Welsh National League (Wrexham Area), Division 1 play at the Wauns, Bradley, near Gwersyllt Cricket Club. Gwersyllt Athletic FC of the Welsh National League (Wrexham Area), Division 1 also play at the Wauns, which has four pitches.

BRECON (Powys) SO0428

Rich Field, in the Watton area of Brecon, is the neat home of Brecon Corinthians (Corries) FC and is named after Herbert Charles Ingram Rich (1821-92), a successful Brecon coach builder who served as mayor of the borough in 1871. Elected to the council in 1865, he was elevated to the aldermanic bench in 1885. He was a prominent Wesleyan Methodist and Freemason. He died on 29 January 1892, and following a service at Lion Street Wesleyan Methodist Church on 3 February, was interred at Brecon Cemetery. His son and grandson, also named Herbert Charles Ingram, served as mayors of Brecon in 1905 and 1926 respectively. The son, educated at Christ College, Brecon, entered his father's business in 1898 and subsequently developed the coach-building firm into the modern business known as Brecon Motors Ltd, which is still based at Rich Way, Brecon. Brecon Corries, once a major force in Welsh League football, now play in the South Wales Senior League, Division 1.

Brecon RFC, one of the founding members of the Welsh

Rich Field, Brecon, home of Brecon Corinthians FC. Photograph: the author.

Rugby Union in 1881, play at Parc de Pugh, in the WRU National Division 3 South East. In 1978, a decision was made to purchase land at Watton Villa from John Prosser Pugh (1939-85), a local farmer and former pupil at Christ College, Brecon, and the field has been named in his honour. The ground boasts an impressive clubhouse, ample car parking, floodlighting, adjacent training pitches and an amusing stone memorial to John Prosser Pugh.

Canolfan Hamdden Aberhonddu/Brecon Leisure Centre also boasts several football and rugby pitches in an impressive complex.

BRICKFIELD RANGERS FC

see WREXHAM

BRIDGEND SN1745

The Brewery Field is the home of Bridgend Ravens, who were recently relegated from the WRU Premier Division, and the Celtic Crusaders Rugby League team who have competed in the Super League from 2009. Rugby has been played at Bridgend since 1878, and the club originally played on Quarella Field. In September 1930, the Welsh Rugby Union, with the support of Bridgend Urban District Council, purchased the Brewery Field, a 12-acre site, for £2,000, with the intention of building a 90,000-capacity Welsh national stadium on the site. It became the home of Bridgend RFC in 1931. As the name suggests, it was previously the site of a brewery, operated by Robert Henry Stiles. The Celtic Crusaders announced ambitious plans in December 2008 to develop a new stadium on the site of the former Island Farm prisoner-of-war camp on the outskirts of Bridgend that would also include facilities for Bridgend Ravens RFC and Bridgend Town FC. The Crusaders made their home debut in the Super League on 21 February 2009, losing 20-28 to Hull in front of 5,272 spectators. In September 2009, the Crusaders announced that they would move to Rodney Parade, Newport, for a two-year period.

Coychurch Road was the home of Bridgend Town FC, founded in 1954. The club played their last game there on 17 February 2007 following their decision to sell the ground to Asda to provide a new superstore for the town. The club has since fulfilled their fixtures at a temporary ground adjacent to Porthcawl Town's Lock's Lane ground with the aid of money provided by the supermarket group, at the University of Glamorgan Ty'n y Wern Fields at Treforest, and latterly at the Brewery Field.

Brewery Field, Bridgend, home of Bridgend Ravens RFC. Photograph: the author.

Bridgend Town played at Coychurch Road for forty-five years. Rugby league, represented by Cardiff Blue Dragons, and cricket have also been played at the ground. Bridgend Town remain committed to finding a permanent ground within the town, and currently play in the Welsh League, Division 1.

Waterton Cross is the home of the South Wales Police rugby team, formed in 1969 following the merger of four police forces in Glamorgan. They play in the WRU National Division 5 South Central. The football ground of the South Wales Constabulary, who once competed in the Welsh League, Division 2, is also located at Waterton Cross which was opened as a playing field on 7 November 1957. Gordon Westcott, in his detailed history of police rugby football in South Wales, notes that the area had been used throughout the Second World War for dumping waste from the vast Royal Ordnance Factory at Bridgend. Because of this involvement the fields were known locally as the 'Burning Ground'.

The extensive Newbridge Fields at Park Court Road, Bridgend are a hive of sporting activity. They are the home of Bridgend Athletic RFC, founded in 1939 and champions of the WRU National Division 2 West in 2008-09; Bridgend Sports RFC, founded in 1938, of the WRU National Division 5 South Central who play at the Bandstand Field; and Great Western Railway FC of the Bridgend District League, Premier Division. Brought up close to Newbridge Fields, the legendary Welsh fullback J P R Williams recalls in his autobiography how his father would take him there at a very young age to kick a rugby ball. Robert Howley, Wales and British Lions scrum half, and current backs coach of the Welsh team, played in a trial match on Newbridge Fields as a nine-year-old.

BRIDGEND CORINTHIANS FC

see COYCHURCH (Bridgend)

BRIDGEND STREET FC

see LLANRUMNEY (Cardiff) and SPLOTT (Cardiff)

BRITANNIA INN FC

see EBBW VALE (Blaenau Gwent)

BRITON FERRY (Neath Port Talbot) SS7394

Founded in 1926, Briton Ferry Athletic FC of the Welsh League, Division 3 play at the Old Road Ground, Briton Ferry, Neath. They played for four seasons in the top flight of Welsh football before being relegated in 1996-97. From 2009-10 the club will merge with Llansawel FC and will be known as Briton Ferry Llansawel FC.

Briton Ferry RFC play in the WRU National Division 3 South West at Ynysmaerdy, a ground provided through the generosity of one of Glamorgan's major landowners, Albert George Child-Villiers, the seventh earl of Jersey (1845-1915).

Baglan Rugby Club, formed in 1962, play at Tŷ Isaf Field, Thorney Road, Briton Ferry in the WRU National League Division 5 South Central.

Giant's Grave FC, founded in 1973, play in the Neath Football League, Premier Division at Parc Newydd Playing Fields, Briton Ferry. Reserve and youth games are played at the Wharf, Giant's Grave.

BRO CERNYW: CPD

see LLANGERNYW (Denbighshire)

BRO FFESTINIOG RFC

see TANYGRISIAU (Gwynedd)

BRO GORONWY: CPD

see MOELFRE (Anglesey)

BRO LLEU: CPD

see LLANLLYFNI (Gwynedd)

BROAD HAVEN (Pembrokeshire) SM8613

Broad Haven FC play in the Pembrokeshire League, Division 3 at Peasy Park, Sandyke Road, Broad Haven.

BROUGHTON (Flintshire) SJ3463

Airbus UK Broughton FC of the Principality Welsh Premier League play at the Airfield, a ground within the confines of the Airbus factory at Broughton. The club, formed in 1946, has played under several names, reflecting the changing ownership of the aerospace factory. It was admitted to the top flight of Welsh football in 2005, playing its first season at Y Morfa, the ground of Conwy United, whilst the Airfield was upgraded to the required standard.

BRUNSWICK FC

see TROEDYRHIW (Merthyr Tydfil)

BRUNSWICK UNITED FC

see SKETTY (Swansea)

BRYMBO (Wrexham) SJ2953

Brymbo FC of the Welsh National League (Wrexham Area), Premier Division play at the Brymbo Sports Complex, Tanyfron, Wrexham.

BRYN ROVERS

see BRYNAMAN (Carmarthenshire)

BRYNAMAN (Carmarthenshire) SN7114

Bryn Rovers of the Neath Football League, Premier Division play at Parc Maes Elwyn, Brynaman. Parc Maes Elwyn is named after John ('Jack') Elwyn Evans (1897-1941), who won one international rugby cap for Wales and subsequently played rugby league for Broughton Rangers. Alun Wyn Bevan, the Welsh rugby referee and commentator, is his great-nephew.

Organised rugby in the village dates from 1897 and the present Brynaman RFC play in the WRU National Division 3 South West, at the Recreation Field, Brynaman, known colloquially as the New Field, a ground purchased by the club and officially opened in 1953. Prior to that date the club had played on the notoriously bad Old Field from 1920. The earliest recorded field was at Ynyscwmgarw, but that had to be relinquished in 1904 as its owner was deeply affected by the religious revival which severely curtailed all sporting activity. After the effects of the revival had largely disappeared the team reconvened and played briefly on Brynaman Common, before moving once again to the rather marshy Waun Esgyrn in 1913.

BRYNAWEL FC

see WINCH WEN (Swansea)

BRYNCAE (Rhondda Cynon Taf) SS9882

Bryncae FC of the Bridgend and District League, Division 1 play at the Opencast Site, Llanharri Road, Bryncae.

BRYNCETHIN (Bridgend) SS9184

Bryncethin RFC, founded in 1890, play in the WRU National Division 5 South Central at the Bryncethin Rugby Field, located behind the Dunraven Hotel, Blackmill Road, Bryncethin.

BRYN-COCH (Neath Port Talbot) SS7499

Bryn-coch RFC, 2008-09 champions of the WRU National Division 4 South West, play at the Memorial Recreational Ground, Tyllwyd Road, Bryn-coch, Neath.

BRYN-CRUG (Gwynedd) SH6003

Tywyn-Bryn-crug, of the Mid Wales League, play at Cae Chwarae Bryn-crug. Tywyn-Bryn-crug first played as an amalgamated club during the 1989-90 season.

see also TYWYN (Gwynedd)

BRYNDEG FC

see CWMBWRLA (Swansea)

BRYNFORD (Flintshire) SJ1774

Brynford United, formed in 1922, of the Clwyd League Premier Division play at Hafod-y-Bryn, Brynford, Holywell.

BRYNHYFRYD (Swansea) SS6595

Cwm Press FC of the Swansea Senior Football League, Division 1; Wern FC of the Swansea Senior District League, Division 3; and Cwm Albion Colts of the Swansea Senior District League, Division 4 all play on pitches at Cwm Level, Brynhyfryd. It was on the Cwm Level pitches that the prestigious talents of Ivor Allchurch (1929-97) were first spotted by an eagle-eyed Swansea Town scout.

BRYNITHEL (Blaenau Gwent) SO2101

Brynithel RFC, formed in 1974, play at Brynithel Recreation Ground in the WRU National Division 5 East.

BRYN-MAWR (Blaenau Gwent) SO1851

Bryn-mawr RFC of the WRU National Division 2 East play at the Recreation Ground.

Nant-y-glo FC play in the North Gwent Football League, Division 1 at the Welfare Ground, Bryn-mawr.

BRYNNA (Rhondda Cynon Taf) SS9883

Brynna FC of the South Wales Amateur Football League, Division 2 play at the Welfare Ground, Brynna, Pontyclun.

BRYNTEG VILLAGE FC

see SOUTHSEA (Wrexham)

BRYNTIRION (Bridgend) SS8880

Bryntirion Athletic of the Welsh League, Division 1 play at Bryntirion Park, Llangewydd Road, Bridgend. Formed in 1956, this ambitious and progressive club initially ground-shared with Bridgend Town at Coychurch Road, before purchasing their own ground in 1997 with the support of the local authority. The ground has since been developed impressively with the support of commercial sponsors, lottery grants and significant personal donations. Floodlighting was also installed in 2008.

BTD STARS FC

see LLANRUMNEY (Cardiff)

BUCKLEY (Flintshire) SJ2764

Football was played at Buckley as early as 1860, and an organised team was established in 1877. Early games were played on Buckley Common and at Mill Lane. Various teams attained a fair measure of success until in 1977, Buckley Town FC was established following a merger between two Welsh league teams, Buckley Wanderers and Buckley Rovers. Initially, the new team played at the Hawksbury, near Elfed High School, before moving to a new purpose-built ground at the Globe, off Liverpool Road. Since the merger, the club has been a major force in the Cymru Alliance League but it surprisingly declined an opportunity to play at a higher level after winning the league in 2005.

BUILTH WELLS (Powys) SO0350

Founded in 1888, Builth Wells RFC of the WRU National League Division 1 West play at the Groe, located on the banks of the Wye, adjacent to the Eisteddfod Gorsedd stones erected in 1933. It is believed that the field was once part of the Thomas Lant estate.

Builth Wells FC and local rivals Builth Wednesdays FC both play in the Mid Wales League (South) at the Lant Fields, Love Lane. The fields are named after Thomas Lant (1865-1945), a native of Bakewell, Derbyshire, the son of John Lant and his wife Mary, who moved to Radnorshire in 1895 to open quarries at Llanelwedd and Llandrindod Wells. Dressed stone from his quarries was used to construct the Elan Valley

Lant Field, Builth Wells, home of Builth Wells FC. Photograph: the author.

dams for Birmingham Water Works, and Lant employed over three hundred men for a decade at the height of the project. He amassed a huge fortune of £133,864 from his business interests, some of which he chose to share with his employees. He also acquired and donated land in Builth and Llandrindod Wells for community recreational use, facilities now administered by Powys County Council. Thomas Lant was buried with his wife at St Matthew's Church, Llanelwedd on 6 February 1945; his wife predeceased him and was buried on 26 November 1926. The Lant Fields are extensive and include many football and rugby pitches. The main football pitch, located in the north-western corner, is an impressive facility with a neat grandstand, floodlighting and unusual galvanized perimeter fencing, with each individual section sponsored by a local business, and identified with separate name plaques.

BULWARK (Monmouthshire) ST5392

Bulwark FC play in the East Gwent Football League, Division 1 at Western Avenue Playing Field, Bulwark, Chepstow.

Chepstow Athletic FC play in the East Gwent Football League, Division 1 at the Mathern Road Ground, Bulwark, Chepstow.

Thornwell Red and White FC play in the East Gwent Football League, Division 1 at Thornwell Park, Bulwark, Chepstow.

BURRY PORT (Carmarthenshire) SN4401

Burry Port RFC of the WRU National Division 4 West and Burry Port FC of the Carmarthenshire League Premier Division play at the Memorial Park.

Porth Tywyn Suburbs played in the Welsh League from 1993 until 2004 at Suburbs Park, Burry Port. They currently play in the Carmarthenshire League, Division 3.

BUTETOWN (Cardiff) ST1874

Butetown/St Mary's FC played until 2009 in the South Wales Senior League, Division 1 at the Marl, Channel View Road, Butetown, Cardiff – as do South Park Athletic FC of the Cardiff Combination Football League, Premier Division.

AFC Butetown of the South Wales Senior League, Division 2 play at Loudoun Square (off Bute Park), Butetown, Cardiff.

BWLCH RANGERS FC

see DAFEN (Carmarthenshire)

BYNEA (Carmarthenshire) SS5499

Bynea RFC play in the WRU National Division 5 West at Tynygraig Road, Bynea, Llanelli.

CADOXTON (Vale of Glamorgan) ST1269

SP Construction FC of the Vale of Glamorgan Football League, Premier Division, and Cadoxton Athletic and AFC Tadross of Division 1, play at Pencoedtre Park.

Witchill Farm Ground in Cadoxton has been cited by Lile and Farmer as the scene of a turbulent football match in 1893 between Barry District and Cardiff.

CADOXTON CONS FC

see DINAS POWYS (Vale of Glamorgan)

CADOXTON IMPS FC

see BARRY (Vale of Glamorgan)

CAEHARRIS SPITE FC

see PENTREBACH (Merthyr Tydfil)

CAER BORDERERS RFC

see HOPE (Flintshire)

CAERAU (Bridgend) SS8594

Caerau FC of the South Wales Amateur Football League, Division 1 play at the Athletic Park, Humphreys Terrace, Caerau. Caerau has a rich football tradition and the club, then known as Caerau Albions, was formed in 1903 largely by immigrants from Cornwall, the Forest of Dean, North Wales and Somerset. In 1969 Caerau gained promotion to the Premier Division of the Welsh League, but within two seasons they found themselves in Division 2 after consecutive relegations. Caerau BC play in the Bridgend and District Football League, Division 1 at Caerau Welfare Park.

CAERAU (ELY) FC/RFC

see ELY (Cardiff)

CAE'R-BRYN (Carmarthenshire) SN5913

Cae'r-bryn AFC of the Carmarthenshire League, Division 2 play at the Cae'r-bryn Welfare Ground, near Llandybïe. The Welfare Association was established in 1934, and is connected with the former Cae'r-bryn Colliery which operated from 1879 until 1928. In 2007 a new welfare hall was officially opened at Cae'r-bryn and, as part of the £130,000 grant-aided project, a new football pitch was laid to replace an earlier field which had been absorbed by open-cast mining.

CAEREINION OLD BOYS RUGBY ASSOCIATION

see MEIFOD (Powys)

CAERGWRLE CASTLE FC

see LLAY (Wrexham)

CAERLEON (Newport) ST3390

Caerleon Town FC, formed in 1889, were admitted to the Welsh League in 1965 and are now established in Division 1. They play at Cold Bath Road, a name with Roman origins which is located close to several architectural remains from that era. They field a reserve side who play in the Newport and District Football League, Premier X Division, at Caerleon School.

Caerleon RFC, formed in 1970, play in the WRU National Division 6 East at the Broadway, Caerleon.

Newport High School Old Boys RFC, formed in 1932, one of the leading community clubs in Wales, play in the WRU

National League Division 3 East. During the club's early years it led a nomadic existence and several locations are recorded as its playing field. These include pitches at the Royal Oak, Bettws, Ponthir, Llanfrechfa and the old Caerleon Racecourse. In 1949 a field at the present site in Yew Tree Lane became available for rent and has since become the club's permanent home.

CAERNARFON (Gwynedd) SH4862

Yr Oval/The Oval, Marcus Street, home of Caernarfon Town FC, founded in 1878, who played in the Welsh Premiership until their relegation in 2009, is one of Wales' most historic grounds. The first game staged at this famous ground dates from 1888. Among the most memorable matches played at Yr Oval were epic battles in the 1986-87 season when the club enjoyed its most successful FA Cup run, defeating Stockport County and York City before losing in the third round to Second Division Barnsley at Oakwell in a replay.

Caernarfon Borough FC, formed in 1985, play in the Caernarfon and District League, Division 1 at Cae'r Aber, located on the foreshore of the Menai Straits.

Caernarfon Wanderers, champions of the Caernarfon and District League, Division 1 in 2008-09, play at Cae Top and will compete in the Gwynedd League from 2009-10.

The field is located close to the town's cemetery, near Llanbeblig Church. In 2006 Gwynedd County Council decided to use Cae Phillips, a field that also adjoins Cae Top, as an extension for the cemetery. Cae Phillips was famously used for filming many scenes in *C'Mon Midffild*, the Welsh-language television comedy.

Caernarfon RFC was established in 1973 and currently play in the WRU National Division 1 North. They play their home games at Y Morfa, a field adjacent to Ysbyty Eryri, which was first used by the club in 1980. Initially, Caernarfon RFC had played on Cae Ysgol Syr Hugh Owen and from 1975 until it acquired Y Morfa it played on a field at Parc Coed Helen.

CAERPHILLY S1586

Virginia Park is the home of Caerphilly RFC, formed in 1887, of the WRU National Division 1 East. The park's name is connected with the Goodrich family, who came to the Energlyn area of Caerphilly via Devon from Virginia in the United States. Virginia Park and Virginia Terrace in Caerphilly continue to provide evidence of this American connection. Virginia Park also hosted Southern League and Welsh League football from 1919-23.

Dafydd Williams Park is used for local football and is named in honour of David Williams (1738-1816), littérateur and political pamphleteer, who was born at Waunwaelod (later the Carpenters' Arms), in the parish of Eglwysilan. His chief claim to fame lies in his establishment of the benevolent Royal Literary Fund (the first meeting was held on 18 May 1790). During his last years he lived at the headquarters of the fund at 36 Gerrard Square, Soho, where he died on 29 June 1816.

Morgan Jones Park, laid out as a public recreation ground in 1934, was named in honour of Morgan Jones (1885-1939), Labour MP for Caerphilly from 1921-39. Jones, a former schoolteacher, was imprisoned as a conscientious objector during the Great War. He served as parliamentary secretary to the Board of Education, and was chairman of the Public Accounts Committee of the House of Commons from 1931-38. Morgan Jones Park is the home of AFC Caerphilly, who play in the South Wales Senior League, Division 2, and is also used by local football sides including Caerphilly Social and RTL Chemicals who play in the Taff Ely and Rhymney Valley Football League.

In his fascinating history of the football clubs of Caerphilly, Dave Collins mentions several other grounds in the town. These include the Malthouse Field, in the town centre, and the Beddau Fields on Nantgarw Road, opposite the Station Inn. The latter site is now given over to housing known as Boundfield Park.

CAERPHILLY TOWN FC

see FOCHRIW (Caerphilly) and LLANBRADACH (Caerphilly)

CAERSWS (Powys) SO0392

Caersws FC, founded in 1878, play in the Welsh Premiership at the compact Recreation Ground which is clearly visible to passing rail passengers on the Cambrian line. Some early games were played at Maesmawr Hall. Caersws have been the most successful village team in Wales and were founder members of the League of Wales. They won the Welsh Amateur Cup in 1962 and the Welsh Intermediate Cup in 1989. They represented Wales in the Intertoto Cup in 2002 losing 3-1 on aggregate to PFC Marek Dupnitsa of Bulgaria. Caersws' home leg, which ended in a 1-1 draw, was played at Park Avenue, Aberystwyth.

CAERWYS (Flintshire) SJ1272

Caerwys FC of the Clwyd League, Division 1 play at Cae Lôn Ysgol, Caerwys.

CAEWERN: AFC

see NEATH ABBEY (Neath Port Talbot)

CALDICOT (Monmouthshire) ST4788

Caldicot Town FC, founded in 1953, of the Welsh League, Division 1 play at Jubilee Way, Caldicot.

Caldicot Castle FC of the Gwent County League, Division 3 play in the Castle Grounds, Church Road, Caldicot.

Tippling Philosopher FC of the East Gwent Football League, Division 2 play at Caldicot Leisure Centre, Mill Lane, Caldicot.

Caldicot RFC play in the WRU National Division 5 East at Longfellow Road, a street named after American poet H W Longfellow (1807-82).

CALSONIC FC

see DAFEN (Carmarthenshire)

CAM GEARS FC

see RESOLVEN (Neath Port Talbot)

CAMBRIAN and CLYDACH FC

see CLYDACH VALE (Rhondda Cynon Taf)

CAMBRIAN WELFARE RFC

see CLYDACH VALE (Rhondda Cynon Taf)

CAMFORD SPORTS FC

see LLANELLI (Carmarthenshire)

CAMROSE (Pembrokeshire) SM9220

Camrose FC play in the Pembrokeshire League, Division 2 at the Folly Ground. B G Charles notes that 'the Folley near Camrose' is recorded in the Court of Great Session records in 1779.

CANTON (Cardiff) ST1676

Canton RFC play in the WRU National Division 5 South East at Lawrenny Road, Canton, Cardiff.

Canton Common was used for football by Riverside FC at the end of the nineteenth century. The club evolved into Cardiff City in 1908.

CANTON LIBS FC

see PONTCANNA (Cardiff)

CARDIFF ST1876

The site of Parc yr Arfau/Cardiff Arms Park was originally a meadow behind the Cardiff Arms Hotel owned by John Patrick Crichton-Stuart, third Marquess of Bute (1847-1900), who decreed that the land should only be used for recreational purposes. The land was sold in 1922 to Cardiff Athletic Club and the Welsh Rugby Union. There are two stadia on the site. The old National Stadium, built in 1969, was demolished in 1977 and the new Stadiwm y Mileniwm/Millennium Stadium – one of the world's most iconic grounds – was built in its place (completed to a north-south alignment in 1999 in time to host the Rugby World Cup). The rugby club still uses the name Cardiff Arms Park for its own ground, which is physically attached to the rear of Millennium Stadium's North Stand, and provides a home for Cardiff RFC who play in the WRU National Premiership League.

The stadium has hosted many stirring events during its long history. Although most famously associated with rugby football it was also host to the British Empire and Commonwealth Games in 1958, and during the period when Wembley Stadium was

Millennium Stadium, Cardiff. Crown Copyright, Royal Commission on the Ancient and Historical Monuments of Wales.

rebuilt it provided a temporary home for the FA Cup and League Cup finals. It was also a popular venue for greyhound racing.

Parc Ninian/Ninian Park, home of Cardiff City, in the Canton area of the city, is named after Ninian Patrick Crichton-Stuart (1907-10), who died at the age of two on 4 February 1910 at Falkland in Fifeshire. His father, Lt Col. Lord Ninian Edward Crichton-Stuart (1883-1915), son of John Patrick Crichton-Stuart, third Marquess of Bute (1847-1900), was educated at Harrow and Oxford before being elected as Unionist MP for Cardiff in December 1910. He served as colonel in the 6th Welch Regiment and became the fifth Member of Parliament to die in the Great War when he was killed in action on 3 October 1915. The ground was built on a former rubbish tip and was going to be called Sloper Park until Lord Ninian assisted the new club with financial guarantees. The ground was officially opened with a defeat in a friendly match against Aston Villa on 1 September 1910. Prior to this time Cardiff City, known as Riverside until 1910, had played at Cardiff Arms Park, Sophia Gardens, Canton Common and at the Harlequins Ground in Roath.

The last competitive match at Ninian Park was held on 25 April 2009 when Cardiff City entertained Ipswich Town in a Championship league match. The result, a very disappointing 0-3 defeat witnessed by 19,129 spectators, was to prove crucial to the Bluebirds' hopes of qualifying for the Premiership promotion play-off games. Cardiff City and Cardiff Blues will share the fine new Cardiff City Stadium from 2009-10 which is being built at a cost of £100m at the adjacent site of the former Cardiff Athletics Stadium at Leckwith. The stadium will have a capacity of around 27,000 with the potential to add a further 8,000 seats if required. As well as the stadium, the project will include a new athletics track together with significant retail, hotel and housing developments. The main contractors are Laing O'Rourke. The inaugural match at the stadium was played on 4 July 2009 when two teams comprising Cardiff City legends, including 65-year-old Jimmy Goodfellow, coached by former managers Lennie Lawrence and Eddie May played an entertaining game in front of almost 5,000 spectators. The first goal at the new stadium was scored by Graham Kavanagh.

During its 99-year history, Ninian Park has witnessed many historic occasions and hosted a variety of sports. It was the venue for showjumping during the 1958 British and Commonwealth Games and, on 14 October 1961, the stadium's record attendance

Ninan Park, Cardiff. Action from a match between Wales and Northern Ireland held on 11 April 1956 which ended 1-1. Photograph: Geoff Charles Collection, reproduced by kind permission of the National Library of Wales.

was set when 61,556 witnessed a 1-1 draw between Wales and England. Ninian Park was the venue on 15 June 1967 for the gallant attempt by Howard Winstone (1939-2000) to wrest the world featherweight championship from Mexican Vincente Salvidar. On 10 March 1971, Cardiff City defeated Real Madrid 1-0 in a European Cup Winners' Cup match at Ninian Park. It was also chosen as the venue for a national youth rally during the historic visit to Wales in June 1982 of Pope John Paul II (1920-2005).

Gerddi Sophia/Sophia Gardens, the home of Glamorgan County Cricket Club, is named after Sophia Rawdon-Hastings, daughter of Francis Rawdon-Hastings (1754-1826), first Marquess of Hastings, and wife of John Patrick Crichton-Stuart, third Marquess of Bute (1847-1900). She was involved in the development of Cardiff, and was concerned with providing open spaces for recreation in the rapidly expanding city in the late 1800s. Opened in 1858, it can possibly lay a claim to being the first urban park in Wales. Now best known as a venue for first-class cricket, some of Cardiff City's early football games were played on the ground. Following a recent sponsorship deal with SWALEC, part of the Scottish and Southern Energy Group, the ground has undergone total refurbishment using considerable private and public funds and has now been re-christened Stadiwm Swalec/Swalec Stadium. Despite being a rather controversial choice for the first test match in the 2009 England v. Australia Ashes series, it hosted the event very successfully and won over most of the sceptical critics who would have preferred to have seen the game at a more traditional test venue. In doing so, the stadium became the 100th ground to be used for a test match.

CARDIFF ACADEMICALS FC

see LECKWITH (Cardiff)

CARDIFF AIRPORT FC

see RHOOSE (Vale of Glamorgan)

CARDIFF ATHLETIC FC

see ELY (Cardiff)

CARDIFF CORINTHIANS FC

see RADYR (Cardiff)

CARDIFF COSMOS ATHLETIC FC

see RHIWBINA (Cardiff)

CARDIFF COSMOS.PORTOS FC

see LLANRUMNEY (Cardiff)

CARDIFF DRACONIANS FC

see GABALFA (Cardiff)

CARDIFF GRANGE HARLEQUINS

see LECKWITH (Cardiff)

CARDIFF HIBERNIANS FC

see PONTCANNA (Cardiff)

CARDIFF HSOB RFC

see WHITCHURCH (Cardiff)

CARDIFF ROVERS FC

see ELY (Cardiff)

CARDIGAN (Ceredigion) SN1746

Cardigan RFC (founded as early as 1876) of the WRU National Division 3 West and Cardigan Town FC of the Ceredigion League, Division 1 play on adjacent pitches at the King George V Playing Fields, Gwbert Road, Cardigan. Cardigan RFC played many of their early games on the County School Field.

Maes Radley is the home of Maesglas FC, founded in 1974, of the Ceredigion League, Division 1. The ground is named in honour of Ivor John Charles Radley BEM DL (1913-92), borough, town and district councillor and a major figure in the public life of Cardigan. He was the founding president of Maesglas FC. Poor drainage has afflicted the pitch during recent seasons, and Maesglas have recently been forced to play some of their home matches on three of their other registered pitches. These include Parc-y-dre, Cilgerran, Tegryn in Pembrokeshire (a pitch formerly used by the defunct Boncath FC) and an all-weather pitch at the West Wales All Terrain Park at Crugmor Farm, in neighbouring Penparc. The pitch at Maes Radley (formerly known as Dôlwerdd), was laid in 1997 during the development of the Afon Mwldan flood alleviation scheme, using waste material from a floodwater diversion tunnel.

CAREW (Pembrokeshire) SNO402

Carew FC of the Pembrokeshire League, Division 2 share the Carew Recreation Ground, Kesteven Close, Carew with the better known Carew Cricket Club.

CARMARTHEN (Carmarthenshire) SN4120

Carmarthen Park, the home of Carmarthen Quins RFC, who were promoted from the WRU National Division 1 West into the Welsh Premiership in 2009, has an interesting history. The 12-acre site was purchased by the borough council in 1899 and opened on Easter Monday 1900. It hosted the National Eisteddfod of Wales in 1911. The rugby pitch is surrounded by the earliest purpose-built cycle track in Wales. However, the first recorded rugby match to take place in the town was against Llandeilo on 3 January 1876 and was played at Picton Court, at the back of Picton Terrace. Other grounds used before the opening of Carmarthen Park include a field near Francis Well (adjacent to the West Wales General Hospital at Glangwili) and Norton's Field (located south of Pentrefelin Street near the slaughterhouse). Henry Norton, a brewer, originally from Derbyshire, twice served as mayor of Carmarthen in 1859 and 1871. A neighbouring field associated with the Morgans Arms in Upper Water Street was also used during the nineteenth century, and this field was used occasionally after the opening of Carmarthen Park. In 1911, the club leased a field behind Waterloo Terrace (on which Myrddin Crescent was later built) which became known as the Carmarthen Harlequins Athletic Ground. In 1962 the club purchased an eight-acre field at Parc-y-deri, near Abergwili, which it still owns and uses for reserve and youth fixtures.

Carmarthen Park in 1900 taken from the tower of St David's Church.
Photograph: J F Lloyd. Reproduced by kind permission of Carmarthenshire
County Museum.

Carmarthen Athletic RFC, founded in 1944, who play in the WRU National Division 1 West, originally shared Carmarthen Park with Carmarthen Quins. Some games were also played at Cillefwr Farm, Johnstown (now the site of an industrial estate) and Glan Tywi Farm, Abergwili. However, by 1965 the club had developed impressive facilities below Carmarthen Park at Five Fields, on land leased from the former Carmarthen Borough Council. Five Fields is now the site of a new Tesco Extra store, opened in November 2006, and the club has gained new facilities in Johnstown but has reverted to playing most of its home games at Carmarthen Park.

Parc Waun Dew/Richmond Park, opened in 1954, is the impressive home of Carmarthen Town FC, a club formed in

1948 who initially played in the Carmarthenshire Association Football League. Alan Latham has described the acquisition of the ground in programme notes, now available on the club's website. He noted that 'it was during the 1953-4 season that the Local Authority acquired the purchase of the Richmond Park ground, which was composed of a large grassland area divided up the middle by a hedge and with an abundance of shrubs, a few trees, and some derelict allotments'. By 1956 plans were well in hand to provide a large covered stand. However, the club encountered little consistent success until it achieved promotion to the Welsh Premiership in 1996. Since that date it has regularly qualified for European football, enjoying some successes and commendable performances. Carmarthen Town won the Welsh Cup in 2007, qualifying once more for the UEFA Cup, and following major improvements to Richmond Park with the opening of an impressive grandstand replacing the one which had served the club well for fifty years, the club was able to stage their first home European tie against Norwegian giants SK Brann of Bergen which they lost 0-8. The name Richmond is derived from *richmead* which in turn comes from the Welsh *waun dew* (rich meadow). This formed part of the common land of ancient Carmarthen.

Carmarthen United FC play in the Carmarthenshire League, Division 1 at Parc Myrddin, the former playing field of Queen Elizabeth Grammar School. For the 2008-09 season they will play under the name Carmarthen Town.

Inter Carmarthen FC play in the Carmarthenshire League, Division 3 at Parc Penllwyn, a ground on which Carmarthen

Athletic Soccer Section, the forerunners of Carmarthen Town, played their first trial match in 1946.

Jays FC (formerly Johnstown Jays) and Johnstown United, both of the Carmarthenshire League, Division 3 play on the Ystrad Fields.

Parc Hinds was established on former priory lands as a recreational area for the eastern end of Carmarthen town and includes a children's playground. The park was given to the town in 1927 by John Hinds (1862-1928), a draper who served as Justice of the Peace, Lord Lieutenant of Carmarthenshire, chairman of the Welsh Baptist Union, mayor of Carmarthen in 1926 and its Liberal Member of Parliament from 1910-22. Parc Hinds has been used to stage junior football matches.

CARMELTOWN (Blaenau Gwent) SO1611

Beaufort RFC play in the WRU National Division 6 East. Rugby was first played in the town from 1948 until 1955 at the Lower Beaufort Welfare Ground, Carmeltown. The present club dates from 1962, playing on a fine pitch developed on the site of an old rubbish tip at the Sports Ground, Carmeltown, Ebbw Vale.

Castle Brierly Hill FC of the North Gwent Football League, Premier Division and Rassau Rangers FC of the North Gwent Football League, Division 1 play at the Beaufort Welfare Ground.

CARNETOWN (Rhondda Cynon Taf) STO794

Grover's Field, Carnetown is the home of Abercynon Athletic FC, established in 1922, who played in the South Wales Amateur

Football League, Division 1 until their withdrawal from the league in August 2007. It is also the home of Carnetown BGC FC who play in the same league. The field is named after Henry Llewellyn Grover (1854-98), a solicitor who lived at Clydach Court, Abercynon and who was appointed deputy coroner of Cardiff. A native of Manchester, he died at a comparatively young age leaving a widow and five children. His brother Montagu was also a practising solicitor.

CARNO (Powys) SO9696

Carno FC of the Mid Wales League play at Tŷ Brith.

CARREG WEN FC

see TRALLWN (Swansea)

CARWAY (Carmarthenshire) SN4606

Carway FC, formerly of the Carmarthenshire League, played at the Carway Welfare Park. The team has re-formed after an absence of three seasons and played in Division 3 of the Carmarthenshire League in 2008-09.

CASCADE FC

see PEN-Y-BRYN (Caerphilly)

CASTELL ALUN COLTS FC

see HOPE (Flintshire)

CASTLE BRIERLY HILL FC

see CARMELTOWN (Blaenau Gwent)

CATHAYS CONSERVATIVES FC

see PONTCANNA (Cardiff)

CATHAYS TENANTS FC

see ELY (Cardiff)

CATHAYS UNITED FC

see PONTCANNA (Cardiff)

CEFN CRIBWR (Bridgend) SS8582

Cefn Cribwr RFC of the WRU National Division 5 South Central and Cefn Cribwr BGC FC of the Port Talbot Football League, Division 1 play on separate pitches at the Cae Gof Recreation Ground. Cae Gof is Welsh for Blacksmith's Field, and two blacksmiths are recorded in the village in the 1880 *Slater's Trade Directory*.

CEFN FFOREST (Torfaen) ST1697

Cefn Fforest FC play in the Gwent County League, Division 1 at the Stute, Cefn Fforest. Reserve team games are played on the Show Field, Cefn Fforest.

CEFN HENGOED (Caerphilly) ST1495

Cefn Hengoed FC play in the Taff Ely and Rhymney Valley Football Alliance, Premier Division. Their ground is situated at Hengoed Road.

CEFN UNITED FC

see RHOSYMEDRE (Wrexham)

CEFN-MAWR (Wrexham) SJ2842

Elements Europe Cefn Druids, founded in 1992 from the amalgamation of Cefn Albion FC and Druids United FC, play in the Welsh Premiership at Plas Kynaston Lane, Cefn-mawr, Wrexham. The team was formerly known as Flexys Cefn Druids when sponsored by Flexys, a major industrial company in the rubber industry operating at Cefn-mawr. For the last six seasons they have been sponsored by the North East Wales Institute of Higher Education (NEWI), Wrexham, and known as NEWI Cefn Druids. From 2009 they will carry the name of their new sponsors, Elements Europe, a construction company based at Oswestry. The team can trace its origins to the famous Druids FC, founded in the 1860s, winners of the Welsh Cup on eight occasions between 1880 and 1904. The Druids played on a field at Plas Madoc in Ruabon. Plas Kynaston Lane has been the home of Druids United and the merged Cefn Druids since 1961. The club has indicated that it wishes to move to a new stadium and plans have recently been approved for a new 3,000-capacity stadium at the Rock, Rhosymedre due for completion by December 2009. The existing ground will become a Tesco supermarket.

Ground plan of the new stadium proposed for Elements Europe Cefn Druids FC at the Rock, Rhosymedre, Wrexham. Reproduced by kind permission of J Ross Developments Ltd, Oswestry.

FC Cefn, champions of the Welsh National League (Wrexham Area), Division 1 and Communities First FC, who also played in Division 1, are both based at Tŷ Mawr Country Park, Cefn-mawr.

CEFNCOEDYCYMER (Merthyr) SO0307

Cefn Coed RFC play in the WRU National Division 5 South East at the Black Patch.

Cefn Coed FC play in the Merthyr Tydfil Football League, Division 1 at Teddington's Field, Cefn Coed. The field is named after Teddington Aircraft Controls who established a factory in Merthyr in 1946 which closed in the early 1970s. The firm was originally established at Teddington, Middlesex in 1928. The Drovers, a team new to Division 2 of the Merthyr Football League in 2008, also play at Teddington's Field.

CEFNEITHIN (Carmarthenshire) SN5513

The local rugby club, founded in 1922, play in the WRU National Division 4 West at Cae Carwyn James, which was completed in 1976. It is named in honour of local boy Carwyn James (1929-83), a Welsh rugby international who famously coached the British Lions to victory over the New Zealand All Blacks in 1971.

CEMAES BAY (Anglesey) SH3693

Cemaes Bay were members of the Welsh Premiership for three seasons, prior to being relegated in 1998, but they now find themselves playing in the bottom tier of the Anglesey League. Football has been played at Cemaes since 1870. The present club was formed in 1976 and initially used the sports and recreational facilities at the nearby Wylfa Power Station before moving to a ground adjacent to the Gadlys Hotel in 1980, staying there for just one season prior to returning to Wylfa. The purchase of the club's present ground, School Lane Stadium, was negotiated in 1988, and the site impressively developed in time to ensure admission to the League of Wales in 1995. It was formerly known as Pen-y-bryn Field.

CERRIGYDRUDION (Conwy) SH9548

CPD Cerrigydrudion of the Clwyd League, Division 1 play at Y Ganolfan, Ysgol Cerrigydrudion.

CHEPSTOW (Monmouthshire) ST5393

Chepstow Town FC, who now play in the Gwent Football League, Division 1, was established in 1878 and were one of six founding members of the Welsh League. They play their home games at the Larkfield Park Playing Fields, part of the former Larkfield Grammar School site.

Chepstow RFC, also probably founded in 1878, play at the Upton Memorial Ground, Western Avenue, Chepstow in the WRU National Division 4 East. Early games are recorded at the Larkfield, the Look-out Field (on top of Mounton Road where Chepstow Community Hospital now stands), Fairfield, where Fairfield Road now stands, and Crossley Crossway Green.

CHEPSTOW ATHLETIC FC

see BULWARK (Monmouthshire)

CHIRK (Wrexham) SJ2937

Chirk AAA FC, founded in 1876, one of the oldest football clubs in Wales, play in the Welsh National League (Wrexham Area), Premier Division. The legendary Billy Meredith (1874-1958) started his illustrious career with the club, and played for the team in two Welsh Cup finals in 1893 and 1894. Their home ground is at Holyhead Road, Chirk. In his club history, Nigel Roberts notes that, prior to the Great War, Lord Howard De Walden had given land at Holyhead Road to the trustees of the newly formed Chirk Amateur Athletic Association. The land was to be used at the discretion of the trustees for sports and games. It became the home of Chirk AAA FC and has remained so ever since.

Informal football games are also played at Brynkinalt Park, a new facility built on the site of the former Brynkinalt Colliery.

CHURCH VILLAGE (Rhondda Cynon Taf)

see LLANTWIT FARDRE (Rhondda Cynon Taf)

CHURCHSTOKE (Powys) SO2794

Churchstoke FC of the Montgomeryshire Amateur League, Division 2 play at the Recreation Field.

CILCENNIN (Ceredigion) SN5260

Cilcennin fielded a team in the Cardiganshire League for three seasons from 1975-78, playing on Cae Bwlch-y-dŵr and Cae'r Groesffordd.

CILFREW (Neath Port Talbot) SN7700

Cilfrew Rovers play in the Neath Football League, Division 1 at the Recreation Ground. The ground is owned by Blaenhonddan Community Council.

CILFYNYDD (Rhondda Cynon Taf) ST0892

Cilfynydd RFC of the WRU National Division 5 South East play at the Welfare Ground.

CILFYNYDD FC

see PONTYPRIDD (Rhondda Cynon Taf)

CILGERRAN (Pembrokeshire) SN1954

A team from Cilgerran has competed intermittently in the Cardiganshire/Ceredigion League from 1947 until 2003. Cilgerran won the title in season 1949-50. Cilgerran Rovers competed in the league until 2003. Matches were played at Parc-y-dre, a pitch that is still occasionally used by Maesglas and St Dogmael's reserve teams in the Ceredigion League.

CIMLA (Neath Port Talbot) SS7609

Cimla RFC, formerly of the WRU National Division 6 West, and Cimla Youth FC of the Neath Football League, Division 1, both play at the Cefn Saeson School Playing Fields.

CLARBESTON ROAD (Pembrokeshire) SN0121

Clarbeston Road FC, founded in 1960, play in the Pembrokeshire League, Division 1 at the Knock Playing Fields. The place-name *Knock* was first recorded in the village in 1331 and refers to a hillock or mound.

CLWB CYMRIC CAERDYDD FC

see PONTCANNA (Cardiff)

CLWB RYGBI CYMRY CAERDYDD

see PONTCANNA (Cardiff)

CLYDACH (Monmouthshire) SO2213

Clydach Wasps, 2008-09 champions of the Gwent County League, Division 1, play at the Clydach Welfare Ground, near Abergavenny.

CLYDACH (Swansea) SN6801

Sunnybank WMC FC play in the Neath and District Premier League at Coedgwilym Park, Pontardawe Road, Clydach. Clydach Sports of the Neath Football League, Division 1 also play at Coedgwilym Park.

INCO FC play in the Neath Football League, Division 2. INCO is the works team of VALE INCO nickel refinery plant, first established at Clydach by German industrialist Dr Ludwig Mond (1839-1909) in 1902, which employed over a thousand workers during the height of its production. The team is the oldest in Clydach and once competed in the Southern League and FA Cup prior to the Great War. It once boasted its own extensive works recreation ground, which also accommodated Glais and Vardre RFC. Much of this land was lost in 1986 to a new bypass, and what was not lost was added to an existing nine-hole golf course. INCO FC have since played at a number of public playing fields including Heol Las, Birchgrove, Ynystawe, Tir Canol, Morriston, Trallwn, Llansamlet and Tir Canol, Morriston.

CLYDACH: FC

see PONTARDAWE (Neath Port Talbot)

CLYDACH VALE (Rhondda Cynon Taf) SS9792

Cambrian and Clydach FC of the Welsh League, Division 1 and Tonypandy Albions FC of the South Wales Senior League, Division 1 both play at King George V New Field, Highfield Road, Clydach Vale.

Max United Falcons FC, a team from the Marxian Club Clydach Vale, also play on King George's Field, Clydach Vale in the Rhondda and District Football League.

Cambrian Welfare RFC play in the WRU National Division 6 Central at the Welfare Ground, Clydach Vale.

CMB FC

see RESOLVEN (Neath Port Talbot)

COACH and HORSES FC

see TREDEGAR (Blaenau Gwent)

COBRA RFC

see MEIFOD (Powys)

COED EVA (Torfaen) ST2793

Coed Eva Athletic FC, formed in 1982, but known as Golden Harvest and then Greenmeadow AFC until 2003, play in the Gwent County League, Division 1 at Penylan Fields.

COED-POETH (Wrexham) SJ2851

Coed-poeth United FC of the Welsh National League (Wrexham

Area) Premier Division play at the Pengelli Playing Fields, Coed-poeth, Wrexham.

COELBREN (Powys) SO8511

Coelbren Athletic play in the Neath District League, Division 2 at Pentwyn.

COGAN CORONATION FC

see PENARTH (Vale of Glamorgan)

COLCOT FC

see BARRY (Vale of Glamorgan)

COLWYN BAY FC

see OLD COLWYN (Conwy)

COLWYN BAY RFC

see RHOS-ON-SEA (Conwy)

COMMUNITIES FIRST FC

see CEFN-MAWR (Wrexham)

CONNAH'S QUAY (Flintshire) SJ2969

GAP Connah's Quay Nomads FC, founded in 1946 by Everton and Wales legend Tommy Jones (1917-2004), play in the Welsh Premiership at the Deeside Stadium, Kelsterton Road, Connah's Quay. Since 2008 they have been known as GAP Connah's

Quay following sponsorship from a major personnel recruitment firm. The club previously played at the Halfway Ground, Coast Road, Connah's Quay until 1997. Reserve matches are played at Dock Road. Their recent proposed merger with Flint Town United proved abortive.

Connah's Quay Albion, formerly of the Clwyd League, played at Golfryn Sports Centre, Deeside.

Wepre Rangers FC of the Clwyd League, Division 2 play at Wepre Park, Connah's Quay.

CONWY SH7777

Conwy United play in the Welsh Alliance League at Y Morfa, Penmaen Road, Conwy. The team was one of the founder members of the League of Wales in 1992, and played in the top flight for eight years.

COOKES UNITED FC

see PENRHYNDEUDRAETH (Gwynedd)

COOPER'S ARMS FC

see MORRISTON (Swansea)

CORNELLY (Bridgend) SS8281

Cornelly United FC of the Port Talbot Football League, Premier Division play at Meadow Street.

CORRIS (Gwynedd) SH7507

Corris United of the Aberystwyth and District Football League, Division 2 play at the King George V Playing Fields in Corris Isaf.

CORUS (STEEL) FC/RFC

see MARGAM (Neath Port Talbot)

CORWEN (Denbighshire) SJ0743

Corwen Amateurs FC of the Welsh National League (Wrexham Area) Premier Division play at the War Memorial Park, Green Lane, Corwen.

Clwb Rygbi Corwen, a Welsh Districts club, play at Parc Dyfrdwy.

COSMOS FC

see NEWPORT

COURT HOUSE FC

see MERTHYR TYDFIL

COWBRIDGE (Vale of Glamorgan) SS9974

Cowbridge RFC play in the WRU National Division 5 South East at the Cowbridge Athletic Ground. Although rugby was played locally as early as 1874 when Cardiff RFC visited Cowbridge Grammar School, the game appears only to have gained popularity in the town after the Second World War.

In the early twentieth century, Cowbridge had two football

teams: Cowbridge Town, who played on the Cricket Field, and the Albions who played on a field adjoining Aberthin Road.

Local football is also played at the Corntown Playing Fields and at the all-weather pitch at Bear Field.

COYCHURCH (Bridgend) SS9379

Brackla FC of the Bridgend and District League, Premier Division, and Bridgend Corinthians FC of the Bridgend and District League, Division 1 both play at the Coychurch Playing Fields.

CPD (CLWB PÊL-DROED)...

see under name of club, e.g. BRO GORONWY

CRANNOG FC

see LLANGRANNOG (Ceredigion)

CRC RANGERS FC

see MORRISTON (Swansea)

CREIGIAU (Cardiff) ST0881

Creigiau FC of the Cardiff and District League, Premier Division play at the Recreation Ground, Creigiau.

CRICKHOWELL (Powys) SO2118

Crickhowell FC play in the Gwent County League, Division 3 at the Elvicta Playing Field. The field takes its name from Elvicta Wood Engineering Ltd, who are based in the town.

CRICKHOWELL RFC

see GLANGRWYNEY (Powys)

CROESERW (Neath Port Talbot) SS8795

Tudor Park, St David's Place, Croeserw, is the home of Maesteg Park FC, formed in 1945, who play in the Welsh League, Division 2, and who were briefly in the League of Wales. The ground is named in honour of Tudor Isaac (1912-99), surveyor and engineer to the Maesteg Urban District Council from c.1926.

Tudor Park was also the home of Croeserw FC, formed in 1992, and Croeserw United, formed in 2004, who play in the Port Talbot Football League, Division 1. However, since 2003 they have played their home games at Caerau Park, Brambles Football Field and Maesteg Swing Park, all in Maesteg. The club returned to Tudor Park in September 2008.

CROESYCEILIOG (Torfaen) ST3096

Croesyceiliog RFC, founded in 1881, of the WRU National Division 3 East play at Woodland Road, Croesyceiliog, Cwmbrân.

Croesyceiliog FC, founded in 1964, of the Welsh League, Division 2 also play at the Woodland Road complex.

The North and Southfield Recreation Ground at Croesyceiliog is also used by several teams from the Newport and District League.

CROMWELL YOUTH FC

see LLISWERRY (Newport); NEWPORT

CROSS HANDS (Carmarthenshire) SN5612

Cross Hands Hotel FC of the Carmarthenshire League, Division 3 play at Cross Hands Park, known also as Cae Pownd.

CROSS INN FC

see LLANRUMNEY (Cardiff)

CROSS KEYS (Caerphilly) ST2291

Cross Keys RFC of the WRU National League Premier Division play at Pandy Park, a field originally known as George Hoare's Field, named in all probability after George H Hoare (b.1847), a native of Whitcombe, Somerset, who worked in the local collieries. Rugby was first played in the area in 1876 and, when Cross Keys RFC was officially formed in 1900, the name of Hoare's Field was changed to Pandy Park, reflecting its geographic location below Pandy Mill. *Pandy* is Welsh for fulling mill.

Cwm-carn Athletic FC play in the Newport and District League, Division 1 at Waunfawr Park, Cross Keys. The park dates from Edwardian times and includes rugby, football and cricket pitches.

CRUMLIN (Caerphilly) ST2198

Crumlin RFC, founded in 1880, of the WRU National League Division 4 East play at the South Celynen Playing Fields, known locally as the Kayfield. Their playing field is located on the site of the former Celynen South Colliery which closed in 1981. Celyn(n)en is Welsh for holly tree.

CRUNDALE (Pembrokeshire) SM9718

West Dragons FC, a newly formed team who compete in the Pembrokeshire Football League, Division 4, play at the Rudbaxton Community Ground, Crundale.

CRYMYCH (Pembrokeshire) SN1833

Crymych RFC play in the WRU National Division 3 West at Parc Lloyd Thomas. The club was formed in 1984 and entered the national league in 1995, playing their matches at Cae London

Parc Lloyd Thomas, Crymych. Reproduced by kind permission of the photographer, Lawrence Hourahane, Tenby.

House which was renamed Parc Lloyd Thomas in 1992 in honour of the club's secretary, David Lloyd Thomas (1946–89). He was born at Mynachlog-ddu, Pembrokeshire, and educated at Crymych Primary School, Narberth Grammar School and the University of Wales, Bangor. After graduating, he returned to his native county, operating his own agricultural and building supplies business, and he was instrumental in ensuring the early success of Crymych RFC as its founding secretary. His parents ran the London House inn at Crymych and owned the adjacent field. He died on 11 November 1989, aged 43, and is survived by his widow, Mary, and sons, David and Daniel.

CRYNANT (Neath Port Talbot) SN7904

Crynant RFC play in the WRU National Division 5 South West. One of their earliest games, recorded in 1898, was played on a field where the present welfare hall now stands. The religious revival of 1904-05 curtailed sporting activities in the village for many years and the club was not re-formed until 1908 when the team played on the Maesmawr Field, which was owned by the club captain, Arthur Jones. The club moved to its present field, adjacent to Maesmawr Field, on 10 April 1956.

CWM (Blaenau Gwent) SO1805

Cwm Sports FC played in the North Gwent League, Division 1 but disbanded in 2007-08. They played at the Cwm Betterment Recreation Field.

Cwm Welfare Youth team, which also disbanded in 2007-08, fielded a senior side in the North Gwent League in 2008-09, and also played at the Cwm Betterment Recreation Field.

CWM ALBION COLTS FC

see BRYNHYFRYD (Swansea)

CWM NI FC

see BLAENRHONDDA (Rhondda Cynon Taf)

CWM PRESS FC

see BRYNHYFRYD (Swansea)

CWM SOCIAL FC

see CWMBWRLA (Swansea)

CWM WANDERERS FC

see CWM-TWRCH (Neath Port Talbot)

CWM WELFARE FC

see BEDDAU (Rhondda Cynon Taf)

CWMAMAN (Rhondda Cynon Taf) ST0099

Cwmaman Institute of the Welsh League, Division 3, founded in 1965 as Ivy Bush FC, play at Canolfan Cwmaman, Glanaman Road, Cwmaman, Aberdare.

CWMAMMAN UNITED FC

see GLANAMAN (Carmarthenshire)

CWMAVON (Neath Port Talbot) SO2607

Cwmavon RFC play in the WRU National Division 3 South West at the Welfare Ground.

Cwmafan Phoenix FC and Cwmafan Welfare, formed in 2004 from the Phoenix's second team, both play in the Port Talbot Football League, Premier Division. Phoenix play at the Welfare Ground, on a pitch that is adjacent to the rugby ground, whilst Welfare play at Parc-y-llyn.

CWM-BACH (Rhondda Cynon Taf) SO0201

Cwm-bach Royal Stars FC play in the South Wales Senior League, Division 1 at the Recreation Ground, Blaennantygroes Road, Cwm-bach.

CWMBRÂN (Torfaen) ST2995

Cwmbrân Stadium, the home of Cwmbrân Town, founded in 1950, is one of the largest and most impressive non-league stadiums in Wales. Originally intended primarily as an international athletics stadium, it has been used by Cwmbrân Town since 1975 and has staged some significant cup ties. Cwmbrân Town were the inaugural winners of the League of Wales and its first representatives in the European Champions' Cup, entertaining and defeating Cork City 3-2 on 18 August 1993 in front of 8,000 spectators. The tie was eventually lost on the away goals rule. Cwmbrân Town currently play in the Welsh League, Division 1.

Cwmbrân Celtic FC of the Welsh League, Division 2 play at Celtic Park, Henllys Way, Cwmbrân, adjacent to Cwmbrân Stadium.

Sebastopol FC, formed in 1973, now play at Cwmbrân Park since their promotion to the Gwent County League, Division 3. Their second team still play at their historic home at Alexandra Road, Sebastopol. Several teams who play in the Newport and District League are also based at Cwmbrân Park: Cwmbrân Centre FYP play in Division 3; Henllys Rangers play in the Premier Division X; St Dials FC, based in the suburbs of Cwmbrân, play in Division 2; and Oakfield FC, near Cwmbrân, play in the Premier Division X. The North and Southfield Recreation Ground at Croesyceiliog are also used by some of these teams.

Lucas Cwmbrân FC play in the Gwent County League, Division 2 at the Lucas Girling Sports Field, Cwmbrân.

Cwmbrân RFC play in the WRU National Division 3 East at the King's Head Ground.

CWMBWRLA (Swansea) SS6595

Bryndeg FC of the Swansea Senior District League, Division 3, and Cwm Social FC of the Swansea Senior District League, Division 3, play at Cwmbwrla Park, Maesglas Road, Cwmbwrla, Swansea, a playing field where John Charles (1931-2004) honed his skills until dusk in the company of his school friends, and where, in August 1948, he was spotted by Leeds United scout Jack Pickard.

CWM-CARN ATHLETIC FC

see CROSS KEYS (Caerphilly)

CWMFFRWDOER SPORTS FC

see PONTNEWYDD (Torfaen)

CWMGORS RFC

see GWAUNCAEGURWEN (Neath Port Talbot)

CWM-GWRACH RFC

see BLAEN-GWRACH (Neath Port Talbot)

CWMLLYNFELL (Neath Port Talbot) SN7412

Cwmllynfell RFC, founded in 1904, of the WRU National Division 1 West play at Bryn Park.

CWMPARC LEGION FC

see TREORCHY (Rhondda Cynon Taf)

CWMRHYDYCEIRW (Swansea)

see MORRISTON (Swansea)

CWMTILLERY (Blaenau Gwent) SO2105

Abertillery Excelsiors, founded in 1910, formerly of the Welsh League, Division 3, play at the Woodland Field, Cwmtillery, which was opened in the mid 1950s. They were relegated to the Gwent County League, Division 1 at the end of the 2008 season.

The Jim Owen Memorial Field was created as a recreational facility in 1994 on the site of the former Cwmtillery Colliery.

The now disbanded Cwmtillery RFC played on this field. They also played on the Bridgend Field, Cwmtillery and on the Woodland Field.

CWM-TWRCH (Neath Port Talbot) SN7511

Cwmtwrch RFC, founded in 1890, play at Glyncynwal Park in the WRU National Division 5 South West. The field is on land which once belonged to Glyncynwal Uchaf Farm, Lower Cwmtwrch.

Cwm Wanderers FC play in the Neath Football League, Premier Division, at the Brynderi Field.

CWRT-Y-FIL FC

see LLANDOUGH (Vale of Glamorgan)

CYMMER (Neath Port Talbot) SS8696

Abercregan Refresh FC of the Port Talbot Football League, Division 1, play at the Red Field, Cymmer. The team takes its name from the Refreshment Rooms, a public house based in the preserved Great Western Railway station.

CYNCOED (Cardiff) ST1880

UWIC FC of the Welsh League, Division 2 and UWIC RFC of the WRU Division 1 East both play at the Cyncoed Campus, Cyncoed, Cardiff.

DAFEN (Carmarthenshire) SN5201

Dafen Welfare Park, or Dafen Park, as it is most commonly known, provides a home for Dafen Cricket Club and Dafen Welfare FC who play in the Carmarthenshire League Premier Division. The football team was formally established in 1925 and as noted by Paul Clement in his detailed historical notes on the club's website, early games were played at Cilsaig and Cae Flat, Pen-y-fan until the Welfare Park was opened.

Calsonic FC of the Carmarthenshire League, Premier Division play at the Calsonic Sports Grounds, Llethri Road, Dafen, Llanelli. Calsonic Kansei Europe PLC is a car parts conglomerate.

Bwlch Rangers formed in 1926 but folded in 1973, only to be re-formed in 1975. They play at Glandafen Park in the Premier Division of the Carmarthenshire League.

DARREN INN FC

see RISCA (Newport)

DEFAID DU FC

see LLANDRINIO (Powys)

DEINIOLEN (Gwynedd) SH5763

Deiniolen FC, formerly of the Caernarfon and District League, played at Y Bwthyn, a relatively new venue opened on 2 July 1994. Prior to that date, the club, which dates from the early 1950s, played its home games at Ysgol Brynrefail, Llanrug. The club recently re-formed after an absence of three years from local football, but again withdrew from the league in 2008 after only one season.

DENBIGH (Denbighshire) SJ0566

Denbigh Town FC, formed in 1880, are considered one of the most historic, successful and ambitious clubs in the region, and were winners of the Welsh Amateur Cup in 1924. They play at Central Park, which has impressive facilities, and the club was promoted to the Cymru Alliance League in 2007, having enjoyed an earlier period at that level between 1996 and 2002.

Caeau Les Phillips Fields are named in honour of the first president and principal driving force behind the formation of Clwb Rygbi Dinbych (Denbigh Rugby Club) who now play in the WRU National League Division 1 North. The fields were formerly known as Graig Fields. The King's Mill Field and Denbigh High School Field were also used by North Wales Hospital RFC, formed in 1972, and Denbigh RFC, formed in 1977, who amalgamated in 1993 to form Clwb Rygbi Dinbych.

David Leslie Phillips was born at Cwm-ffrwd, near Carmarthen, on 11 November 1921. Educated at the Queen Elizabeth Grammar School, Carmarthen, he graduated from St David's College, Lampeter in 1947, having had his education interrupted by war service in the Middle East and North Africa, where he rose to the rank of major in the Royal Horse Artillery. He undertook a postgraduate qualification in teaching at the University College of Wales, Aberystwyth, and spent the rest of his career in that profession, becoming headmaster of Ysgol Fron-goch, Denbigh. Phillips was a remarkable sportsman:

he played first-class rugby for Llanelli and for English premier club Waterloo, and he was also Welsh shot-put champion in 1947. He served many organisations with distinction, including the Commonwealth Games Committee for Wales, the Royal Welsh Agricultural Society, the Urdd National Eisteddfod and the Church in Wales where he was a lay-preacher. His wife, Margaret, a local Justice of the Peace, pre-deceased him. Leslie Phillips died aged 68 on 27 February 1990. He is survived by his three sons.

DENTICARE TONNA FC

see NEATH ABBEY (Neath Port Talbot)

DEPORTIVO CENTRICA FC

see ELY (Cardiff)

DERI (Caerphilly) SO1201

Deri Broncos RFC play in the WRU National Division 5 South East at Parc Deri Newydd.

DEVAUDEN GREEN FC

see SHIRENEWTON (Monmouthshire)

DEWI STARS FC

see LLANDDEWIBREFI (Ceredigion)

DINAS POWYS (Vale of Glamorgan) ST1571

Dinas Powys RFC, formed in 1882, play in the WRU National Division 5 South East. Early games were played on Dinas Powys Common, and the area has since remained the home of the club. Considerable work was undertaken to level the pitch in the 1970s in order to rid it of its famous slope, work that was completed in time for the 1979-80 season. The club used its reserve pitch at Parc Bryn-y-don during this period.

Dinas Powys FC, founded in 1974, of the Welsh League, Division 1 play at the Murch Field, Sunnycroft Lane, Dinas Powys. The club also played at Dinas Powys Common prior to moving to the Murch Field.

Cadoxton Cons FC of the South Wales Senior League, Division 2, Elec Tec FC formerly of the Vale of Glamorgan League, Premier Division and Glenbrook (Division 1) also play at Parc Bryn-y-don.

DINAS ROCK FC

see ABERDARE (Rhondda Cynon Taf)

DOLGELLAU (Gwynedd) SH7217

Dolgellau AAFC were champions of the Aberystwyth and District League, Division 1 in 2009 and were promoted to the Mid Wales League. They play at Y Marian Mawr, along with Dolgellau RFC of the WRU National Division 2 North, although on a separate pitch. Y Marian is a large, open green space, given in trust to the town in 1811, and has been the focus of the town's recreational facilities for several generations. It included a bowling green in the sixteenth century and was also a popular venue for cockfighting and street fairs as depicted by Marion Eames in her novel *Y Stafell Ddirgel*. It was the site of the National Eisteddfod in 1948, commemorated by the Gorsedd stones which remain a prominent feature of the park. Y Marian has also served as the venue for the popular annual music festival, Sesiwn Fawr Dolgellau.

DOLWYDDELAN (Gwynedd) SH7355

Clwb Rygbi Bro Ffestiniog, established in 1973, played their early games at Cae Pont-y-Pant, Dolwyddelan.

DOWLAIS (Merthyr Tydfil) SO0707

Dowlais RFC play in the WRU National Division 4 South East at Blaen Dowlais.

The Lord Raglan FC, a team new to Division 2 of the Merthyr Football League in 2008, also play at Blaen Dowlais.

DREFACH FELINDRE (Carmarthenshire) SN3538

Parc Puw is the home of Bargod Rangers FC who play in the Ceredigion League, Division 2. The impressive gates to the park were donated by D L James, Gilwen View, Dre-fach in 1973. Earlier games were played at Llysnewydd. The club, formed in 1897, was a founder member of the Cardiganshire League in 1921 and has produced many players who later went on to play Welsh league football. John Davies, an exceptional goalkeeper, went from Bargod to play in the football league with Cardiff City, before joining Hull City in 1980. Davies has remained with

Hull City and is the club's Football in the Community manager. Alun Ffred Jones, the present Welsh Culture Minister, also played in goal for Bargod Rangers. The club changed its name from Bargoed Rangers to Bargod Rangers in January 1975.

DROVERS FC

see CEFNCOEDYCYMER (Merthyr Tydfil)

DUFFRYN (Newport) ST2985

Duffryn FC played in the Newport and District Football League, Premier Division X at Duffryn High School, Lighthouse Road, Duffryn, Newport, but disbanded at the end of 2008.

DUGOUT: FC

see EBBW VALE (Blaenau Gwent)

DUI DRAGONS FC

see PONTPRENNAU (Cardiff)

DUNVANT (Swansea) SS5993

Dunvant RFC, formed in 1887, of the WRU National Division 2 West play at Broadacre. Early games were played at Upper Killay and Cae Banel, the team relocating to a field at Cwm-y-glo Farm in the 1930s, before moving to a field on the edge of a quarry at Penlan Farm and 'to the infamous slope of Heaslelands Chicken Farm at Goytre Fawr'. The team finally settled at their present home at Broadacre in 1969, which has subsequently been developed into an impressive facility.

DYFFRYN: CLWB RYGBI

see VALLEY (Anglesey)

DYFFRYN BANW FC

see LLANGADFAN (Powys)

EBBW VALE (Blaenau Gwent) SO1609

Eugene Cross Park, Newchurch Road, Ebbw Vale is the home of Ebbw Vale RFC, who play in the WRU National League Premier Division, as well as cricket clubs, and was the home of Ebbw Vale FC whilst they competed in the League of Wales from 1991 to 1998. It was also home to the short lived Ebbw Vale rugby league side that played from 1907–12. The field, originally known as Bridgend Field in the mid nineteenth century, was later

Eugene Cross Park, Ebbw Vale. Reproduced by kind permission of the photographer, Richard Whitcome, Ebbw Vale.

purchased by the Ebbw Vale Steel, Iron and Coal Company who realised the importance of healthy recreation for their employees. To this end they formed the Ebbw Vale Welfare Association in November 1919, which bought the Bridgend Field and associated lands extending to 26 acres. The Bridgend Field then became known as the Beaufort Welfare Ground.

In 1973 its name was again changed to Eugene Cross Park in honour of Sir Eugene Cross (1896-1981), the influential and long-standing chairman of the welfare trustees. Cross was born on 13 September 1896 at 15 Gantra Row, Ebbw Vale, the eldest son of Eugene Cross, a first-generation Irish immigrant whose father William Cross was a native of Cork. He served in the Great War at Gallipoli and in France, and was awarded the Military Medal. He was a founder member of the Ebbw Vale Labour Party, served as a justice of the peace from 1941, was awarded the MBE in 1954 and was knighted in 1979. In 1967-68 he served as vice chairman of the Welsh Hospital Board. He died on 27 November 1981.

RTB (Ebbw Vale) RFC, formed in 1953 as a works team at the Richard Thomas and Baldwin steelworks, of the WRU National Division 5 East, and RTB Ebbw Vale FC of the Gwent County League, Division 1, both play at the Hilltop Stadium.

Britannia Inn FC, based in the Newtown area of Ebbw Vale, and FC Dugout, both of the North Gwent Football League Division 1, also play at the Hilltop Stadium.

EFAILNEWYDD (Gwynedd) SH3535

Pwllheli RFC, formed in 1972, play in the WRU National League Division 1 North at Parc Bodegroes.

ELEC TEC FC

see DINAS POWYS (Vale of Glamorgan)

ELEMENTS EUROPE CEFN DRUIDS FC

see CEFN-MAWR (Wrexham)

ELY (Cardiff) ST1376

The Glamorgan Wanderers, a WRU National Premier League rugby team, play at the Memorial Ground, Ely, on the western fringes of Cardiff. The club was founded in October 1893 by a group of ex-pupils of Monkton House School, and the name Glamorgan Wanderers Rugby Football Club was adopted in 1913 in preference to Old Monktonians. The Wanderers certainly lived up to their new name well, playing at seven different grounds, including Sophia Gardens, Tydraw Road (Penylan), Bishop's Field (Llandaff), and several locations in Whitchurch and Llandaff North until they settled at their present ground in 1952. This was purchased by raising money through various appeals in post-war Cardiff. As its name implies, the Memorial Ground is dedicated to all those players who lost their lives in the two world wars.

Caerau (Ely) of the Welsh League, Division 2, founded in 1955, play at Cwrt-yr-Ala, Ely, Cardiff. Grange Harlequins of the Welsh League, Division 2 are also using the ground as a temporary home. It was also the home of AFC Cardiff, once of the Welsh League, National Division. Caerau (Ely) RFC of the WRU National Division 6 Central also play at the same complex.

Fairwater Rebels and Trelai FC of the Cardiff and District

Football League, Premier Division; Cardiff Rovers FC and Deportivo Centrica FC of Division 1; Cathays Tenants FC and St Joseph's OB FC of Division 2; Sporting Llandaff of Division 3 and Inter Cardiff FC of Division 4 all play at Trelai Park. The park, a facility opened in 1933, is also home to several teams who play in the Cardiff Combination Football League. These include Avenue Hotspurs FC of the Premier Division, Fairwater Hotel FC (since relegated from that division), RAFA Boys FC, who clinched the Division 1 title in 2009, and the 4th Home Guard Ely FC.

ELY RANGERS FC

see WENVOE (Cardiff)

ENTO ABERAMAN ATHLETIC FC

see ABERAMAN (Rhondda Cynon Taf)

EVANS and WILLIAMS FC

see LLANELLI (Carmarthenshire)

EVANSTOWN (Rhondda Cynon Taf) SS9789

Gilfach-Goch Athletic FC of the South Wales Amateur Football League, Division 2 play at the Abercerdin School Field, Kenry Street, Evanstown.

FAIRFIELD UNITED FC

see TALYWAIN (Torfaen)

FAIROAK FC

see HEATH (Cardiff)

FAIRWATER (Cardiff) ST1377

Fairwater FC, founded in 1978, were champions of the South Wales Senior League, Division 1 in 2008-09 and play at Poplar Park, Fairwater, Cardiff. Their present facilities do not meet the criteria for promotion to the Welsh League, and a possible move to Canton High School is being explored.

Fairwater RFC play in the WRU National Division 3 South East at Waterhall Park, behind Fairwater Leisure Centre.

FAIRWATER HOTEL FC

see ELY (Cardiff)

FAIRWATER REBELS FC

see ELY (Cardiff)

FAIRWOOD (Swansea) SS5919

Killay AFC, formed in 1972, play their home games in the Carmarthenshire League, Division 3 at the Swansea University playing fields at Fairwood Common, Gower Road.

FALL BAY RFC

see SCURLAGE (Swansea)

FELIN-FACH (Ceredigion) SN5255

Felin-fach FC play in the Ceredigion League, Division 2 at Cae Chwarae Felin-fach.

FELIN-FOEL (Carmarthenshire) SN5202

The Felinfoel Recreation Ground (King George Playing Field), owned by Llanelli Rural Council, is home to the local cricket, football and rugby teams.

Felinfoel RFC play in the WRU National Division 1 West, while Felinfoel FC play in the Carmarthenshire League, Division 1.

FELINHELI (Gwynedd) SH5267

Although football has been played in the village since the nineteenth century, the present CPD Felinheli was founded in 1977. The team play in the Caernarfon and District League, Division 1 at Cae Seilo, Ffordd Bangor. The former Seilo Welsh Congregational Chapel is adjacent to the ground.

FERNDALE (Rhondda Cynon Taf) SS9997

Rugby was first played at Ferndale in the Rhondda Fach Valley in 1882 at Darran Park until the team disbanded in 1921. It was re-formed in 1989 and games were played initially at Blaenllechau Park. The club now play in the WRU National Division 4 South East at Greenwood Park, once the site of the infamous Banana tip, which was eventually landscaped in the 1980s.

Ferndale FC enjoyed a very prosperous period in the 1960s

when they were one of the strongest teams in the Welsh League. During that period they also played at Darran Park, and were one of the first clubs in Wales to install an artificial pitch. The club now play in the Rhondda and District Football League and have relocated to neighbouring Maerdy. Ferndale Boys' Club play in the South Wales Amateur Football League, Division 2 at Maerdy Field, Rowley Terrace, Maerdy.

FERNHILL FLYERS FC

see MOUNTAIN ASH (Rhondda Cynon Taf)

FFAIR-FACH (Carmarthenshire) SN6323

Llandeilo FC play in the Carmarthenshire League, Division 2 in the neighbouring village of Ffair-fach, on a field behind Heol Myrddin.

FFOSTRASOL (Ceredigion) SN3747

Ffostrasol Wanderers FC of the Ceredigion League, Division 1 play at Parc Troedyrhiw.

FFYNNONGROYW (Flintshire) SJ1382

Point of Ayr FC of the Clwyd League, Division 1 play at Ffynnongroyw Playing Fields.

FIELDS PARK PONTLLAN-FRAITH FC

see PONTLLAN-FRAITH (Caerphilly)

FISHGUARD (Pembrokeshire) SM9537

Fishguard Sports FC of the Pembrokeshire League, Division 2 play at St Mary's.

Fishguard and Goodwick RFC of the WRU National Division 5 West play at the Moors.

FLEUR DE LYS (Caerphilly) ST1596

Fleur De Lys RFC, formed in 1966, of the WRU National Division 3 East play at Trelyn Park, Victoria Road, Fleur De Lys.

FLEUR DE LYS FC and FLEUR DE LYS WELFARE FC

see BLACKWOOD (Caerphilly)

FLEXYS CEFN DRUIDS FC

see CEFN-MAWR (Wrexham)

FLINT (Flintshire) SJ2472

Flint Town United, founded in 1886, play in the Cymru Alliance League at Cae-y-Castell, in the shadow of the thirteenth-century Edwardian castle. Flint Town United were founder members of the League of Wales in 1993, but were relegated after five seasons in the top flight. They have played at Cae-y-Castell since 1994. The team originally played at Strand Park, before moving in 1924 to a new ground in Holywell Road where they stayed until 1993. Their recent proposed merger with GAP Connah's Quay proved abortive.

Flint RFC, a Welsh Districts club, play on an adjoining field at Cae-y-Castell.

FOCHRIW (Caerphilly) SO1005

Fochriw FC, founded in 1987, play in the South Wales Senior League, Division 1 at the Fochriw Welfare Ground.

Caerphilly Town FC of the South Wales Senior League, Division 2 play at Fochriw Welfare Ground and Llanbradach Park.

FORGESIDE RFC

see BLAENAVON (Torfaen)

FOUR CROSSES (Powys) SJ0508

Four Crosses of the Mid Wales League have excellent facilities at Foxon Manor.

4TH HOME GUARD ELY FC

see ELY (Cardiff)

FURNACE (Carmarthenshire) SN5102

Furnace United RFC, founded in 1883, play in the WRU National Division 5 West at Cae Castell.

GABALFA (Cardiff) ST1678

Cardiff Draconians, 2008-09 champions of the South Wales Amateur Football League, Division 2, play at Llanidloes Road, Gabalfa, Cardiff.

GADLYS ROVERS FC

see ABERDARE (Rhondda Cynon Taf)

GAERWEN (Anglesey) SH4871

Gaerwen FC play in the Gwynedd League at Lôn Groes. The team formerly played at Plas Newydd.

GALAXY: AFC

see BARRY (Vale of Glamorgan)

GAP CONNAH'S QUAY NOMADS FC

see CONNAH'S QUAY (Flintshire)

GARDEN VILLAGE FC

see GORSEINON (Swansea)

GARDEN VILLAGE YOUTH FC

see BRADLEY (Wrexham)

GARNDIFFAITH (Torfaen) SO2605

Garndiffaith RFC of the WRU National Division 2 East play their home games at Lasgard View. The club, formed in 1922, has an illustrious early history but disbanded during the Second World War. It re-formed in 1946, playing on Pen-y-lan Fields.

GARNLYDAN (Blaenau Gwent) SO1612

Garnlydan FC play in the North Gwent League, Division 1 at the Recreation Ground.

GARW ATHLETIC FC

see PONTYCYMMER (Bridgend)

GELLIDEG (Merthyr Tydfil)

Gellideg Foundation FC of the Merthyr Tydfil Football League, Division 1, CPD Llew Goch [*sic*] and Park View FC (a new entrant in 2008), both of Division 2, play at the Gellideg School pitch.

GEORGETOWN BGC FC

see ABERFAN (Merthyr Tydfil)

GIANT'S GRAVE FC

see BRITON FERRY (Neath Port Talbot)

GILFACH-GOCH (Rhondda Cynon Taf) SS9889

Gilfach-Goch RFC, established in 1889, play at the Welfare Ground, in the WRU National Division 2 East.

GILFACH-GOCH ATHLETIC FC

see EVANSTOWN (Rhondda Cynon Taf)

GILWERN (Powys) SO2414

Gilwern and District FC play in the Gwent Central League, Premier Division at the Gilwern Playing Fields, Common Road, Gilwern.

GLADESTRY (Powys) SO2355

Vale of Arrow FC, formerly of the Mid Wales (South) League, played at Gladestry Football Field.

GLAIS (Swansea) SN7000

Glais RFC, founded in 1896, play in the WRU National League Division 5 South West on a field located behind their clubhouse, but they once played at the INCO Recreational Fields in Clydach.

GLAMORGAN TAP FC

see TREDEGAR (Blaenau Gwent)

GLAMORGAN WANDERERS RFC

see ELY (Cardiff)

GLAN CONWY (Conwy) SH8075

Glan Conwy FC of the Welsh Alliance Football League play at Cae Ffwt, Llanrwst Road, Glan Conwy.

GLANAMAN (Carmarthenshire) SN6714

Grenig Park, Glanaman, is the home of Cwmamman United FC, founded in 1976, who play in the Welsh League, Division 3. The Afon Grenig is a tributary of the river Aman.

Amman United RFC, founded in 1903, who play in the WRU National League Division 4 West, play at Cwmamman Park. Early games were played on land that belonged to Brynlloi Farm, where Bethania Presbyterian Chapel was subsequently built in 1906.

GLANCYNON FC

see HIRWAUN (Rhondda Cynon Taf)

GLANGRWYNEY (Powys) SO2416

Crickhowell RFC play in the WRU National Division 6 East at Parc Broyd, Glangrwyney, opened in 1986 and named in honour of the club's president, the late Bob Broyd (1923-2008). Broyd, a native of Essex who settled in the area in the 1970s, farmed Penrhiw in Llangenny, and was the main driving force behind the development of the club's facilities.

GLANNAU: CPD

see ST ASAPH (Denbighshire)

GLANTRAETH FC

see BODORGAN (Anglesey)

GLYNCEIRIOG (Wrexham) SJ2038

Glynceiriog FC of the Welsh National League (Wrexham Area), Division 1 play at the Cross, Glynceiriog.

GLYNCOCH (Rhondda Cynon Taf) ST0792

Glyncoch RFC play in the WRU National Division 6 Central at Coed-y-lan Road, Glyncoch, Pontypridd.

GLYNCOED CORRIES FC

see PONTPRENNAU (Cardiff)

GLYNCORRWG (Bridgend) SS8799

Glyncorrwg RFC, formed in 1880, play in the WRU National Division 4 South West at Ynysgorrwg Park, a new playing field opened in 1953 after considerable work was undertaken to level the former site of Ynysgorrwg Colliery. In common with many other mining villages, Glyncorrwg found it difficult to find a level piece of land for recreational use. Earlier locations where rugby was played include fields at Heol-y-Deryn, Dunraven Street and the top of Tŷ'n-y-Pant mountain.

Glyncorrwg Hall FC, who play in the Port Talbot Football League Premier Division, also play at Ynysgorrwg Park.

GLYN-NEATH (Neath Port Talbot) SN8706

Founded in 1889, Glyn-neath RFC played at several venues including Angel Field, Pontneddfechan, Pentre Maelwod, Cae Elias (Newtown), Cae Pentre (Lamb and Flag), Cae Butchers, Cae Mrs John and Cae Maesmarchog before settling at their present home, Abernant Park, in 1901. The team play in the WRU National Division 3 South West.

The football team, known as Aberpergwm during its early

days, was formed around 1912 and was based in the Lamb and Flag area of the village but moved to the Welfare Field in the early 1930s and changed its name to Glynneath Welfare. The club enjoyed a successful period in the 1960s when it competed in the Welsh League. In 1984, following a change in local government status, the team adopted the name Glyn-neath Town. They now play in the Neath Football League, Premier Division.

GODRE'R-GRAIG (Neath Port Talbot) SN7507

Godre'r-graig FC play in Neath Football League, Division 2 at Carreg-yr-Afon Recreation Ground.

GOGINAN (Ceredigion) SN6881

Goginan FC, a village team who competed in the Aberystwyth and District League from 1970 to 1992, played at Cae Penbryn, also called Cae Cleifer, Goginan, by permission of the farmer Mr John Roberts, Penbryn. The Welsh *cleifer* indicates that the field was shaped like a butcher's cleaver. Goginan also fielded a team in the same league for three seasons from 1949 until 1952, playing at Troedyrhiw Farm, Melindwr.

GOODWICK (Pembrokeshire) SM9437

Goodwick United FC of the Pembrokeshire League, Division 1 play at Phoenix Park. Earlier games were played at Penrhiw Field.

GORDON LENNOX FC

see ABERFAN (Merthyr Tydfil)

GORS FC

see TOWNHILL (Swansea)

GORSEINON (Swansea) SS5898

Garden Village FC, founded in 1922, of the Welsh League, Division 1 play at Stafford Common, Victoria Road, Kingsbridge, Gorseinon. The origin of the name Stafford is uncertain, but the archives of the Badminton estate and the diaries of Lewis Weston Dillwyn (1778-1855) of Penlle'r-gaer frequently mention Mynydd Stafford and other common lands as early as 1658.

Gorseinon Athletic FC play in the Carmarthenshire League, Premier Division at Parc-y-werin, Alexandra Road, Gorseinon.

Gorseinon RFC, founded in 1884, play in the WRU National Division 3 West at the Welfare Ground. The Welfare Ground was known as King's Holme prior to the Great War. After the war the club re-formed under the name of St Catherine's Church and games were played at Pencefnadra at the rear of Whittington Terrace. Between 1918 and 1931 the ground was redeveloped and the team changed its name to Grovesend Welfare. The name was again changed to Gorseinon in the early 1950s.

Kingsbridge Colts FC of the Swansea Senior District League, Division 3 play at Garden Village, Myrtle Road, Kingsbridge, Gorseinon.

GOVILON (Monmouthshire) SO2613

Govilon FC, 2008-09 champions of the Gwent County League, Division 2, play at the Recreation Ground, Govilon, near

Abergavenny. The popular Butch's Bank provides an elevated view of the pitch.

GOWER SPORTS FC

see RHIWBINA (Cardiff)

GOWERTON (Swansea) SS5996

Gowerton RFC, formed in 1884, play in the WRU National Division 5 South West at the Athletic Ground, Victoria Road. The land was originally owned by Sir John Talbot Dillwyn-Llewelyn, first baronet of Penlle'r-gaer, and formed a part of the Trafle Mill Farm Estate.

Gowerton FC of the Swansea Senior Football League, Division 2 play at the Elba Sports Complex, Gorseinon.

GOYTRE (Neath Port Talbot) SS7889

Glenhafod Park Stadium in the village of Goytre, near Port Talbot, is the home of Goytre United FC, founded in 1953, who play in the Welsh League, Division 1. The name Glenhafod is taken from a disused coal mine in the surrounding hillside. The stadium has a capacity of 4,000. In 1990 the impressive 350-seater Boris Suhanski grandstand was built, with floodlights being installed in 2000. The grandstand, named after the secretary and main driving force behind the development of the club, includes seating from the old Cardiff Arms Park. The club has twice declined the opportunity of playing in the Welsh Premiership.

GOYTRE FC

see PENPERLLENI (Torfaen)

GRAIG FC

see PONTYPRIDD (Rhondda Cynon Taf)

GRAIGWEN JUNIORS FC

see PONTYPRIDD (Rhondda Cynon Taf)

GRAIG-Y-RHACCA (Caerphilly) ST1989

Graig-y-Rhacca FC play in the Newport and District League, Division 2 at the Addison Way Playing Fields. Formed in 2002, a senior side first competed in 2007–08, winning promotion at its first attempt. Many streets in Graig-y-Rhacca have been named after English literary figures including Dickens, Gray, Herrick, Longfellow, Milton and Shelley. Addison Way is named after Joseph Addison (1672-1719), poet, essayist and man of letters.

GRANGE ALBION FC

see LECKWITH (Cardiff)

GRANGE HARLEQUINS FC

see LECKWITH (Cardiff)

GRANGETOWN (Cardiff) ST1774

Grangetown Catholics Old Boys FC and St Patrick's FC of the Cardiff and District League, Premier Division, and Legal and General Rams FC of Division 4 all play at Sevenoaks Park, Grangetown. The park is known locally as the Tan, as it was once the site of a tannery. The park is bordered by seven oak trees.

GREAT WESTERN RAILWAY FC

see BRIDGEND

GREENFIELD (Flintshire) SJ2077

Greenfield FC, re-formed in 2005, of the Clwyd League Premier Division, are currently playing at Ffordd Marion in Gronant whilst they upgrade their pitch at the former Courtaulds site to meet Welsh Alliance League criteria. They have also played at Holywell High School in past seasons. Their forerunners, Courtaulds Greenfield FC, the works team based at the rayon and nylon factory, enjoyed considerable success in the Welsh League during the 1970s before folding in the 1980s following the closure of the plant.

GRESFORD (Wrexham) SJ3535

Gresford Athletic FC, founded in 1946, play in the Cymru Alliance League at Clapper's Lane, named in turn after Clapper Farm. A *clapper* is a form of bridge made from stepping stones.

GRIFFITHSTOWN (Torfaen) ST2999

Griffithstown is the home of Panteg FC who now play in the Gwent County League, Division 2, having been relegated from the Welsh League in 2000. Panteg FC was formed in 1947 under the name RTB Panteg FC as a works team representing the local

Richard Thomas and Baldwin steelworks, and home games were played at the RTB Sportsground, but the grounds were sold in 1981 for road improvements. The club relocated to Panteg House Sportsground where they have played since that date. The team was re-named Panteg in 1972.

PILCS FC, the works team of the Pilkington's Group PLC factory at Griffithstown, Pontypool, play in the Gwent County League, Division 3 at the PILCS Sports and Social Club located between Griffithstown and New Inn.

GROVE PARK FC

see PORT TALBOT (Neath Port Talbot)

GROVESEND (Swansea) SN5900

Pengelli United FC play in the Carmarthenshire League Premier Division at Golden Grove Park, Grovesend.

GUILSFIELD (Powys) SJ2211

Guilsfield FC were formed in 1957, but football has been played in the village since the early 1930s. As the village expanded, a new community centre was built that also included a football pitch, Community Centre Ground, which remains the home of this progressive club. Plans are afoot to move to a new ground.

GURNOS (Merthyr Tydfil) SO0408

Gurnos Rangers SC FC of the Merthyr Tydfil Football League, Division 1 play at the Prince Charles Hospital Field, Gurnos, Merthyr Tydfil.

White Horse FC, a team new to Division 2 of the Merthyr Tydfil Football League in 2008, play at Pen y Dre School Pitch, Gurnos.

GWAELOD-Y-GARTH (Cardiff) ST1183

Gwaelod-y-garth FC of the Cardiff and District Football League, Division 1 play their home games at a ground located near Main Road.

GWALCHMAI (Anglesey) SH3975

Gwalchmai FC, promoted to the Gwynedd League in 2008 from the Anglesey League, play at Cae Maes Meurig. They formerly played at the Bodwina Ground.

GWAUNCAEGURWEN (Neath Port Talbot) SN7011

Cwmgors RFC, founded in 1927, play in WRU National Division 5 South West at Parc-y-werin, Gwauncaegurwen. The club initially played at Parc Howard, Cwmgors, but in the early 1950s the ground was requisitioned for opencast coal mining to meet post-war energy shortages.

Gwauncaegurwen FC play in the Neath Football League, Division 2 at the Maerdy Playing Field, Clwyd Road, Gwauncaegurwen.

GWERNYFED RFC

see TALGARTH (Powys)

GWERSYLLT ATHLETIC FC

see BRADLEY (Wrexham)

GWILI ROVERS FC

see LLANPUMSAINT (Carmarthenshire)

GWYNFI UNITED FC

see BLAENGWYNFI (Neath Port Talbot)

HAFOD (Swansea) SS6594

St Joseph's FC, founded in 1921, and Maltsers Sports FC, both of the Swansea Senior Football League, Division 2, play at Pentrehafod, Pentremawr Road, Hafod, Swansea.

HAFOD BROTHERHOOD FC and HAFOD RANGERS FC

see SKETTY (Swansea)

HAKIN (Pembrokeshire) SM8905

Hakin United FC, 2008-09 champions of the Pembrokeshire League, Division 1, play at the Observatory Field. The field is named after the astronomical observatory established at Hakin by Charles Francis Greville (1749-1809). The stone structure of the planned observatory building remains, and there are street names in Hakin such as Observatory Close and Observatory Avenue.

Milford Haven RFC of the WRU National Division 4 West also play on a separate pitch at the Observatory Field.

HALKYN (Flintshire) SJ2171

Halkyn United, founded in 1945, play in the Welsh Alliance League at Pant Newydd, Pentre Road, Halkyn. The club spent five years in the Cymru Alliance League until they were relegated in 2006. Halkyn previously played on a field adjacent to the Village Park in Pentre Halkyn.

HARLECH (Gwynedd) SH5831

Harlech RFC, founded shortly after the Second World War, play in the Gwynedd League at Cae Ysgol Ardudwy, Harlech.

Harlech Town, formerly of the Gwynedd League (1986-89) and the Caernarfon and District League (1963-86), played at King George Field, Beach Road, Harlech.

HARP ROVERS FC

see SKEWEN (Neath Port Talbot)

HARTRIDGE RFC

see LLAN-WERN (Newport)

HAVERFORDWEST (Pembrokeshire) SM9515

Haverfordwest County FC, who play in the Welsh Premiership, can trace their origins back to 1899, although the team did not enter the Welsh League until 1936. They played at the Bridge Meadow, but in 1994 the club decided to sell their ground to supermarket chain Safeway, who agreed in return to provide them with a new ground, now known as the New Bridge Meadow.

The team had to withdraw from the Welsh Premiership for three seasons whilst their new ground was prepared, but their decision has been vindicated as they can now boast much improved facilities at their premises. During that period they played at the Haverfordwest RFC ground at Pembroke Road. In 2004 the club qualified for the UEFA Cup but lost both legs to Fimleikafélag Hafnarfjarðar of Iceland, who subsequently went on to defeat Dunfermline Athletic in the next round. Haverfordwest's home leg was played at Ninian Park on 15 July 2004 as the New Bridge Meadow did not meet UEFA criteria.

Prendergast Villa FC of the Pembrokeshire Football League, Division 1 play at Ysgol Sir Thomas Picton School, Haverfordwest.

Haverfordwest Cricket Club play in the Pembrokeshire Football League, Division 2 at Haverfordwest Cricket Field, Dale Road, Haverfordwest. The cricket club is the oldest in Wales, having been founded in 1824.

HAVERFORDWEST RFC

see MERLIN'S BRIDGE (Pembrokeshire)

HAWARDEN (Flintshire) SJ3165

Hawarden Rangers of the Welsh National League (Wrexham Area), Premier Division play at the Gladstone Fields, which are named in honour of William Ewart Gladstone (1809-98), four-time prime minister of Great Britain. Gladstone married Catherine Glynne (1812-1900), daughter of Sir Stephen Richard Glynne (1780-1815), eighth baronet of Hawarden Castle,

Flintshire, and made his home at Hawarden Castle in the village, where his descendants still live.

HAY-ON-WYE (Powys) SO2242

G L Fairs has noted that football was played at Hay-on-Wye as early as 1879-80 but that the first club ended in financial failure. A new club was founded by the Revd J J de Winton and members of St Mary's Church Choir, and this is the club that remains in existence today. Hay St Mary's FC of the Mid Wales League (South) have played at the Brecon Road Playing Fields since 1969, but during the last three years the club has acquired two new pitches at neighbouring Forest Road. The club, which runs several teams, has an impressive website and has obvious ambitions to play at a higher level. The site notes that 'Hay are now developing new pitches and have recently played under floodlights for the first time. They have also … got two portable stands which will allow access to higher leagues … when the opportunity presents itself.' Hay St Mary's were declared league champions in 2008-09.

HEATH (Cardiff) ST1799

St Joseph's RFC, formed in 1959, play in the WRU National League Division 4 East at Heath Park, Cardiff. Fairoak FC, Heath Park Rangers FC and Memory Lane FC of the Cardiff and District Football League, Division 4, and Heath Park United of the Cardiff Combination Football League, Premier Division also play at Heath Park.

St Joseph's FC of the South Wales Senior League, Division 1 play at Maesycoed Road, Heath, Cardiff.

HENDY (Carmarthenshire) SN5803

Hendy RFC, formed in 1881, play in the WRU National Division 4 West at Hendy Park, which was opened on 11 September 1972 by Carwyn James (1929-83). Earlier games were played at Fforest Lane, Cae Bryn Môr, Talyglun Canol and, prior to Hendy Park, at Ystumenlle.

Hendy FC of the Carmarthenshire League, Division 1 play at Cae Ynystomenlle, colloquially known as Cae Ystumenlle, a field named after the neighbouring farm, which is now the home of broadcaster Garry Owen and his wife, who was raised on the farm.

HENLLYS RANGERS FC

see CWMBRÂN (Torfaen)

HEOLGERRIG (Merthyr Tydfil) SO0306

Heolgerrig SC FC play in the Merthyr Tydfil Football League, Division 1 at Heolgerrig Village Field, Cwmglo Road, Heolgerrig.

HEOL-Y-CYW (Bridgend) SS9484

Heol-y-Cyw RFC, founded in 1905, play in the WRU National Division 3 South East. Their ground is located off High Street.

HERBRANDSTON (Pembrokeshire) SM8707

Herbrandston FC play in Division 1 of the Pembrokeshire League at the Sports Field, Little Castle Grove, Herbrandston.

HIGHCROFT: AFC

see LLANRUMNEY (Cardiff)

HIRAEL (Gwynedd) SH5872

Rhiwlas FC, promoted to the Gwynedd League in 2008 from the Caernarfon and District League, Division 1, play at the King George V Playing Field, Beach Road, Hirael.

HIRWAUN (Rhondda Cynon Taf) SJ1361

Hirwaun RFC of the WRU National Division 5 South Central, and Hirwaun Welfare FC of the South Wales Amateur Football League, Division 2, both play at the Welfare Ground, Manchester Place.

Glancynon FC, founded in 1998, play in the Aberdare Valley Football League, Premier Division at Cefndon Fields.

HOLT (Denbighshire) SJ4053

Holt Nomads of the Welsh National League (Wrexham Area), Division 1 play on a field adjacent to Maes-y-llan School.

HOLTON ROAD FC

see BARRY (Vale of Glamorgan)

HOLYHEAD (Anglesey) SH2482

Holyhead Hotspur, founded in 1990, play in the Cymru Alliance League and are the heirs of a long tradition of strong football teams emanating from this town. They play at the New Oval

Stadium, Kingsland, Holyhead, a stadium officially opened in July 2007. Cae Mwd was the ground used by Holyhead Town, who were a major force in Welsh football during the 1950s and 1960s. The site of Cae Mwd, off Turkeyshore Road, is now the fast-ferry service car park. Wartime matches were played at the Recreation Ground.

Holyhead Gwelfor Athletic, formerly of the Anglesey League, played at Morawelon but announced their resignation from the league at the end of the 2008–09 season.

Rugby and football fields for local activities are also provided at the Millbank Playing Fields, a major development costing £1 million, which opened in 2005.

HOLYHEAD RFC

see VALLEY (Anglesey)

HOLYWELL (Flintshire) SJ1875

Holywell Town can trace their roots to 1893 with the founding of Holywell Acodians. Early games were played at Ffordd Fer. Following the Second World War, football was established at Halkyn Road, the present home of the club. The club became a major force in non-league football in the 1950s when the Welsh League (North) title was won in 1953, and in 1962 over 3,000 spectators witnessed a narrow away win for Swansea Town in a close-fought Welsh Cup tie. Holywell Town were founder members of the Cymru Alliance League in 1992 and were also inaugural members of the League of Wales in 1992. Since 1998, the club's fortunes have dwindled, and they now play in the Welsh Alliance League.

HOPE (Flintshire) SJ3058

Castell Alun Colts FC of the Welsh National League (Wrexham Area) Premier Division play at Castell Alun Sports and Leisure Centre, Hope. The centre also provides a pitch for the Caer Borderers RFC, a Welsh Districts side.

HOPKINSTOWN (Rhondda Cynon Taf) ST0590

Hopkinstown FC play in the South Wales Senior League, Division 2 at the Great Western Field.

HUBBERSTON FC

see THORNTON (Pembrokeshire)

HUNDLETON (Pembrokeshire) SM9600

Hundleton FC, formed in 1989, play in the Pembrokeshire League, Division 2 at the Hundleton Playing Fields. The club were crowned league champions in 2008-09.

INCO FC

see CLYDACH (Swansea)

INTER CARDIFF FC

see ELY (Cardiff)

INTER CARMARTHEN FC

see CARMARTHEN (Carmarthenshire)

ISLAND MARINE FC

see BARRY (Vale of Glamorgan)

JAYS FC

see CARMARTHEN (Carmarthenshire)

JOHNSTON (Pembrokeshire) SM9310

Johnston FC play in the Pembrokeshire League, Division 2 at Glebelands.

JOHNSTOWN (Carmarthenshire) SN3919

Johnstown FC play in the Carmarthenshire League, Premier Division at Johnstown Park and Welfare Field.

JOHNSTOWN (Wrexham) SJ3046

Johnstown Youth FC of the Welsh National League (Wrexham Area), Division 1 play at the Moreton Playing Fields, Heol Kenyon, Johnstown, in the Rhos area of Wrexham. The name Moreton is derived from Moortown – the element *moor* being the equivalent of the Welsh *rhos* in Rhosllannerchrugog.

KENFIG HILL (Neath Port Talbot) SS8483

Kenfig Hill RFC of the WRU National Division 3 South West and Kenfig Hill FC of the South Wales Amateur Football League, Division 1, play on adjacent pitches at the Central Athletic Ground, Crofft Goch, Kenfig Hill. These fields were requisitioned for recreational use by Pen-y-bont Rural District

Council in 1944 and were originally known as the Pisgah Field, as they were located behind the Welsh Baptist chapel of that name in North Avenue.

Tony Lewis' detailed history of the rugby club makes reference to several fields used during its formative years. These include Cae Rhys, a field christened by the returning Great War soldiers as 'the Somme'. This field was also used at an early date for association football. The rugby club also briefly used the field upon which Park Street was built, and a field known as Cae Eithyn located near the Stormy Pistyll was used from 1912-14.

KERRY (Powys) SO1490

Kerry FC play in the Mid Wales League at Dolforgan Park. The local Dolforgan estate was once owned by the eminent antiquarian and railway engineer John Bancroft Willans (1881-1957).

KIDWELLY (Carmarthenshire) SN4006

Kidwelly RFC, who play in the WRU National Division 2 West, and Kidwelly Town FC of the Carmarthenshire League, Division 3, both play at Parc Stephens, which is named after Sir Alfred Stephens (1871-1938), a local industrialist and mayor of the borough of Kidwelly. Stephens also unsuccessfully contested the Carmarthen constituency as a Conservative candidate in the 1923 general election and at the by-election of 1924.

KILGETTY (Pembrokeshire) SN1207

Kilgetty FC, established in 1924, play in the Pembrokeshire

League, Division 1 at the King's Moor Sports Ground, James Park, Kilgetty. The name King's Moor dates from the early eighteenth century.

KILLAY (Swansea) SS6093

Swansea Uplands RFC, formed in 1919 at the Uplands Hotel, Swansea, acquired their present ground at Upper Killay in 1952. They now play in the WRU National Division 5 West. Prior to purchasing their ground at Killay, they played at a variety of locations in the city including St Helen's (1919-1952), Singleton Park, and a field near the Bible College of Wales at Derwen Fawr, Sketty.

KILLAY FC

see FAIRWOOD (Swansea)

KILVEY UNITED FC

see PENLAN (Swansea)

KINGSBRIDGE COLTS FC

see GORSEINON (Swansea)

KNAP FC

see BARRY (Vale of Glamorgan)

KNIGHTON (Powys) SO2872

Knighton Town, formed in 1887, play in the Mid Wales League (South) at the Showground. The ground is located at Bryn-y-

Castell, Ludlow Road, Knighton, and is referred to by Wales and Liverpool fullback Joey Jones in his autobiography as a ground where he, Bryan Flynn and Mickey Thomas played in a Welsh Schoolboys trial match.

KRUF FC
see AMMANFORD (Carmarthenshire)

LAMB INN FC
see ABERDARE (Rhondda Cynon Taf)

LAMPETER (Ceredigion) SN5748
The Memorial Field, North Road, home of Lampeter Town RFC, who play in WRU National Division 3 West, was purchased by the old borough council and named in memory of those who died during the Second World War. The Lampeter Club, founding members of the WRU in 1881, possibly dates from as early as 1875, and rugby was almost certainly brought to the town through the influence of St David's College. Some early games were played on Lampeter's Show Field.

Lampeter Town of the Ceredigion League, Division 1 play on an adjacent field that is part of the Memorial Field (sometimes referred to as Maes–y–felin owing to the proximity of the housing estate of that name). Lampeter competed in the Aberystwyth and District League after the Second World War, playing their games at the Show Field. Lampeter Town's student neighbours from the University of Wales Trinity St David, Lampeter, who compete in Division 2 of the same league, are based at the College Fields.

LAMPHEY (Pembrokeshire) SN0100

Lamphey FC play in the Pembrokeshire League, Division 3 at the Lamphey Playing Fields.

LANDORE (Swansea) SS6595

North End FC of the Swansea Senior Football League, Division 2, and Landore FC of the Swansea Senior District League, Division 4, both play at RTB Landore, Beaufort Road, Landore, Swansea. The Liberty Stadium, home of Swansea City FC and the Neath–Swansea Ospreys RFC is also located in this area of the city.

LAUGHARNE (Carmarthenshire) SN3010

Laugharne RFC, founded in 1893, play in the WRU National Division 3 West at Wooford Park. George Tremlett notes that the club used a field known as the Pluds until 1945, when it moved to the Cricket Ground, a field at the top of the lane by the entrance to Glan-y-Môr, owned by Tudor Williams who kindly allowed the club to use it until 1951 when it moved to Wooford Field, later re-named Wooford Park.

LAWRENNY (Pembrokeshire) SN0106

Lawrenny FC play in the Pembrokeshire League, Division 3 at the Lawrenny Sports Playing Fields.

LECKWITH (Cardiff) ST1574

Cardiff Grange Harlequins, founded in 1935, of the Welsh League, Division 2 played at Cardiff Athletics Stadium/Leckwith Stadium, Cardiff, in the shadow of Ninian Park. In 2004-05, they were members of the Welsh Premier League. They have now relocated to Cwrt-yr-Ala in Ely owing to the building of Cardiff's new stadium on that site. Cardiff Grange Harlequins FC also field a team in the local Cardiff and District League, Division 2, playing at Jubilee Park in Sloper Road, a ground also used by other local teams such as Canton Libs.

Grange Albion play in the South Wales Senior League, Division 1 at Coronation Park, Sloper Road, Leckwith, Cardiff.

Cardiff Academicals FC of the Cardiff and District League, Premier Division play at Fitzalan High School, Lawrenny Avenue, Leckwith and also at Heath Park.

LEGAL and GENERAL RAMS FC

see GRANGETOWN (Cardiff)

LETTERSTON (Pembrokeshire) SM9329

Letterston FC play in the Pembrokeshire League, Division 2 at the Commons.

LEWIS MERTHYR FC

see TREHAFOD (Rhondda Cynon Taf)

LEWISTOWN (Bridgend) SS9388

Lewistown FC play in the South Wales Senior League, Division 1 at the Lewistown Welfare Ground. Pantyrawel FC, formed in 1986, of the Bridgend and District Football League, Premier Division also play at the Lewistown Welfare Ground.

LEX XI FC

see WREXHAM

LISVANE (Cardiff) ST1883

Lisvane/Llanishen FC play in the South Wales Senior League, Division 2 at Heol-y-Delyn, also known as the Village Field.

LISWERRY

see LLISWERRY (Newport)

LITTLE BLUE UNITED FC

see SPLOTT (Cardiff)

LLAN-ARTH (Monmouthshire) SO3710

Llan-arth FC play in the Gwent Central League, Premier Division. Their field does not have a name but is located near Llan-arth Village Hall.

LLANBADARN FAWR (Ceredigion) SN6080

The university playing fields at Blaendolau are best known for their association with the hugely successful and influential Wales International Football Tournament, formerly known as the Ian Rush Tournament, first held in 1985 and played annually since 1986. Many young players such as Steven Gerrard, Michael Owen and Andriy Shevchenko have developed into household names since their appearances at Llanbadarn. Blaendolau also plays host to several teams in the Aberystwyth and District Football League, including the university's second and third reserve teams, together with FC Phoenix. It also hosted Llyfrgell Gen., the short-lived team based at the National Library of Wales, which folded in 2009 after only two seasons. At the time of writing, press reports have speculated that a major retailer may be interested in acquiring a section of the 50-acre Blaendolau Fields.

Cae Llety Parc, opposite Blaendolau, which adjoins Llety Parc (Park Lodge) Hotel, is often used for junior football by kind permission of the owner.

On land to the north-east of Blaendolau, located between the main Aberystwyth to Shrewsbury railway line and the Vale of Rheidol narrow gauge railways, is Cae Llety Gwyn, home of Padarn United FC, who play in the Aberystwyth and District League, Division 1. During the pre-war seasons, the team played on a field known as Gay Meadow, located on farmland at Felin Person, now a caravan park, which overlooks the Glan-yr-afon Industrial Estate. It is also known that a team under the name Padarn United played several games on the Vicarage Field, Aberystwyth, before that land was acquired by the university in 1906.

It is also worth noting that on Cae Halog (desecrated field), which is adjacent to Cae Llety Gwyn and close to the present-day railway crossing, it was customary for the young men of Llanbadarn to spend Sunday, Christmas Day and other holidays engaged in a variety of sports, such as wrestling and cockfighting. Sometimes other young men from neighbouring parishes would come to fight with the Llanbadarn boys. They fought with swords and double-pointed sticks and played a game known as *torri cleddyf Arthur* (snapping Arthur's sword), which involved turning a somersault in the air while hanging on to a bar. It is also known that football matches were played on the field.

LLANBERIS (Gwynedd) SH5760

Llanberis FC of the Welsh Alliance League play at Cae Ffordd Padarn. Arwel Jones, in his detailed history of the club, has noted that competitive football was played at Llanberis as early as 1895, the early games being held at Cae'r Ddôl. It appears that the first game played on the Padarn Road Field, then known as the Padarn Villa Hotel Field, took place in December 1909. The club has played continuously at that venue since the late 1950s, purchasing the field in the 1970s and improving the facilities. Prior to that, other fields were used such as Maes Padarn and the Dolbadarn Hotel Field where the National Slate Museum now stands.

LLANBOIDY (Carmarthenshire) SN2123

Llanboidy FC of the Ceredigion League, Division 1 play at Cae Dan Dre.

LLANBRADACH (Caerphilly) ST1490

Llanbradach Social FC withdrew from the South Wales Senior League, Division 1 in 2009. They played at Llanbradach Park. Their reserve side continue to play at Trosnant, Pen-y-bryn, near Hengoed.

Caerphilly Town FC of the South Wales Senior League, Division 2 play at Fochriw Welfare Ground and Llanbradach Park.

LLANDAFF / LLANDAFF NORTH (Cardiff) ST1577/8

Llandaff RFC, formed in 1876, play in the WRU National Division 4 East, and were crowned champions in 2008-09. Since their foundation, they have always played at the Bishop's Field, Llandaff.

Llandaff North RFC play in the WRU National Division 3 South East at Hailey Park. The Villa FC of the Cardiff and District Football League, Division 1 also play at Hailey Park. The park, opened in 1926, is named after the Cardiff coal owner Claude Percival Hailey (b.1875).

Junior teams in the Cardiff and District League use the Blackwier Fields at the northern end of Bute Park. The Bute family presented Bute Park to the city in 1947.

Llandaff Fields were purchased for Cardiff Council by the influential mill owning Thompson family in 1898. The park is located on the historically important route between the city centre and the cathedral in Llandaff. Pope John Paul II (1920–2005) celebrated mass at Llandaff Fields during his visit to Wales in June 1982. Another John – John Toshack – raised in the neighbouring suburb of Canton, has stressed the importance of these playing fields to his personal development as a footballer. The fields are used for local football.

Sporting Llandaff FC play in the Cardiff and District League, Division 3 at Trelai Park, Ely.

LLANDARCY (Neath Port Talbot) SS7195

Neath Athletic AFC, a club that was formed in 2005 following the merger of Neath AFC and Skewen, played at the impressive

Llandarcy Park complex until the end of the 2006-07 season. Since August 2008 they have shared the Gnoll, the historic home of Neath RFC.

An oil refinery was sited at Llandarcy near Skewen by the Anglo-Persian Oil Company Limited in 1921, and opened in 1922 by Prime Minister Stanley Baldwin (1867-1947). It was built in order to treat imported mineral crude oil and was the first large commercial oil refinery to be established in Britain. The village derives its name from the entrepreneur William Knox D'Arcy (1849-1917), one of the main founders of the oil industry in Persia (now Iran) and a director of the Anglo-Persian Oil Company which later grew into British Petroleum (BP).

BP Llandarcy RFC of the WRU National Division 2 West, and Llandarcy FC of the Neath Football League, Division 2 also play on other pitches at Llandarcy Park.

LLANDDEWI BREFI (Ceredigion) SN6655

Dewi Stars FC, promoted in 2009 as runners-up of Division 2 of the Ceredigion League, are based at the Llanddewi Playing Fields. The village has a long sporting tradition with the Stars well established by the mid 1920s. The Revd Dr D Ben Rees, in his history of the parish, notes several locations where football has been played in the locality. These include Dôl Garth, Cae Mawr (which belonged to the vicarage), Dôl-gam, Dôl-felin and Cae Pontllanio, near Glanteifi.

LLANDEGFAN (Anglesey) SH5673

Llandegfan FC play in the Anglesey League. Their ground has no specific name.

LLANDEILO (Carmarthenshire) SN6222

Cae William, home of Llandeilo RFC, champions of the WRU National Division 4 West in 2008-09, is named after Francis William Rice, fifth Baron Dynevor (1804-1878). Rice was educated at Westminster School, matriculated at Oxford in 1826 and was awarded his MA in 1847. From 1827 to 1878 he was the vicar of Fairford, Gloucestershire. In 1869, upon the death of his cousin, he succeeded to the title of Baron Dynevor. He died on 3 August 1878, aged 74.

Rugby was played in Llandeilo as early as 1871 at the Bridge Field. The club, founded in 1881, was represented at the inaugural meeting of the Welsh Rugby Union held in that year. Cae William, the gift of the Dynevor family, became the home of Llandeilo RFC in 1919 after a brief period during the pre-war years when the club played at the Gurrey Fach Field.

To mark the millennium, a new combined 100-seater stand and clubhouse was opened at Cae William. Cae William also has a second pitch that has been used temporarily by the local football team, who now play at Ffair-fach.

LLANDEILO FC

see FFAIR-FACH (Carmarthenshire)

LLANDOUGH (Vale of Glamorgan) ST1673

Cwrt-y-Vil FC of the Cardiff and District League, Division 1, formed in 1950, play at Llandough. Their ground is amusingly described on the club's website as Fortress Llandough and prospective spectators are told that different options are available to view matches at this venue: they 'can choose to sit in the all seater Car Park End stand (on the benches), stand on the Bob Berry Bank or in the more friendly family stand (swings, slide and climbing frame)'!

LLANDOVERY (Carmarthenshire) SN7634

Llandovery RFC, formed in 1881, and one of the founding members of the WRU, play in the WRU National League Premier Division at the Church Bank Playing Fields, an area described as lying outside the chartered borough in 1485. The fields were acquired in 1979 and were officially opened by Hermas Evans, WRU district representative and past president of the union, on 9 September 1985. The opening ceremony was followed by a match against Crawshay's Welsh XV. Early games were played at Cae Glas y Bwci on the outskirts of the town and other venues used include Barlow's Field and the Castle Fields. Barlow's Field was acquired by the town's improvement committee in 1956 and is named after Arthur Barlow. He was recorded in the 1901 census as a 37-year-old clogger, born at Newtown, Montgomeryshire, and living with his young family and parents, both Lancastrians, at 1 Cross Street, Llandovery.

Towy Valley FC of the Carmarthenshire League, Division 2 play at the Castle Fields, Llandovery.

LLANDRINDOD WELLS (Powys) SO0561

The Broadway, Lant Avenue, is the home of Llandrindod Wells AFC and Llandrindod Colts FC, who both play in the Mid Wales League (South), and Llandrindod Wells RFC, formed in 1972, who play in the WRU National League Division 6 Central. Thomas Lant (1865-1945) was a native of Bakewell, Derbyshire, the son of John Lant and his wife Mary, who moved to Radnorshire in 1895 to open quarries at Llanelwedd and Llandrindod Wells. Dressed stone from his quarries was subsequently used to construct the Elan Valley dams for Birmingham Water Works, and Lant employed over 300 men for a decade at the height of the project. He amassed a huge personal fortune of £133,864 from his business interests, some of which he chose to share with his employees. He also acquired and donated land in Builth and Llandrindod Wells for community recreational use, including the land on which these two clubs play, which is now administered by Powys County Council. Thomas Lant was buried with his wife at St Matthew's Church, Llanelwedd on 6 February 1945; his wife pre-deceased him and was buried on 26 November 1926.

In 1871 the Revd Francis Kilvert noted in his famous diary that 'men played … football until it grew dusk' in neighbouring Clyro, but organised football at Llandrindod dates from 1883 where matches were played against other local teams such as Knighton, Newbridge and Rhayader on the Rock House Ddôl, which also doubled up as a race track.

After 1921 the Rock House Ddôl was no longer available and the team acquired a new field at Waterloo Road, which was called the Dinam in recognition of the financial support given towards its purchase by Baron David Davies (1880-1944) of Llandinam. The field was first used on 1 December 1921 and provided a home for Llandrindod for 30 years, later becoming the site of a carpet factory, Mid Wales Yarns.

LLANDRINIO (Powys) SJ2917

Defaid Du FC, founded in 2004, of the Montgomeryshire
Amateur League, Division 2 play at Llandrinio Recreation
Ground.

LLANDUDNO (Conwy) SH7881

Football in Llandudno dates from 1878, and in 1898 a full
international between Wales and Ireland was staged on the
Council Field. Llandudno Town, founded in 1921, were founder
members of the Welsh National League (North) in 1921, and the
club moved to its present ground at Maesdu Park, Builder Street
West, Llandudno after the Council Field was used to construct
a new Asda store in the late 1970s. The club has played in the
Cymru Alliance League since 1992 and has ambitions to play at
Welsh Premiership level.

Llandudno RFC, founded in 1952, compete in the WRU
National Division 1 North. The club played its early games
at away venues before it leased Y Morfa, home ground of the
disbanded Conwy Football Club. Since 1957 the club has played
at the Maesdu Road Recreational Ground.

Real Llandudno play in the Gwynedd League at the Oval,
Lloyd Street, Llandudno.

Penrhyn United FC formerly of the Clwyd League, Division
2 played at Ysgol John Bright, Llandudno for two seasons, but
announced their resignation at the end of the 2008-09 season.

LLANDUDNO JUNCTION (Conwy) SH7978

Llandudno Junction FC of the Welsh Alliance League play at the Flyover, Victoria Gardens, Llandudno Junction. The club previously played at Victoria Avenue and at the Recreation Ground, Llanfairfechan.

Although football has been played at the Junction since 1910, the present team has its origins in works team Hotpoint FC, formed in 1975. However, the town has an illustrious and romantic football history. After 40 years of moderate success playing at Nant-y-Coed, Llandudno Junction FC merged in 1954 with neighbouring Conwy Borough to form Borough United FC, a team fondly remembered as the Welsh representatives in the European Cup Winners' Cup in 1963 after surprisingly dismissing Newport County in the Welsh Cup final. Borough progressed through the preliminary round, defeating Maltese side Sliema Wanderers before bowing out to the mighty Slovan Bratislava of Czechoslovakia. Both Borough's home legs were played at Wrexham's Racecourse Ground, attracting a total of almost 28,000 spectators. In spite of this success, the club folded in 1969 after it was evicted from its Nant-y-Coed ground.

LLANDYBÏE (Carmarthenshire) SN6115

Llandybïe RFC play in the WRU National Division 5 South West. Although rugby was probably played at Llandybïe in the nineteenth century, the club was officially founded in 1901. Early games were played on Cae Coed, a field that was owned by the Red Lion, whose landlord was an enthusiast for the game. After a few seasons the club began to use Cae Fallen, a field where the present primary school stands, and subsequently several other locations, including Gelliforynion, Gelli Road, Llangwyddfan, Cilyrychen and Ty-Isaf on the outskirts of the village, until the club was given a permanent home. This opened in 1950 through the efforts of the Llandybïe Playing Fields Association, established under the King George V Foundation.

LLANDYGÁI (Gwynedd) SH5970

Mynydd Llandygái FC of the Caernarfon and District League, Division 1 play at Cae Cymunedol Penrhiw.

Since 1995, Bangor RFC of the WRU National Division 5 North have played at Cae Milltir, Llandygái.

LLANDYRNOG (Denbighshire) SJ1065

Llandyrnog United FC, founded in 1972, play at Cae Nant, Llandyrnog. They were relegated from the Cymru Alliance League in 2008, and will play in the Welsh Alliance League from 2009-10.

LLANDYSUL (Ceredigion) SN4140

Llandysul FC, champions of the Ceredigion League, Division 2 in 2008-09, play at the Memorial Park, a pleasant complex that also includes a cricket field and a bowling green. Prior to opening the Memorial Park, Llandysul played for many years at Cae Wilkes Head, a field opposite the public house of that name. The field is now a small industrial estate.

LLANEDEYRN BULLDOGS FC

see PENTWYN (Cardiff)

LLANEFYDD (Conwy) SH9870

CPD Llanefydd of the Clwyd League, Division 2 play at Cae Llanefydd.

LLANELLI (Carmarthenshire) SN5000

Parc y Strade/Stradey Park was, until October 2008, the world-famous home of Llanelli RFC, who play in the WRU National League Premier Division, and the regional side Scarlets. Francis Jones has documented the history of the house that gave its name to the ground, noting that the place-names *Straddy, Park Estradey* and *Park Ystradey* can be found in documents from the Muddlescombe Estate, Kidwelly, dating from 1552. Until 1610, these lands on the border of Pembrey and Llanelli parishes were owned by yeomen farmers before becoming the property of the Vaughans of Derwydd, Llandybïe. John Mansel, the son of Sir Francis Mansel of Muddlescombe, married Mary, daughter of Sir Henry Vaughan of Derwydd and came to live at Stradey, although it remained the property of the Vaughan family until 1673, when it was sold to the Mansel family. The house was substantial and boasted no less than 15 hearths in 1670. The Mansel family continued to occupy the house for a century and a half until the death in 1808 without issue of Mary Anne Mansel, the widow of E W R Shewen. She bequeathed the estate to Thomas Lewis (*d.*1829) of Llandeilo, Carmarthenshire. Despite major improvements made to the mansion in the period 1820-

30, David Lewis, the son and heir of Thomas Lewis, decided in 1844 to build a new mansion on higher ground. Stradey Castle was completed and the old Stradey house completely demolished in 1855. The Mansel Lewis family remained at Stradey until the last quarter of the twentieth century.

Llanelli RFC's first recorded match against another club took place on New Year's Day 1876 at the People's Park, Llanelli, where the town hall now stands. Rugby was first played at Stradey Park in 1879, but the field was known as the Stradey Grounds during those early years. Llanelli were represented at the founding meeting of the WRU in 1881. During the ensuing 125 years, Stradey Park witnessed many historic occasions, including Llanelli's 9-3 victory over the New Zealand All Blacks on 31 October 1972 and, more recently, the funeral of the legendary Ray Gravell (1951-2007), who played in that match, held on 15 November 2007. The last game played at Stradey Park was an EDF Cup tie against Bristol on 24 October 2008, which resulted in a resounding 27-0 home win for the Scarlets. The occasion was an emotional one for the capacity crowd of 10,500 and the match was televised live on BBC2 Wales. The historic match received a great deal of publicity on a day when one of the great Stradey Park heroes, Phil Bennett, also celebrated his 60th birthday.

The site occupied by Stradey Park will be re-developed for housing by Taylor Wimpey. The famous scoreboard can be found in the club's shop at Llanelli's new stadium at Pemberton which has been christened Parc-y-Scarlets, and was built at a cost of £23 million. The capacity of the stadium constructed by Andre Scott Ltd is 14,870, which can be increased to 15,180 if required. The first game at Parc-y-Scarlets was played on 15

November 2008 when Llanelli defeated Cardiff 32-3 in a WRU premiership match. The crowd was restricted for safety reasons to 4,832. Parc-y-Scarlets was officially opened on 31 January 2009 when the Scarlets entertained and defeated the Barbarians 40-24 in front of a near-capacity crowd of 14,497. The new ground has also accommodated association football fixtures including the 2009 Welsh Cup Final in which Bangor City beat Aberystwyth Town 2-0 on 4 May 2009, a 1-0 victory for Wales in a full international friendly against Estonia on 29 May 2009, and Llanelli's 0-3 second leg defeat against Motherwell in the Europa Cup, first qualifying round on 9 July 2009.

Llanelli Wanderers RFC, formed in 1951, play in the WRU National Division 3 West at a ground adjacent to Stradey Park which will not be affected by developments proposed for the stadium.

New Dock Stars RFC play in the WRU National Division 5 West at St George's Field, Trostre Road, Llanelli.

Llanelli FC, founded in 1896, of the Welsh Premiership League, play at their impressive Stebonheath Park home, a ground that they purchased in 1922 to further their ambitions of gaining membership to the English Football League. The club website notes that association football was brought to this rugby stronghold by migrant workers from Staffordshire, with early games being played at Cae Blake in the Furnace area of the town and at the People's Park in Llanelli town centre. From 1904 the team entered the Swansea and District League. Home matches were played initially at Tunnel Road and later at Penyfan Fields. Success led to a further move to more impressive facilities at

Halfway Park, where the team played in the Southern League until they acquired their present ground. The town council has been the owner of Stebonheath Park since 1977. Llanelli were founder members of the League of Wales, but they enjoyed little success until 2005 when they became full-time professionals. In 2007-08 this bold move finally bore dividends as they were crowned league champions, qualified for the Champions League and recorded a famous 1-0 victory over Latvian champions FK Ventspils at Stebonheath Park on 15 July 2008.

Penygaer Park, north-east of the town centre, has several football pitches that host teams from the Carmarthenshire League. These include Camford Sports FC, Evans and Williams FC and Llanelli Steel FC of the Premier Division, West End United FC and Llan Rads (Llanelli Radiators) of Division 2. In 1962, Penygaer Park hosted a very wet National Eisteddfod of Wales, which is still considered one of the most successful festivals ever.

Penyfan United of the Carmarthenshire League, Division 2 play at Penyfan Fields. Penyfan, a large housing estate, is sited on the land that was once part of the now demolished Penyfan Mansion.

Seaside FC of the Carmarthenshire League, Premier Division play at Crown Park, Caroline Street, Llanelli.

Tafarn United, founded in 2007 and based at Tafarn y Felin, Swiss Valley, Llanelli, play in the Carmarthenshire League, Division 3 at Coedcae School, Trostre Road, Llanelli.

Trallwm FC of the Carmarthenshire League, Division 1 play at Trallwm Park.

Trostre Sports FC play in the Carmarthenshire League,

Division 1 at the Trostre Sports Ground.

Wellfield Athletic FC, formed in 1975, of Carmarthenshire League, Division 1, play at Parc y Bobl/People's Park, Park Crescent, Llanelli.

LLANFAIR CAEREINION (Powys) SJ1006

Llanfair United play in the Montgomeryshire Amateur League, Division 1 at Mount Field.

LLANFAIRFECHAN (Conwy) SH6874

Llanfairfechan Town FC play in the Gwynedd League at the Recreation Ground.

LLANFAIRPWLL (Anglesey) SH5371

Llanfairpwll FC, formed in 1899, of the Cymru Alliance League played at Y Gors until 2009. The club has recently moved to a new field at Maes Eilian.

LLANFARIAN (Ceredigion) SN5877

Llanfarian (Rovers) has fielded teams in the Aberystwyth and District League during three periods: 1935-36, 1947-52, and 1962-68. During the earliest period, games were played on Cae Pâl (also known as Cae Figure Four), located opposite the Royal Oak Inn, part of which has since been utilised for housing. The post-war team played initially at the Black Lion Field, Llanrhystud, before acquiring the use of a field at Tyllwyd Farm through the generosity of a local farmer who was also a prominent figure in the club. The re-formed team of the 1960s played at Cae'r Felin, in neighbouring Rhyd-y-felin. The field takes its name from a twelfth-century mill located on land adjacent to the ford at Nant Paith.

LLANFECHAIN (Powys) SJ1820

Llanfechain FC play in the Montgomeryshire Amateur League, Division 2 at the Recreation Field.

LLANFOIST (Monmouthshire) SO2813

Llanfoist FC play in the Gwent Central League, Premier Division. Their ground is located behind the Cedars.

LLANFYLLIN (Powys) SJ1419

Llanfyllin Town FC, founded before 1885, play in the Mid Wales League at Cae Llwyn.

LLANGADFAN (Powys) SJ0110

Dyffryn Banw FC were founded in 1990 and played in the Montgomeryshire Amateur League, Division 1 at Cae Morfa, Llangadfan until they were promoted to the Mid Wales League in 2008.

LLANGADOG (Carmarthenshire) SN7028

Llangadog RFC play in the WRU National Division 6 West at Cae Baron's Court. The field formed part of Baron's Court Farm before it was acquired for community use.

LLANGEDWYN (Powys) SJ1824

Llangedwyn FC play in the Montgomeryshire Amateur League, Division 1 at the School Field.

LLANGEFNI (Anglesey) SH4675

Llangefni Town FC, founded in 1897, were relegated to the Cymru Alliance League at the end of the 2007-08 season after playing for one season in the Welsh Premiership. They have played at Cae Bob Parry, Talwrn Road, Llangefni since 2000. Auctioneer Bob Parry gifted the field to Cwmni Tref Llangefni. Llangefni had previously played at several locations including Cae Comrades, Cae Rice (where the industrial estate is located), a field at Pencraig (now the site of Coleg Menai), and Cae Lôn Newydd at Isgraig which is still used for reserve and youth games.

Llangefni RFC play at Cae Smyrna, Glanhwfa Road, Llangefni in the WRU National Division 1 North. The field lies in close proximity to Smyrna Welsh Congregational Chapel.

LLANGEINOR (Bridgend) SS9287

Llangeinor FC of the Welsh League, Division 2 play at Llangeinor Park, Bettws Road, Bridgend. Football was played in the village before the Second World War and the club's website notes that early games were played at Pandy Woods and Llangeinor Common. After many years in junior football the club was admitted to the Welsh League in 2006.

LLANGENNECH (Carmarthenshire) SN5601

Llangennech Park plays host to the local cricket, football and rugby teams. The park was opened in 1904 after a former major landowner in the village, Mr David Evans, had dedicated the land to the parish council in 1897. It is recorded that one of the earliest rugby games was played on the Pencoed Grounds, although the exact location of this field remains a mystery. Kenny Bevan, the club historian, notes that 'the most likely explanation is that the team played on some fields near the village that were owned by Pencoed Farm'. Tradition also notes that some games were also played on Cae Tatws, near Glanmwrwg Farm.

Llangennech RFC play in the WRU National Division 1 West. Llangennech FC play in the Carmarthenshire League, Division 2.

LLANGERNYW (Denbighshire) SH8767

CPD Bro Cernyw of the Clwyd League, Division 2 play at Canolfan Addysg Bro Cernyw, Llangernyw.

LLANGOED (Anglesey) SH6079

Llangoed and District FC play in the Anglesey League at the Llangoed Village Playing Field. An earlier field was known as Tyddyn Paun.

Clwb Rygbi Llangoed play at Cae Rygbi Llangoed. A prestigious annual rugby sevens tournament, established in 1992, is held in the village in June, with international participation. This is held at Cae Rygbi Llangoed and at the Llangoed Village Playing Field.

LLANGOLLEN (Denbighshire) SJ2141

Llangollen Town FC, formed in 1908 and champions of the Welsh National League (Wrexham Area) Premier Division in 2008-09, play at the Tower Farm Fields, Dinbren Road, Llangollen. The picturesque Castell Dinas Brân, which overlooks the ground, presumably accounts for its name.

Llangollen RFC, a Welsh Districts side, play at the School Field, Dinbren Road, Llangollen.

LLANGRANNOG (Ceredigion) SN3154

Crannog FC of the Ceredigion League, Division 1 play at Gwersyll yr Urdd, Llangrannog.

LLANGWM (Pembrokeshire) SM9909

Llangwm RFC, founded in 1885, and Llangwm Cricket Club both play at the Green. Llangwm RFC compete in the WRU National Division 5 West. Games are also played at the Pill Parks Field.

LLANGYFELACH FC

see MORRISTON (Swansea)

LLANGYNWYD (Bridgend) SS8588

Llangynwyd FC of the Bridgend and District Football League, Premier Division play at the Llan (Llangynwyd) Playing Fields. The field is also still known as the Harlequins Field due to its past connections with Maesteg Harlequins RFC.

LLANHARAN (Rhondda Cynon Taf) ST0083

The home of Llanharan RFC, formed in 1919, who play in the WRU National Division 1 East, is called Maes Llaethdy/Dairy Field because of its past proximity to the adjacent CWS milk depot which closed in the late 1960s after half a century of milk processing. The club purchased the ground in 1989, having played all its previous seasons at the Welfare Ground. The first game on the new field was played against Aberavon Quins to mark the opening of the 1990-91 season, with the home team winning by 43-18. A 440-seater grandstand, partly funded by a members' debenture scheme and incorporating spacious changing rooms, was added to a covered terrace two years later, with floodlights soon following, to make it an impressive venue.

Llanharan FC play in the Bridgend and District Football League at the Welfare Ground.

LLANHARRY (Bridgend) ST0080

Llanharry FC of the Bridgend and District Football League, Division 1 play at the Recreation Ground.

LLANHILLETH (Caerphilly) SO2100

Llanhilleth RFC of the WRU National Division 5 East have impressive facilities at Llanhilleth Park.

Llanhilleth Athletic FC of the Gwent County League, Division 2 also play at Llanhilleth Park.

LLANIDLOES (Powys) SN9584

Llanidloes Town FC, formed in 1875, were once a significant force in Welsh football, twice winning the Welsh Amateur Cup in 1922 and 1964. They were also founding members of the League of Wales in 1992, but were relegated after only one season in the national league. Llanidloes currently play in the Montgomeryshire League, Division 1, but a club with their fine facilities at Victoria Avenue and illustrious pedigree is surely worthy of a higher standard of football.

Llanidloes RFC of the WRU National Division 4 North were formed in 1975 and have rapidly developed impressive facilities at Cae Hafren on the eastern outskirts of the town where they have five pitches and a new spectator stand.

LLANILAR (Ceredigion) SN6275

Llanilar FC of the Aberystwyth and District League, Division 1 play at Castle Hill Park, a field below Castle Hill, seat of the Loxdale family. Ystwyth Rovers FC, who played in the same league from 1958 to 1963, also played on this field.

LLANISHEN (Cardiff) ST1781

Llanishen RFC of the WRU National Division 3 South East play at Usk Road.

LLANLLYFNI (Gwynedd) SH4751

Llanllyfni FC of the Welsh Alliance League, formed in 2005, play on the King George V Playing Field, and have had a meteoric rise during their comparatively short history. They were promoted

Cae y Brenin Siôr V / King George V Playing Field, Llanllyfni.
Reproduced by kind permission of the photographer, Donna Sherret,
Llanllyfni and CPD Llanllyfni FC.

to the Welsh Alliance League in 2008-09 as champions of the Gwynedd League.

CPD Bro Lleu played at the Ozanam Centre, Tŷ'n Pwll, Llanllyfni and at Ysgol Dyffryn Nantlle, Pen-y-groes when they were members of the Caernarfon and District League. Ozanam is an American-based charity, established by Joseph Ozanam (1813-53) to assist children with behavioural problems.

LLANMARTIN (Newport) ST3989

Underwood Social Club FC of the Gwent County League, Division 3 play at Llanmartin Leisure Centre.

LLANMILOE (Carmarthenshire) SN2508

Pendine FC play in the Pembrokeshire League, Division 2 at the Llanmiloe Playing Fields.

LLANNERCH-Y-MEDD (Anglesey) SH4184

Llannerchymedd FC play in the Anglesey League at Cae Tan Parc.

LLAN-NON (Ceredigion) SN5167

Football at Llan-non dates from 1948 when the village first entered a team in the Aberystwyth and District League. The team was discontinued after four seasons, revived in the 1970s as a Cardiganshire League club, and later rejoined the Aberystwyth-based league in 1990. Initially, Llan-non FC played at Cae Penlon close to the centre of the village. The present team, who operate in the Aberystwyth and District League, Division 2, play at Morfa Esgob. This low-lying land on the Ceredigion coastline is located between the rivers Perris and Cledan and was apparently given to the Bishop of St David's by Lord Rhys, Rhys ap Gruffudd (1132-97) in 1190, accounting for its episcopal name meaning 'Bishop's Seashore'.

LLANPUMSAINT (Carmarthenshire) SN4129

Gwili Rovers, who were established in 1981, played in the Cardiganshire League until they were disbanded in 2004. Their playing field was purchased from Colonel FitzSimon of Pantycelyn with the financial support of the Sports Council of Wales and Carmarthen District Council. The field on which they played was known as Cae Pantycelyn or Cae Chwarae Pantycelyn. It is still well maintained in expectation that the club might reform.

LLANRHAEADR-YM-MOCHNANT (Powys) SJ1226

Llanrhaeadr-ym-Mochnant FC play in the Mid Wales League at the Recreation Field, Tan Llan, Llanrhaeadr-ym-Mochnant.

LLANRHYSTUD (Ceredigion) SN5369

Llanrhystud FC, formed in 1991, play in the Aberystwyth and District League, Division 1. Their playing field is located at the western end of the village along Church Lane. E Aled Jones has chronicled the history of football in the village in some detail. He has noted that a local team existed as early as 1878, and games were played on a fairly regular basis until 1889. Llanrhystud also played for one season in the league from 1947–48, home games being played on the Black Lion Field. This field was also used for a brief period by Llanfarian Rovers. It is now used for a Sunday market.

Cae Eithin Duon, Llanrug. Reproduced by kind permission of the photographer, Kevin Wyn Owen, and CPD Llanrug United FC.

LLANRUG (Gwynedd) SH5363

Llanrug United FC of the Welsh Alliance League have played their football at Cae Eithin Duon since 1968, but several other fields have hosted the team since its formation in 1922. These include Cefn Llwyd (1922-30), the Recreation Ground (1930-31), and Cae Plwy (1931-37 and 1945-46 when football resumed after the war). The years 1947-48 saw the team play their games at Cae Bailey, a field named after Henry Bailey Williams (1805-79), rector of Llanrug (1843-1879), who lived at Pantafon, Llanrug, and who held other property in the parish. During the early 1950s the club used at least three different fields at Tan'rwylfa, Pontrhyddallt, Dôl Helyg and Parc y Rhos.

LLANRUMNEY (Cardiff) ST2208

Rumney RFC of the WRU National Division 1 East and Llanrumney United FC of the South Wales Senior League, Division 1 both play at Riverside Park, Hartland Road, Llanrumney, Cardiff.

Splott Albion FC of the South Wales Amateur Football League, Division 1; Cardiff Cosmos Portos FC of the Cardiff and District Football League, Division 1; Llanrumney OB FC of Division 2; Cross Inn FC of Division 3 (based at Ye Olde Cross Inn, Llanrumney) and Llanrumney RFC of the WRU National Division 6 Central all play at the University Playing Fields, Llanrumney, a 33-acre site that includes five football and four rugby pitches. Several teams from the Cardiff Combination Football League also play on these fields, including BTD Stars FC (formed in 1966 by staff members of the British Transport Docks

Board), AFC Highcroft and STM (St Mellon's) Sports FC, who all play in Division 1.

Until 2008 Bridgend Street FC of the South Wales Amateur Football League, Division 1 also played at the University Playing Fields, but in August 2008 they returned to their roots at Splott Park.

Old Illtydians RFC, formed in 1928, of the WRU National League Division 3 South East, play at the Recreation Ground, Eastern Leisure Centre, Newport Road, Cardiff. From 1932 until 1966 they played at the Blackweir Playing Fields, Bute Park.

LLANRWST (Conwy) SH8061

Llanrwst United FC, founded in 1983 from the amalgamation of two teams, Llanrwst Athletic and Llanrwst United, play in the Welsh Alliance League at Gwydir Park. The place-name Gwydir dates from the fourteenth century and is associated with the low-lying land south-west of Llanrwst which belonged to the Wynn family of Gwydir Castle. It is interesting to note that when Accrington Stanley famously resigned from the English Football League in 1962 and eventually folded in 1966 as a Lancashire Combination side, a stand from their Peel Park ground was later acquired by Llanrwst and re-erected at Gwydir Park. It is still in use and has recently been refurbished. Llanrwst United is a progressive club and has ambitions to play at a higher level.

LLANSAMLET FC

see MORRISTON (Swansea)

LLANSANNAN (Conwy) SH9365

CPD Llansannan play in the Clwyd League, Premier Division, and their ground is located at Cae Chwaraeon, Maes Gogor, Llansannan.

LLANSAN(T)FFRAID-YM-MECHAIN (Powys) SJ2220

Y Dreflan was home to Llansantffraid FC (later Total Network Solutions (TNS) FC) until they merged with Oswestry Town to create the New Saints. The New Saints, who play in the Welsh Premiership, are now based at Park Hall, Oswestry. In March 2007 a new club known as Llansantffraid Village was formed, which has competed with great success in the Montgomeryshire Amateur League, Division 1. Promotion as champions of Division 2 was achieved during their first season.

LLANSAWEL FC

see NEATH ABBEY (Neath Port Talbot)

LLANSTEFFAN (Carmarthenshire) SN3510

Llansteffan FC of the Carmarthenshire League, Division 2 play at Y Morfa/The Green, Llansteffan.

LLANTRISANT (Rhondda Cynon Taf) ST0483

Llantrisant RFC, formed in 1891, of the WRU National Division 2 East play at St David's Place, Llantrisant.

LLANTWIT FARDRE (Rhondda Cynon Taf) ST0886

The club's website provides a detailed record of all the playing fields associated with rugby football in the village since the first record of a game being played as early as 1886 on the Duffryn Bach Field, off Station Road. Rugby continued to be played there until 1908, when the team moved to Tynywaun Field, opposite the Hollybush public house (Maesycelyn), where they played until the outbreak of war in 1914.

Little rugby was played in the village between the two world wars, but occasional matches were organised and played on the Bryn Field (behind the New Inn public house) and the Vicarage Field, which was associated with St Illtud's Church.

The present day club, who play in the WRU National Division 2 East, was founded in 1946, and until 1949 home fixtures were played on fields at Duffryn Dowlais Farm. At the beginning of the 1949-50 season, the team transferred to the Vicarage Field, but a major step forward took place in 1951 when the Llantrisant and Llantwit Fardre Rural District Council made a field available at Cae Fardre, Church Village. It was officially opened on 1 September 1951 with Pontypridd Rugby Club providing the opposition. Cae Fardre, immortalised by Neil Jenkins in his autobiography as his practice ground, is still used by the second XV, but the firsts now play at Parc Canol/Central Park, Church Village, acquired in September 1972. Both grounds are part of the same complex.

Llantwit Fardre FC, founded in 1958, of the Welsh League, Division 3 play at Tonteg Park, Llantwit Fardre.

LLANTWIT MAJOR (Vale of Glamorgan) SS9768

Llantwit Major RFC, founded in 1889, play in the WRU National Division 4 South East at the Recreation Ground. Vivian Kelly has noted that the club also played some games on the Crooked Shoard and on fields behind Ham Lane and West House.

Llantwit Major AFC play at Windmill Lane in the South Wales Amateur Football League, Division 1. The former windmill at SS9769 is a prominent local landmark.

LLANUWCHLLYN (Gwynedd) SH8730

Llanuwchllyn FC of the Welsh National League (Wrexham Area), Division 1, formed in 1956, play at a ground adjacent to Y Neuadd Bentref (village hall), known locally as Cae Ffwtbol. This field was acquired in 1988 and used from 1990 onwards. Previously, the team played on Cae'r Prys, a field on the land of Prys Mawr Farm on the outskirts of the village.

LLAN-WERN (Newport) ST3688

Llan-wern AFC, formed in 1963, play in the Welsh League, Division 2 and share their ground with Newport County at Spytty Park.

Hartridge RFC, champions of the WRU National League Division 6 in 2008-09, play at the Corus Llanwern Sports Ground, Newport.

LLANWDDYN FC

see ABERTRIDWR (Powys)

LLANYBYDDER (Carmarthenshire) SN5244

Cae OJ/OJ Park, home of Llanybydder RFC who play in the WRU National Division 3 West, is named in honour of Oriel Jones, a local businessman, councillor and president of Llanybydder RFC.

LLANYBYDDER FC

see ALLTYBLACA (Ceredigion)

LLANYSTUMDWY (Gwynedd) SH4738

Llanystumdwy FC play in the Gwynedd League at Parc Dwyfor.

LLAY (Wrexham) SJ3355

Llay Welfare of the Welsh National League (Wrexham Area), Premier Division play at the Ring, Llay, Wrexham.

Caergwrle Castle FC, formerly of the Welsh National League (Wrexham Area), Division 3, played at Nant-y-gaer, Llay until they folded in 2008.

LLEW GOCH (sic): CPD

see GELLIDEG (Merthyr Tydfil)

LLISWERRY (Newport) ST3348

Lliswerry FC of the Gwent County League, Division 2 play at the Newport International Sports Village Pitch.

Lliswerry FC of the Newport and District League play

at Lliswerry School. Several teams in the District League play all or some of their games at Lliswerry Recreational Ground, including Cromwell Youth (Premier Y), Riverview Hibernians and Spencer Old Boys FC (Division 2).

LLWYDCOED (Rhondda Cynon Taf) SN9904

AFC Llwydcoed, founded in 1948, who play in the Welsh League, Division 2 are based at the Llwydcoed Welfare Ground, Merthyr Road, Llwydcoed, Aberdare.

LLWYNYPIA (Rhondda Cynon Taf) SS9993

AFC Llwynypia play in the South Wales Senior League, Division 2 at Ynyscynon Park.

LLYFRGELL GEN. FC

see LLANBADARN FAWR (Ceredigion)

LÔN-LAS YOUTH FC

see SKEWEN (Neath Port Talbot)

LORD RAGLAN FC

see DOWLAIS (Merthyr Tydfil)

LOUGHOR (Swansea) SS5798

Loughor Rovers play in the Carmarthenshire League, Division 1 at Parc Williams, Castle Street, Loughor. According to local historian Sheila Francis, Parc Williams is named after a generous benefactor who emigrated to the United States. I am very much indebted to alderman Morlais Thomas who provided me with a great deal of additional information on the benefactor, J C Williams. He was born at Bryn Road, Loughor, the son of Thomas and Elizabeth Williams. He emigrated to the United States at the end of the nineteenth century, where he was initially engaged in the silkworm farm industry with his wife Frances Courtney, a native of Waunarlwydd, near Swansea, who tragically died in a garden fire at the family home. Williams later went into the steel industry, becoming a millionaire. In his will he left a substantial legacy to his native town in the form of a scholarship and bursary, and donated land that was subsequently named Parc Williams in his honour.

Football has been played in Loughor since 1920 and several other fields are noted on the club's website that have played host to the predecessors of the present team including Cae Globe, behind the Globe Inn. During the 1930s football was also played on land opposite Loughor Foundry and at Pen-y-beili.

Rugby was first played at Loughor in 1882 and the local club play in the WRU National Division 2 West at Villa Field, Belgrave Road, Loughor. Rugby was also played on Cae Globe and the Rectory Field.

LOVELL'S ATHLETIC FC

see NEWPORT

LOWER NEW INN FC

see NEW INN (Torfaen)

LUCAS CWMBRÂN FC

see CWMBRÂN (Torfaen)

MACHEN (Caerphilly) ST2189

Rugby was played at Machen as early as 1870 on a sloping field known as Cae'r Fforwm, and the club were founder members of the Welsh Rugby Union. The present team compete in the WRU National Division 4 East and play at the Welfare Ground, Machen.

Tradesman's Arms FC, a team based at the public house of that name at Chatham, Machen, play in the Newport and District League, Premier Division X.

MACHNO UNITED FC

see PENMACHNO (Conwy)

MACHYNLLETH (Powys) SH7400

Machynlleth FC, founded in 1885, a team with an illustrious history and twice winners of the Welsh Amateur Cup in 1902 and 1932, now play in the Aberystwyth and District League, Division 1 at Cae Glas, adjacent to Plas Machynlleth and Bro Ddyfi Leisure Centre on land given to the town by the marquess of Londonderry in 1948. Cae Glas was officially opened in 1976, but had been used by the club since the beginning of the 1975-76 season. The club formerly played at the renowned Newlands Park until the early 1970s, a ground that was subsequently developed for housing. David Wyn Davies' history of the club records that the team first played on Isaac Evans' field in the Garsiwn. The approach to the field was through Garsiwn Square and spectators were asked to pay one penny admission at the kissing gates near Brickfield House. The team also played on Cae Third (the Goat Inn Field), on a field between Tanrallt and the cemetery, on the Rectory Field alongside Newtown Road, on Cae Maenllwyd and on the Plas Grounds. However, shortly after the Great War the club settled at its new home, Newlands Park, which developed into a fine ground hosting seven prestigious Welsh Amateur Cup final matches and regularly attracting crowds in excess of 3,000. The last game played at Newlands Park was held on 29 April 1973.

Machynlleth RFC, who play in the WRU National League Division 2 North, also play at Cae Glas on an adjoining Plas Grounds pitch.

MACKWORTH FC

see ABERDARE (Rhondda Cynon Taf)

MAERDY (Rhondda Cynon Taf) SS9798

Ferndale, once a major force in Welsh League football, now play in the Rhondda and District Football League and have relocated to Maerdy Field, Rowley Terrace, Maerdy.

Ferndale Boys' Club who play in the South Wales Amateur Football League, Division 2 also play at Maerdy Field.

MAESGLAS FC

see CARDIGAN (Ceredigion)

MAESTEG (Bridgend) SS8591

Maesteg RFC, formed in 1877, play in the WRU National League Division 2 West at Llynfi Road. The ground was opened in 1900 and was created from a tip of the Llynvi iron works.

Maesteg Harlequins RFC, formed in 1936, play in the WRU National Division 3 South West at the South Parade Playing Fields, Maesteg. They moved to this ground when it was opened in 1962 as a new municipal field sited on a former brickworks. Prior to that date they had led a very nomadic existence and their official website records that their home grounds included Maesteg RFC's Llynfi Road, Llangynwyd Playing Fields, Coytrahen – the old playing field that was situated behind Maesteg hospital, home to Nantyffyllon RFC and still referred to as Nanty's 'old field' – and the Hurling Field, a ground built for a large Irish community to enjoy their favourite pastime.

Maesteg Celtic RFC of the WRU National Division 4 South West play at the Garth Welfare Park, Maesteg.

FC Maesteg of the Bridgend and District Football League, Premier Division also play at South Parade Playing Fields.

MAESTEG PARK FC

see CROESERW (Neath Port Talbot)

MALPAS (Newport) ST3090

Malpas Gladiators FC play in the Gwent County League, Division 2 at Westfield Park, Malpas. Malpas FC, who play in the Newport and District League, Premier Division X, also play at the same location where two pitches are available. They also play at Shaftesbury Park, Newport. Some other defunct teams in the Newport and District League, such as Parc-y-Prior FC, have also used the same playing field.

MALTSERS SPORTS FC

see HAFOD (Swansea)

MANORBIER (Pembrokeshire) SSO697

Manorbier United FC play in the Pembrokeshire League, Division 3 at the Manorbier Playing Fields.

MARDY (Monmouthshire) SJ3015

Mardy FC of the Gwent County Football League, Division 1 play at Mardy Park, Mardy, near Abergavenny.

MARGAM (Neath Port Talbot) SS8038

Corus RFC of the WRU National Division 1 West and Corus Steel FC, newly promoted to the Welsh League, Division 3, both play at the Corus Sports Ground, Margam, Port Talbot.

Margam YC FC play in the Port Talbot Football League, Premier Division at the Groeswen Playing Field.

MARKHAM (Caerphilly) SO1601

Markham RFC play in the WRU National Division 6 East at King George's Field.

MARSHFIELD (Newport) ST2758

Marshfield FC play in the Newport and District League, Premier Division X. Matches are played on the playing fields in Wellfield Road located behind Marshfield Village Hall. Plans to drain and adapt an adjacent field for junior football are currently under consideration.

MARTYRS FC

see PENYDARREN ((Merthyr Tydfil)

MASTER MARINERS FC

see BARRY (Vale of Glamorgan)

MATHERN (Monmouthshire) ST5291

Mathern Wanderers, formed in 2003, play in the East Gwent Football League, Division 1 at the Mathern Athletic Football Ground.

MAX UNITED FALCONS FC

see CLYDACH VALE (Rhondda Cynon Taf)

MAYHILL (Swansea) SS6494

West End FC, founded in 1964, who play in the Welsh League, Division 1, are based in the Mayhill area of Swansea. Their ground is Pryderi Park Stadium. During their early days in the Swansea Senior League they played at Paradise Park, a red ash pitch in the Townhill area of the city.

MEIFOD (Powys) SJ1512

Meifod FC play in the Montgomeryshire Amateur League, Division 1 at the King's Head Field. An earlier venue was the Pentre Go Field.

COBRA (Caereinion Old Boys Rugby Association) RFC play at Cae COBRA, Meifod in the WRU National League Division 2 North.

MEINCIAU (Carmarthenshire) SN4610

Meinciau FC were a force to be reckoned with in the Carmarthenshire League during the early 1960s. Their playing field, located in the centre of this Gwendraeth Valley village, now looks rather sad and neglected.

MELIDEN (Flintshire) SJ5199

Meliden FC returned to the Clwyd League, Division 2 in 2008–09 after an absence of ten years. Home games are played at Ffordd Pennant, Meliden.

MEMORY LANE FC

see HEATH (Cardiff)

MENAI BRIDGE (Anglesey) SH5572

Menai Bridge RFC, a Welsh Districts side, play at Llyn y Felin, Coed Cyrnol, Menai Bridge.

Menai Bridge Tigers FC once fielded a very successful senior side in the Anglesey League. The club still has an active junior section operating six teams. Games are played on King George's Field, Menai Bridge. They re-entered the Anglesey League in 2009-10.

MERLIN'S BRIDGE (Pembrokeshire) SM9414

Merlin's Bridge of the Pembrokeshire League, Division 1 play at the Racecourse.

Haverfordwest RFC, founded in 1875, of the WRU National Division 3 West, play at Pembroke Road, Merlin's Bridge, Haverfordwest.

MERTHYR TYDFIL (SO0506)

Penydarren Park is the historic home of Merthyr Tydfil FC, founded in 1945, who play in the Southern League, Premier Division. In the late 1940s and early 1950s they won no less than five league championships, and in 1947 they attracted a record crowd of over 21,000 for an FA Cup tie against Reading. In the early 1990s they enjoyed two seasons in the English Football Conference and still harbour ambitions of entering the Football League. Plans have been drawn up for a possible new stadium on the outskirts of the town, in the hope that they can again bring league football back to the town and emulate Merthyr Town FC, a club with no direct connections to the present team, who graced the Third Division from 1920 until it folded in 1934. Merthyr Town FC also played at Penydarren Park. However, recent serious and well-publicised financial problems appear to be threatening the future of the club, and the economic downturn which has had severe effects on major employers such as the

*Penydarren Park, Merthyr Tydfil. Action from an FA Cup first round tie
drawn 2-2 between Merthyr and Ipswich Town on 29 November 1951.
Photograph: Geoff Charles Collection, reproduced by kind permission of the
National Library of Wales.*

Hoover Candy Group is further adding to the club's difficulties.
After a High Court hearing in June 2009 the club was placed into
administration at the request of the Supporters' Trust.

Merthyr Saints (formerly Hoover Sports), founded in the
1950s, play in the Welsh League, Division 3 and are based at the
ICI Rifle Field, Bryniau Road, Pant, Merthyr Tydfil. Originally,
Hoover Sports played on a ground adjacent to the Hoover factory
at Pentrebach.

Bluebirds FC, Court House FC and Morlais Tavern FC
(disbanded in 2008), based in Dowlais, of the Merthyr Tydfil
Football League, Premier Division, play at the Oval, Mountain

Hare, as do Baili Glas FC, a team based at the Baili Glas Inn, Twynyrodyn Road, Merthyr Tydfil, who play in the league's First Division, together with Quar Park Rangers, based at the Quar Park Inn, Brecon Road, who were relegated from the Premier Division to Division 1 in 2008.

Merthyr Tydfil RFC, one of the founding members of the WRU in 1881, play in the WRU National League Division 1 East at the Wern in Ynysfach, Merthyr. The club's website records several venues used by the club until it settled at its present ground in 1958. These include Plymouth Ground at Pentrebach, used before the Great War, Gwynne's Field, Cefncoedycymer and Penydarren Park. After the Second World War, Dix's Field, Danydarren and Glyndyrus Field, Abercannaid were used before the present ground was acquired.

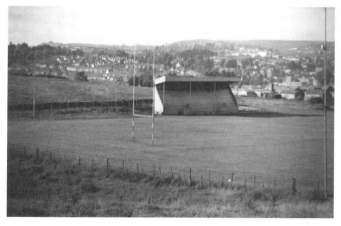

Wern Field, Merthyr Tydfil in the 1960s, home of Merthyr RFC.
Photograph reproduced by kind permission of Alan George and Michael
Donovan, Merthyr. http://www.alangeorge.co.uk/

Rugby league was also played briefly at the Rhydycar Ground by the Merthyr Tydfil rugby league team from 1909-11. The club failed to survive in the face of stiff competition from the more popular association football and rugby union codes.

METAL BOX FC

see RESOLVEN (Neath Port Talbot)

MID-RHONDDA FC/RLFC

see TONYPANDY (Rhondda Cynon Taf)

MILFORD HAVEN (Pembrokeshire) SM9005

Milford United FC, once a major force in Welsh League football, play at Marble Hall in the Pembrokeshire League, Division 2.

Milford Athletic FC play in the Pembrokeshire League, Division 2 at Pill Lane.

MILFORD HAVEN RFC

see HAKIN (Pembrokeshire)

MISKIN: AFC

see MOUNTAIN ASH (Rhondda Cynon Taf)

MOCHDRE (Conwy) SH8278

Mochdre Sports FC play in the Clwyd League, Premier Division at the Mochdre Sports Ground, Blackmarsh Fields, Mochdre.

see also BETWS-YN-RHOS (Conwy)

MOELFRE (Anglesey) SH5186

CPD Bro Goronwy play in the Anglesey League at Caeau Gleision Farm, Moelfre.

MOLD (Flintshire) SJ236

Mold Alexandra FC, founded in 1929, promoted from the Welsh National League (Wrexham Area), Premier Division to the Cymru Alliance League in 2008, play at Alyn Park. Mold Alex, as they are affectionately known, were founder members of the League of Wales in 1992 but survived only three seasons in the top flight before being relegated in 1995. The possibility that the ground, which is owned by Synthite, a chemical company based at the town for over 50 years, may be developed for housing has apparently been explored, with the promise that Synthite would provide a new ground on land that they own on the outskirts of the town at Ffordd Pennant.

Mold Juniors play in the Welsh National League (Wrexham Area), Division 1 at Mold Sports Centre.

Mold RFC play at Chester Road and compete in the WRU National Division 1 North.

MONKTON (Pembrokeshire) SM9701

Monkton Swifts FC play at Monkton Lane in the Pembrokeshire League, Division 1.

MONMOUTH (Monmouthshire) SO5012

Monmouth RFC play in the WRU National Division 4 East at the Old Druid's Mead. It is recorded that a team from Monmouth played neighbouring Chepstow at the Dixton in November 1887.

Monmouth Town FC, established in 1930, of the Welsh League, Division 3 play at Monmouth Sports Ground, Chippenham, Monmouth.

MONTGOMERY (Powys) SO2296

Football was played in the nineteenth century in the town, and Caerhowell is recorded as the location of a match held in 1894. The current team, Montgomery Town of the Montgomeryshire League, Division 2, play at Clostanymur (enclosure beneath the wall), a name reflecting its location in the shadow of the town walls built by Edward I in 1279-80.

MORLAIS TAVERN FC

see MERTHYR TYDFIL

MORRISTON (Swansea) SS6698

Morriston Rugby Club, founded in 1876, is one of the oldest clubs in Wales. They play at the Maes Collen Playing Fields, Heol Gwernen, Cwmrhydyceirw in the WRU National Division 3 West. Among their many playing fields can be counted the site of the defunct Duffryn Steelworks, the Old Worcester Field, Midland Field, Lan Field, and a field near Morriston golf course. They acquired their present ground in 1961.

Morriston Town FC, founded in 1926, of the Swansea Senior League, Division 1, play at the Dingle, Clydach Road, Morriston. The club was relegated in 2008 after competing for over 50 years in the Welsh League.

Morriston Olympic FC of the Swansea Senior Football League, Division 1; Cooper's Arms FC and Llangyfelach FC of Division 2; CRC (Cwmrhydyceirw) Rangers FC of Division 3 and Llansamlet FC of Division 4 all play on several pitches at Tir Canol, Chemical Road, Cwmrhydyceirw, Morriston.

MOSTYN (Flintshire) SJ1580

Maes Pennant, the home of Mostyn Dragons FC, 2008-09 champions of the Clwyd League, Division 2, is named after Thomas Pennant (1726-98), the eminent naturalist and antiquary of Downing Hall, Flintshire, who married Ann, daughter of Sir Thomas Mostyn (1704-58) of Mostyn Hall.

MOUNTAIN ASH (Rhondda Cynon Taf) ST0499

Mountain Ash RFC, founded in 1875, have an illustrious history. They defeated a touring Canadian side in 1904 and toured the south of France with success as early as 1911. They currently play in the WRU National Division 2 East at Parc Duffryn Pennar. From 1909 to 1995 they played at the Recreation Ground; earlier games were played on the Washery Field.

Abercynon RFC play in the WRU National League Division 2 East at Parc Abercynon, Mountain Ash.

Mountain Ash Town play in the Aberdare Valley Football League, Premier Division at Peace Park and Caedrawnant Fields. Osborne Athletic, a team based at the Osborne Hotel, Penrhiwceibr, but now known as Penrhiwceiber Con Athletic, also played in the Aberdare Valley Football League, Premier Division at Caedrawnant Fields. Pentwyn Fields in Mountain Ash was the home ground for Fernhill Flyers FC, another Aberdare Valley Football League, Premier Division side that failed to reform for the 2008-09 season.

Pentwyn Fields is also home to Perthcelyn United FC who, in 2008, entered two new teams in the Aberdare Valley Football League, Division 1. Perthcelyn United 'A' were crowned league champions.

Mountain Ash Athletic FC of the Aberdare Valley Football League, Division 1 play at Deep Duffryn.

AFC Miskin of the Aberdare Valley Football League, Division 1 have used both Deep Duffryn and the Caedrawnant pitches.

MOUNTAIN RANGERS FC

see RHOSGADFAN (Gwynedd)

MUMBLES (Swansea) SS6188

Underhill Park (originally known as Underhill Field), Newton Road, is the home of Mumbles RFC, founded in 1887, who currently play in the WRU National Division 2 West. Underhill lies at the foot of Llanmadoc Hill, one of the highest points on Gower and the site of an Iron Age hill fort.

Mumbles Rangers FC of the Swansea Senior Football League, Division 3 also play at Underhill Park.

MURTON (Swansea) ST0581

Murton Rovers FC of the Swansea Senior District League, Division 3 play at Murton, near Bishopston, Gower.

MYNYDD LLANDYGÁI FC

see LLANDYGÁI (Gwynedd)

MYNYDDISA (Flintshire) SJ2564

Mynyddisa FC, founded in 1976, of the Cymru Alliance League play at Argoed Sports Ground, Snowden Avenue, Bryn-y-Baal, Mynyddisa. The club's website notes that football was probably first played in the village in 1931 and that the home pitch at this time was on the Wylfa Hill Field. Other pitches used were opposite the stone cottages in Chambers Lane, Field Bron, Wylfa Farm, Argoed Small Holding and also the Wilcox and Jones Estate Field located opposite the garden centre.

After 33 years of existence, and a very successful last season, the club rather surprisingly announced in May 2009 that it was folding.

MYNYDD-Y-GARREG (Carmarthenshire) SN5050

Mynydd-y-garreg RFC, founded in 1985, of the WRU National Division 6 West, play at Parc Gwenllian. The park is named in honour of Princess Gwenllian (*d.*1136), who fell in battle against the Normans at neighbouring Maes Gwenllian, Kidwelly. The village will always be synonymous with the late Ray Gravell (1951-2007), the Llanelli, Wales and British Lions rugby legend.

NANT CONWY: CLWB RYGBI

see TREFRIW (Conwy)

NANTGAREDIG (Carmarthenshire) SN4921

Nantgaredig RFC, formed in 1966, of the WRU National Division 6 West, play at Cae'r Ystrad, a field the club purchased in 1973. Since that date the club has invested heavily in improved facilities, including new changing rooms and floodlighting.

NANTLLE VALE FC

see PEN-Y-GROES (Gwynedd)

NANTYFFYLLON (Bridgend) SS8592

Nantyffyllon RFC of the WRU National Division 3 South West play at Blosse Street, Nantyffyllon. The name Blosse is associated with the Lynch-Blosse family of Galway, who were significant local land and coalmine owners. The club approached Mr Lynch-Blosse and negotiated a reasonable price with him for allotment land at Blosse Street, which was converted into a first-class playing pitch and clubhouse, officially opened in September 1963.

Today the family is represented by the seventeenth baronet Sir Richard Hely Lynch-Blosse (b.1953), a medical practitioner, who succeeded to the title in 1971.

The club traces its origins to the late nineteenth century with the formation of Spelters RFC, reflecting the place-name of that part of the village. The original Spelters Field is very close to the present field, but rugby was also played at other locations in the village, notably Ton Hir, shared with Nantyfyllon AFC after the Great War, and the Hospital Field, opened in 1933, which was later shared with Maesteg Park FC in the mid 1950s.

NANT-Y-GLO (Blaenau Gwent) SO1910

Nant-y-glo RFC play in the WRU National Division 4 East at Porters Road. Local rugby is also played at Banna Park, Nant-y-glo.

PFS Athletic FC play in the North Gwent Football League, Division 1 at Nant-y-glo Leisure Centre.

NANT-Y-GLO FC

see BRYN-MAWR (Blaenau Gwent)

NANTYMOEL (Bridgend) SS9392

Nantymoel RFC play at Nantymoel Park in the WRU National Division 4 South East.

Nantymoel FC, once of the Welsh League but now of the Bridgend and District Football League, Division 1, play at the Aber Fields.

NARBERTH (Pembrokeshire) SN1014

Narberth RFC of the WRU National Division 1 West, formed in 1879, play at the Lewis-Lloyd Ground. Rugby was played in Narberth from the 1870s until around 1909, with the game being revived in 1926 through a public meeting and the acquisition of a field, Bloomfield Meadow, through the generosity of Miss Lewis-Lloyd, the landowner. In 1945 the ground was given as an outright gift to the club. It was officially opened on 16 September 1948, and the field re-named the Lewis-Lloyd Ground in recognition of her generosity. In 1965 the club adopted the

Lewis-Lloyd Ground, Narberth RFC. Reproduced by kind permission of the photographer, Elwyn Davies, Narberth and Narberth RFC.

otter as its emblem to further acknowledge Miss Lewis-Lloyd's support for local rugby as she was a staunch follower of the otter hunt. In the late 1980s major levelling and drainage work was undertaken on the field and a new 500-seater stand was built which incorporated wheelchair access. The club also built a new clubhouse with a viewing balcony, and the addition of floodlighting in 2008 makes it one of the most modern and impressive rugby grounds in Wales.

Narberth FC of the Pembrokeshire League, Division 1 play at Jesse Road.

NAVAL and MILITARY FC

see ST THOMAS (Swansea)

NEATH (Neath Port Talbot) SS7597

The Gnoll is the home of Neath RFC, who play in the WRU National League Premier Division. Dr Andrew Hignell has recorded the history of the ground in some detail. The Gnoll, a seventeenth-century house, was from 1710 the home of the Mackworth family, wealthy industrialists, who made a fortune from copper smelting. It is likely that the name *Gnoll* is derived from *Knoll*, a hillock, and it is recorded that a hillock on the eastern extremities of the estate was written as *La Knolle* in 1570. References to *Cae'r Gnol* and *Heol y Gnol* also occur before 1685. In 1811 the Gnoll Estate was bought by Henry Grant, who later became the first mayor of the town. Grant sold off some of the land for building purposes and allowed ball games to be played on the fields below Gnoll House.

Cricket was played on this land as early as the 1840s, and rugby followed from 1871 with the formation of Neath RFC, one of the founding clubs of the WRU in 1881. The south-western part of the sports field was devoted to rugby, with cricket being played in the north-eastern half.

In 1923 the Neath Corporation became the new owners of the Gnoll Estate, and decreed that the ruins of the Gnoll House and gardens should be the town's war memorial, and that the rugby and cricket ground should be preserved and developed for sporting activities. Although Gnoll House itself became unsafe and was later demolished in 1957, the strategy succeeded and first-class county cricket was staged at the ground for many decades. The venue continues to host rugby of a high standard.

From 2008 the Gnoll will also host Neath FC's home games

in an ambitious move by the soccer club to meet UEFA ground criteria. Previously, association football had only been played on a handful of occasions at the Gnoll. In 1987 the actor Dennis Waterman captained a team of celebrities which included England World Cup winners Geoff Hurst and Martyn Peters in a charity football match.

NEATH ABBEY (Neath Port Talbot) SS7397

The Cwrt Herbert Playing Fields are situated on what was once part of the estate of Neath Abbey. Following the dissolution of the monastery in 1539 by Henry VIII the abbey lands were dispersed, and by the late sixteenth century the abbot's house was converted into an impressive home by the new owner Sir John Herbert (*d.*1617).

Several clubs are based at Cwrt Herbert, including Llansawel FC of the Welsh League, Division 3 (who have now merged with Briton Ferry Athletic to form Briton Ferry Llansawel FC) and AFC Caewern, founded in 2000, who play in the Neath Football League, Premier Division. Initially, they played at Pontardawe Leisure Centre. FC Nedd, who compete in the same division, also play at Cwrt Herbert. Bear FC and Borough Arms FC, who play in Division 1, and Oxford Arms FC and Denticare Tonna FC, who play in Division 2, are also based at Cwrt Herbert.

Neath Athletic RFC of the WRU National Division 5 South West also play at Cwrt Herbert.

NEATH ATHLETIC FC

see LLANDARCY (Neath Port Talbot)

NEFYN (Gwynedd) SH3040

Nefyn United of the Welsh Alliance League play at Cae'r Delyn.

NELSON (Caerphilly) ST1195

Nelson RFC play in the WRU National Division 3 East at the Park, Nelson.

Nelson Cavaliers FC, founded in 1972, play in the South Wales Senior League, Division 2 at Wern Field. The team used the Park and the Welfare Ground during its first three years of existence.

NEW BRIGHTON (Wrexham) SJ2750

New Brighton FC of the Welsh National League (Wrexham Area), Division 1 play at the Community Centre, New Brighton.

NEW DOCK STARS RFC

see LLANELLI (Carmarthenshire)

NEW INN (Torfaen) ST3099

New Inn FC of the Gwent County League, Division 3 play at Woodfield Road, New Inn, south of Pontypool. Lower New Inn FC field a side in the Gwent Central League, Premier Division.

New Panteg RFC play in the WRU National League Division 6 East at New Road, New Inn.

NEW PANTEG RFC

see NEW INN (Torfaen)

NEW RADNOR (Powys) SO2160

Radnor Valley FC play in the Mid Wales League (South). Their field is located in School Lane, New Radnor.

THE NEW SAINTS FC

see OSWESTRY (Shropshire)

NEW TREDEGAR (Caerphilly) SO1403

New Tredegar RFC, founded in 1977, of the WRU National League Division 4 East, and Tredegar Arms FC, originally founded as a Sunday League team in 1992, play in the North Gwent Football League, Division 1 at Grove Park, New Tredegar.

NEWBOROUGH (Anglesey) SH4265

Newborough FC, once of the Anglesey League, played at Tir Bodfail. They were a considerable force in local football, winning the League title on no fewer than eight occasions between 1954 and 1973.

NEWBRIDGE (Torfaen) ST2197

Formed in 1888, Newbridge RFC of the WRU National Division 1 East play at the Welfare Ground, Bridge Street, Newbridge. According to Terry Powell, the club historian, Newbridge RFC moved to the Welfare Ground in 1921 from Waen Bwdr, its fifth venue in a space of 30 years. Its first ground was known as Dr Richards' Field – Richards was the first president of the club. In 1890 the club moved to a field on Tŷ Isaf Farm and shortly afterwards moved again to Top Flats, where the Treowen Housing estate now stands. From 1901 the club played at the Show Field, where Alexandra Palace is located.

Treowen Stars, formed in 1926, play in the Gwent County League, Division 1 at Bush Park, Uplands, Newbridge.

Pentwynmawr Athletic FC play in the Gwent County League, Division 1 at the Welfare Ground.

NEWBRIDGE-ON-WYE (Powys) SO0158

Newbridge of the Mid Wales League play at Penbont Field, Penbont Farm, Newbridge-on-Wye. There is also a small football pitch in the centre of the village administered by Powys County Council.

NEWCASTLE EMLYN (Carmarthenshire) SN3040

Parc Emlyn is the impressive home of ambitious Newcastle Emlyn FC, a club formed in the early twentieth century, who play in the Welsh League, Division 2, having gained promotion in 2008. The record attendance of 1,800 was set in a friendly match with Chelsea in 1991. The derivation of the word Emlyn is uncertain, but it might have come from Emelinus – a Roman chieftain who may have been in some way connected to the site of the castle.

Dôl Wiber (field of the viper/serpent), on the Ceredigion side of the river Teifi, is the home of Newcastle Emlyn RFC, who play in the WRU National Division 3 West. The club, formed in 1977, played its early games at Cae Gelligatti near the town cemetery before moving to Cwrcoed Meadows in 1978. Both fields take their names from adjacent farms. In 1991 the club purchased its present ground at Dôl Wiber, which was officially opened on 27 August 1992 with a prestigious fixture against Neath RFC. The field was called Dôl Wiber after the late J Ainsleigh Davies (*d.* 2002) who won a competition to suggest a suitable name for the club's new venue. The (*g*)*wiber* refers to the legend of the Emlyn wyvern successfully slain by a brave local after it had threatened to overcome the population of the town. It is a fine venue with good parking facilities, several pitches, floodlighting and a sizeable grandstand on the main pitch.

NEWCASTLE-ON-CLUN (Shropshire) SO2482

Newcastle FC play in the Mid Wales League (South) at the Mill Field.

NEWI CEFN DRUIDS FC

see CEFN MAWR (Wrexham)

NEWPORT ST3178

Newport RFC played their early games on the Marshes, an area now known as Shaftesbury Park. In 1877 Godfrey Charles Morgan (1831-1913), second Baron Tredegar, granted use of land at Rodney Parade at a 'peppercorn rent' to Newport Cricket and Athletic Club. The area, which eventually grew to 15 acres, was purchased for £7,026 from the Tredegar Estate in 1923. It is worth noting that as a young captain in the Crimean

War, Morgan participated in the Charge of the Light Brigade in 1854.

Rodney Parade, famous home of Newport RFC who play in the WRU National Premier League, and regional side Dragons, is situated off Rodney Road in Newport and is named after Charles Rodney Morgan (1828-54), the son of Sir Charles Morgan Robinson Morgan (1792-1875), first Baron Tredegar, who died at the young age of twenty-five. The origins of the name Rodney in the family can be traced to Sir Charles' mother-in-law, Sarah Bryges Rodney (c.1780-1871), daughter of Admiral Sir George Brydges Rodney (1718-92). It has witnessed many historic matches

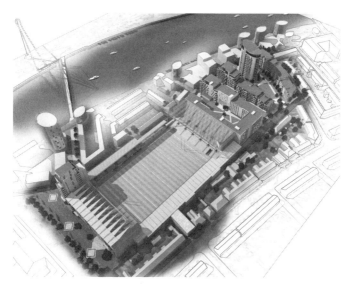

Rodney Parade, Newport. An archictectural vision of the proposed redevelopment, reproduced by kind permission of Robert Guy, Arturus Architects, Bristol.

including the unforgettable win over Sir Wilson Whineray's otherwise undefeated Fifth All Blacks in 1963 when John Uzzell dropped his winning goal to record an unlikely 3-0 win.

Plans were recently announced to refurbish the ground and increase its capacity to 15,000 spectators. Approval for the plans were given the go ahead in March 2009.

Newport Saracens, who play in the WRU National Division 2 East, played at Mount Pleasant Park, Beech Grove St Brides Wentlooge, Newport. They moved to their new Maesglas ground on 26 January 2008.

St Julian's HSOB RFC play in the WRU National Division 6 East.

Newport also has a famous soccer tradition and Somerton Park, opened in 1912, was the home of Newport County FC who played in the English Football League for 68 years. A club record crowd of 24,268 was recorded for the visit of arch-rivals Cardiff City in a league encounter in October 1937. The club struggled for most of the post-war period, but did have a successful run in the European Cup Winners' Cup in 1980 after winning the Welsh Cup for the first and only time in its history. After defeating teams from Northern Ireland and Norway, County finally succumbed to defeat at Somerton Park against Carl Zeuss Jena of East Germany in front of over 18,000 fans. Following its failure to gain re-election to the Football League, the club folded in February 1989 after failing to meet its commitments to the Conference League. Somerton Park was also a popular venue for greyhound and speedway racing.

The club was re-formed in June 1989 and after a few years

playing in exile, is now established at Spytty Park (Newport Stadium), with an expressed wish to try and regain its English Football League status. The club currently plays in the Conference League South. Llanwern AFC, formed in 1963, who play in the Welsh League, Division 2 share the ground with Newport County at Spytty Park.

Somerton Park was demolished in 1993 and redeveloped for housing.

Crindau Park, in the Shaftesbury area of the city, is home to Albion Rovers who have an interesting history. Albion Rovers FC was formed by Scottish coal miners who moved to Wales to seek work in 1937. They named the team after the Coatbridge team who now play in the Scottish League, Division 3. They currently play at Crindau Park (also known as Kimberley Park, named after the terrace of the same name built shortly after the Boer War siege of 1899-1900). The club has also played at Lliswerry Recreation Ground and shared Spytty Park with Newport County during the period from 1993 to 2005 when they played in the Welsh League. However, they were relegated to the Gwent County League in 2005 and currently play at that level in Division 1, but have had a good season, comfortably winning the league title in 2008-09.

Shaftesbury Youth FC play in the Newport and District League, Division 1 at Shaftesbury Park. Malpas FC also play some games at Shaftesbury Park.

Newport YMCA FC, founded in 1973, of the Welsh League, Division 2 play at Mendalgief Road, Newport.

Rexville, Newport was the home of Lovell's Athletic FC –

one of Wales' most famous clubs. The club, based at the Lovell's toffee factory in Newport, was formed in 1917 and played with considerable success in the Western League, Southern League and Welsh League until it folded in 1969. It once attracted a crowd in excess of 10,000 for a cup match in 1945. The ground was located at the junction of Albany Street and Alderney Street adjacent to the factory. The factory has now been relocated and its site and the football ground developed into a housing estate aptly named the Turnstiles. Dave Twydell has chronicled the fascinating history of this club in some detail.

Newport Corinthians play in the Gwent County League, Division 2 at Coronation Park, a ground overshadowed by Newport's famous transporter bridge. Racing Club Newport FC of the Newport and District League, Division 3 also play at Coronation Park. Ship and Pilot FC also play some games at the Park.

Cromwell Youth FC of the Gwent League, Division 2 play at Hartridge Comprehensive School, Newport.

St Julian's Youth FC play in the Newport and District League, Premier Division X at Glebelands.

Cosmos FC play in the Newport and District Football League, Division 2 mainly at Tredegar Park. The park is also the venue used by other local teams, such as Newport Eagles (Division 2) and Tŷ-Sign FC (Division 3). The 2004 National Eisteddfod of Wales was held within the confines of the park.

Spencer Youth and Boys FC of the Gwent County League, Division 1, and Spencer Old Boys FC of the Newport and District Football League, Division 1, play at Ringland Park.

Villa Dino/Christchurch FC play in the Gwent County League, Division 3 and are based in the Christchurch area of the city.

NEWPORT (Pembrokeshire) SN0553

Maes Chwarae Trefdraeth/Newport Playing Fields, purchased through a community initiative in 1950, are managed by a joint committee of sporting clubs under the jurisdiction of Newport Town Council as custodian trustees. The fields have developed considerably since their acquisition over half a century ago, to include tennis courts, a multi-usage games area, changing rooms and the site of Ysgol Bro Ingli. The site of the school was once known as Bryn Gast. Newport Lions FC, a football team which withdrew from the Pembrokeshire League in 2008, played at this venue as did the short-lived Newport Borough FC who withdrew from the Cardiganshire League in 1950 after only two seasons. Today, the playing fields provide a home for Newport RFC, a junior club formed in 1983, as well as hosting the annual popular Newport Barbarian Sevens tournament. An earlier successful junior rugby team played on the Royal Oak Field, now a housing estate.

NEWPORT CIVIL SERVICE FC

see BETTWS (Newport)

NEWPORT HIGH SCHOOL OLD BOYS RFC

see CAERLEON (Newport)

NEWQUAY (Ceredigion) SN3859

Parc Arthur, impressive home of Newquay FC, who play in the Ceredigion League, Division 1 is named in honour of Arthur Thomas, a former chairman of the club. The field was originally known as Cae Gwair, and formed part of Towyn Farm.

NEWTON WANDERERS FC

see PORT TALBOT (Neath Port Talbot)

NEWTOWN (Powys) SO1191

Football in Newtown dates from 1875 and early games were played on a field known as the Cummings, now the location of Newtown Bowls Club in Back Lane. Latham Park became the home of Newtown in the late 1940s, and is named after George Latham (1881-1939), a Welsh international footballer who was born at Newtown on New Year's Day 1881. He played for Newtown in 1897-98 before leaving to fight in the Boer War until 1901. After the war, he returned for a brief spell with his home club before signing for Liverpool in 1902. He spent seven years at the club but only played 18 first team games. He also had brief spells with Wrexham, Southport, Stoke City and Cardiff City, and won a total of ten international caps. He enlisted with the Royal Welch Fusiliers in the Great War, serving as a captain, and was decorated with the Military Cross in 1917 for his bravery in Turkey. He is best remembered as a coach, being influential in preparing the Great Britain XI for the Paris Olympics of 1924 and the victorious Cardiff City team for the 1927 Cup Final. Latham suffered a serious motorcycle accident in 1936 which

Latham Park, Newtown. Photograph by Kevin Hughes. Reproduced with the kind permission of the photographer and Barry Gardner, Newtown Football Club.

curtailed his coaching activity. He retired to Newtown and died on 9 July 1939. Latham Park, now called G F Grigg Latham Park following a sponsorship deal with a local construction firm, is one of the most picturesque grounds in the Welsh Premiership. Because of its high seating capacity it has frequently been used by other Welsh Premiership clubs as a venue for European matches.

Newtown RFC of the WRU National Division 2 North play at the Recreation Ground, off the Welshpool Road.

NEYLAND (Pembrokeshire) SM9605

Neyland RFC, founded in 1885, play in the WRU National Division 5 West at John Street.

Neyland Athletic FC play in the Pembrokeshire League, Division 1 at the Neyland Athletic Ground.

NORTH END FC

see LANDORE (Swansea)

OAKDALE (Caerphilly) ST1899

Oakdale RFC play in the WRU National League Division 5 East at the Recreation Ground, Oakdale.

OAKFIELD FC

see CWMBRÂN (Torfaen)

OGMORE VALE (Bridgend) SS9390

Ogmore Vale RFC play in the WRU National Division 5 South Central at Ogmore Park.

OLD COLLEGE INN (OCI) FC

see BARRY (Vale of Glamorgan)

OLD COLWYN (Conwy) SH8678

Colwyn Bay FC, founded in 1881, play their football in the Northern Premier League, Division 1 North. Early games were played at Pendorlan, Penrhos Field, Llanerch Road by Tan-y-Bryn, the Marine Hotel Field and Eirias Park where they played a strong Manchester United team in 1922. They also played briefly at Mochdre after the Second World War, before moving back once more to Eirias Park where the Bay's record attendance of 5,000 was set in 1964 during an encounter with local rivals Borough United. Since 1984 they have played at Llanelian Road, Old Colwyn which has a capacity of 2,500.

Eirias Park was designated in December 2008 as the official home of the Gogledd Cymru (North Wales) WRU fifth development region.

OLD ILLTYDIANS RFC

see LLANRUMNEY (Cardiff)

OLD PENARTHIANS RFC

see PENARTH (Vale of Glamorgan)

ONLLWYN (Neath Port Talbot) SN8410

Onllwyn FC, who play in the Neath Football League, Premier Division at the Onllwyn Recreation Ground, were founded in 1988, but football has been played by several teams in this mining village since the early years of the twentieth century. The Welfare Association was established in 1922, and its first priority was the creation of a football pitch.

OSBORNE ATHLETIC FC

see PENRHIW-CEIBR (Rhondda Cynon Taf)

OSWESTRY (Shropshire) SJ2922

The New Saints FC of the Welsh Premiership now play their home games at Park Hall, Oswestry, a ground first used by the club in 1993. It has a FIFA-approved artificial playing surface, and hosted its first ever European tie on 9 July 2009 when the New Saints were defeated 1-2 by Icelandic side Fram Reykjavic in the second leg of the Europa Cup, first qualifying round.

OVERTON (Flintshire) SJ3741

Overton Recreation FC of the Welsh National League (Wrexham Area), Premier Division play at the Overton-on-Dee Recreation Ground.

OXFORD ARMS FC

see NEATH ABBEY (Neath Port Talbot)

PADARN UNITED FC

see LLANBADARN FAWR (Ceredigion)

PANDY (Monmouthshire) SO3322

Pandy FC play in the Gwent Central League, Premier Division at Wern Gifford.

PANTEG FC

see GRIFFITHSTOWN (Torfaen)

PANTSIDE (Caerphilly) ST2197

Pantside FC play in the North Gwent League, Premier Division at the Pantside Football Ground.

PANTYFFYNNON (Carmarthenshire) SN6210

Pantyffynnon RFC of the WRU National Division 6 West play at Pantyffynnon Park.

PANTYRAWEL FC

see LEWISTOWN (Bridgend)

PANTYSCALLOG VILLAGE JUNIORS FC

see PENYDARREN (Merthyr Tydfil)

PARC-Y-PRIOR FC

see MALPAS (Newport)

PARK LAWN FC

see RHIWBINA (Cardiff)

PARK TRAVELLERS FC

see SKEWEN (Neath Port Talbot)

PARK VETS FC

see BARRY (Vale of Glamorgan)

PARK VIEW FC

see GELLIDEG (Merthyr Tydfil)

PEMBREY (Carmarthenshire) SN4201

Pembrey FC of the Carmarthenshire League, Division 3 play at
Pembrey Park.

PEMBROKE (Pembrokeshire) SM9801

Pembroke Rugby Club dates from 1896 and was admitted to

the Welsh Rugby Union in 1919. The team play in the WRU National Division 4 West at Crickmarren Field, Upper Lamphey Road, Pembroke. The name Crickmarren is recorded as early as the twelfth century, but its origins are obscure. Later forms appear to suggest two elements: *crug* and *myharen*, giving the meaning 'mound of the ram'.

PEMBROKE DOCK (Pembrokeshire) SM9603

Pembroke Boro FC play in the Pembrokeshire League, Division 2 at London Road, Pembroke Dock. Boro were once one of the strongest teams in Wales, and they graced the Welsh League South upper division for many years. Following a disastrous season in 1994-95 they withdrew from the Welsh League.

Pennar Robins FC of the Pembrokeshire Football League, Division 1 play at Bush Camp, Pembroke Dock.

Pembroke Dock is also home to Pembroke Harlequins RFC. Rugby was first organised as a sport in the town by local dockers and early games were played at the Barrack Hill Ground. During the early years of the twentieth century the name Harlequins was adopted. Several other venues were used by the club, including Britannia Field and the Green in neighbouring Pembroke, which involved moving the posts for every game from Pembroke Dock! The club also had the use of Bierspool Field after the Great War until 1926 when it again moved to the Corporation Field, which was requisitioned for military use in 1936. The club used the Bush Field for the ensuing three years prior to the outbreak of war. After the war, the club again played at the Bierspool and, in 1956, after protracted negotiations, purchased a sufficient area of the field to enable it to develop a first class pitch with excellent facilities. The Quins compete in the WRU National Division 4 West.

PENALLTA RFC

see YSTRADMYNACH (Caerphilly)

PENARTH (Vale of Glamorgan) ST1871

Penarth RFC play in the WRU National Division 3 South East and are based at the Athletic Field, Lavernock Road, Penarth. The club was once a major force in Welsh rugby and, for 85 years from 1901 until 1986, hosted the Barbarians in an annual Good Friday fixture.

Old Penarthians RFC, formed in 1923, play in the WRU National Division 5 South East at Cwrt-y-Vil Fields. They previously played at the Cogan Recreational Ground and initially at the Stanwell Road School Field.

Cogan Coronation FC, founded in 1960, of the South Wales Senior League, Division 1, play at the Cogan Recreation Ground, Andrew Road, Penarth.

Penarth Town, champions of the Vale of Glamorgan Football League, Division 1 in 2007-08 now play in the South Wales Amateur League, Division 2 at the Cwrt-y-Vil Fields.

PENCADER (Carmarthenshire) SN4436

Pencader United FC of the Ceredigion League, Division 1 play at Parc Pencader.

PENCLAWDD (Swansea) SS5495

Penclawdd RFC, formed in 1888, play in the WRU National Division 3 West. Since 1922 the club has played at the Welfare Ground, known locally as the Rec. Ann Roberts, a local historian, notes that earlier games were played at several venues including the Dunraven Field, Cae Dono and a field at Graig-y-Coed.

Penclawdd FC of the Swansea Senior District League, Division 3 play at Station Road, Penclawdd. The team originally played on a field at Abercedi, before acquiring a new home in the 1970s at Dan-y-graig after an old copperworks reservoir was drained.

PENCOED (Bridgend) ST9581

Pencoed RFC, founded in 1888, play in the WRU National Division 2 West. The clubhouse, which adjoins the field, was formerly a private house of note known as the Verlands, and this name is now also generally used to refer to the club's playing field.

Pencoed Athletic FC of the South Wales Amateur Football League, Division 2 play at Felindre Road.

PENDINE FC

see LLANMILOE (Carmarthenshire)

PENGELLI UNITED FC

see GROVESEND (Swansea)

PENIEL (Carmarthenshire) SN4324

Peniel FC, formed in 1949, largely through the efforts of the late David Dilwyn Davies, played friendly games until 1958 (with the exception of 1953-55) when they elected to enter a team in the Cardiganshire League, only to withdraw in January 1959 after playing only 13 games. Their pitch was located on Cae'r Ysgol, the field on which the new Peniel Primary School was built in 1957. As a result, when Peniel joined the Cardiganshire League they were forced to look for a new venue. Their home matches were then played at neighbouring Alltwalis which also offered better changing facilities. The last Cardiganshire League match for Peniel was a 3-5 home defeat on 3 January 1959 against Llandysul, when one of the goal posts snapped in half. After suffering many heavy defeats, financial difficulties, a lack of officials, and the loss of key players to national service, this incident was possibly the last straw that triggered their withdrawal from the league, leading to the demise of a successful and vibrant club that offered regular football to many local youngsters.

PENLAN (Swansea) SS6496

Penplas FC and Penlan Club FC of the Swansea Senior Football League, Division 1; Plough Colts FC, Rockspur FC and Treboeth United FC of the Swansea Senior Football League, Division 2; Kilvey United FC of Division 3 and Blaenymaes FC of Division 4 all play at the Mynydd Newydd Playing Fields, Heol Gwyrosydd, Penlan, Swansea. Kilvey had previously played at Maestag Park in the Port Tennant area of the city until 1997, prior to adopting Ashlands in the St Thomas area as their new venue.

Penlan RFC, formed in 1967, champions of the WRU National League Division Six West in 2008-09, play at Mynydd Newydd Playing Fields.

PENLEY (Flintshire) SJ4139

Penley FC of the Welsh National League (Wrexham Area), Division 1 play at Maelor School, Penley.

PENLLE'R-GAER (Swansea) SS6198

Penlle'r-gaer FC play in the Carmarthenshire League, Division 3 at Penlle'r-gaer Park.

PENMACHNO (Conwy) SH7950

Machno United of the Caernarfon and District League, Division 2 play at Cae Tŷ'n Ddôl .

PENMAEN-MAWR (Conwy) SH7176

Penmaen-mawr Phoenix of the Clwyd League, Premier Division play at Cae Sling, Bangor Road, Penmaen-mawr. Phoenix were recent members of the Welsh Alliance League.

PENNAR ROBINS FC

see PEMBROKE DOCK (Pembrokeshire)

PENPARCAU FC

see ABERYSTWYTH (Ceredigion)

PENPERLLENI (Monmouthshire) SO3204

Goytre FC, who play in the Welsh League, Division 3, are based at Plough Road, Penperlleni, Pontypool.

PENPLAS FC

see PENLAN (Swansea)

PENRHIW-CEIBR (Rhondda Cynon Taf) ST0597

Penrhiwceiber Rangers, founded in 1961, of the Welsh League, Division 2, and Tynte Rovers of the Aberdare Valley Football League, Premier Division play at Glasbrook Field, Penrhiw-ceibr, Mountain Ash. The name Glasbrook is associated with the Swansea family who became significant coal owners in the South Wales coalfield. In the late 1930s a delegation of workers from the Penrhiw-ceibr Colliery successfully approached the management of the colliery, which was then owned by Powell Duffryn, requesting the use of a portion of land for recreational purposes for the villagers of the area of Penrhiw-ceibr – a piece of land that eventually became known as the Glasbrook Recreational Field. The two football teams who had initial use of the field were Penrhiwceiber Powell Duffryn and Tynte Rovers. Penrhiwceiber are now called Penrhiwceiber Rangers.

Osborne Athletic FC, a team founded in 1986 and based at the Osborne Hotel, Penrhiw-ceibr played in the Aberdare Valley Football League, Premier Division at Caedrawnant, Mountain Ash until 2008. They have also played at the Pentwyn Fields, Penrhiw-ceibr. They are now known as Penrhiwceiber Con Athletic.

PENRHIW-FER (Rhondda Cynon Taf) ST0090

Penrhiw-fer FC, founded in 1967, play in the South Wales Senior League, Division 2 at Penrhiw-fer Park. They played in the Welsh League, Division 3 from 2004 until relegated in 2008.

PENRHOS FC

see PENYRHEOL (Caerphilly)

PENRHYN UNITED FC

see LLANDUDNO (Conwy)

PENRHYN-COCH (Ceredigion) SN6484

Cae Baker, the home of Penrhyn-coch FC, formed in 1965, who play in the Cymru Alliance League, is named after John Baker (1830-1902), a native of Stafford who settled at neighbouring Bow Street with his wife Ann and family in the 1880s where he farmed Rhydypennau. John Baker and his family are buried in Llanfihangel Geneu'r Glyn Church. Several references are made to the family by the author Tom Macdonald in his acclaimed autobiography *Y Tincer Tlawd*. The stretch of road that runs through the village of Bow Street had at that time a slight incline which locals referred to as *Rhiw Baker* (Baker's Hill). He was also the tenant of the field in Penrhyn-coch village which still bears his name, and which at that time formed a part of the Gogerddan Estate and part of Tymawr Farm. Today, Cae Baker is council owned and boasts excellent facilities including floodlights, a small stand seating 50 people, and a spacious neighbouring clubhouse opened in July 1981 by Mike England, the former Tottenham Hotspur and Wales centre half.

Reserve games are played at Cae Cwmbwa. The farm Cwmbwa has an interesting connection with the medieval poet Dafydd ap Gwilym (*fl.* 1340). Cwmbwa was the home of Y Bwa Bach, the hunchback husband of Morfudd, to whom Dafydd directed so much of his poetical attention.

PENRHYNDEUDRAETH (Gwynedd) SH6139

Penrhyndeudraeth FC of the Caernarfon and District League, Division 2 play at Maes-y-Parc.

Cookes United FC were the formidable works team of Cooke's Explosives Works, Penrhyndeudraeth, part of the ICI empire. They competed in the prestigious Cambrian Coast League from 1951 until 1958. Their playing pitch at Cae Cookes is now a piece of derelict land. The works closed in the 1990s.

PENTRAETH (Anglesey) SH5278

Pentraeth Nurseries FC, champions of the Anglesey League in 2008-09, play at Cae Panton. The field is named after the landed Panton family of Plas Gwyn, Pentraeth. Caeau Bryniau/Bryniau is also recorded as an earlier playing field. Referee Gwyn Pierce Owen refers to Bryniau as his spiritual home during his playing days for Pentraeth in the Anglesey League in the early 1960s. Pentraeth Nurseries FC will compete in the Gwynedd League from 2009-10.

PENTRE (Rhondda Cynon Taf) SS9696

Wyndham FC, a team based at the Wyndham Hotel, Tynewydd, play in the Rhondda and District Football League, Premier Division at Pentre Park (Astroturf). They have since gained promotion to the South Wales Amatuer Football League and now play under the name Cwm Ni FC.

PENTREBACH (Merthyr Tydfil) SO0603

Caeharris Guest Club FC (formerly Caeharris Spite FC), established in 1991, and Pentrebach Labour Social FC of the Merthyr Football League, Premier League both play at the Pentrebach Playing Fields.

Plymouth Ground, Pentrebach was once an early venue used by Merthyr RFC.

PENTWYN (Cardiff) ST2081

Pentwyn (and Llanedeyrn) Dynamos, established in 1975, play in the Welsh League, Division 2 at Parc Coed-y-Nant, Bryn Celyn Road, Pentwyn, Cardiff.

Llanedeyrn Bulldogs FC, a community club established in 2000, field a senior team in the Cardiff Combination Football League, Premier Division and play at Llanedeyrn High School Field.

PENTWYNMAWR ATHLETIC FC

see NEWBRIDGE (Torfaen)

PEN-TYRCH (Cardiff) ST1081

Pentyrch RFC play in the WRU National Division 3 South East. In 1882 informal rugby games were played on the Forlan Fields at Cefn Bychan and an organised game was also played on a field adjoining Ynys House. In 1883 a club was formally established and they moved to land at Y Dwrlyn (between the council estate at Bronllwyn and the Bovis Estate), where they remained until the turn of the twentieth century. The club led a nomadic life for the next five years and some games were played on a field near the railway line at Creigiau and on Penygarn Field until a more permanent home was found at Clawdd Siôn, a boggy field, through an arrangement with the Wingfield Estate. The club remained there until 1952 when it transferred to its present home at Parc-y-Dwrlyn, which boasts cricket and bowls facilities and which is also used for junior football. In 1993 Parc-y-Dwrlyn staged a one-day first-class cricket match between Glamorgan and Northants.

PEN-Y-BANC (Carmarthenshire) SN6124

Pen-y-banc RFC play in WRU National Division 6 West at Waun Goch Fach.

PEN-Y-BONT (Powys) SO1164

Pen-y-bont Athletic and Pen-y-bont United FC play in the Mid Wales League (South) at the Racecourse Ground. Horse racing is held on the ground in August.

PEN-Y-BRYN (Caerphilly) ST1396

Llanbradach Social FC play in the South Wales Senior League,

Division 1 at Llanbradach Park. They also play at Trosnant, Pen-y-bryn, near Hengoed.

Cascade FC of the South Wales Senior League, Division 2 also play at Trosnant.

PEN-Y-CAE (Wrexham) SJ2845

Pen-y-cae of the Welsh National League (Wrexham Area), Premier Division play at Afoneitha Recreation Ground.

PENYDARREN (Merthyr Tydfil) SO0507

Penydarren BGC FC of the South Wales Senior League, Division 1 play at the Bont, Rocky Road, Penydarren, Merthyr Tydfil.

Martyrs FC of the Merthyr Tydfil District, Premier League play at the Greenie, Penydarren.

Pantyscallog Village Juniors FC's senior side play in the Merthyr Tydfil Football League, Premier Division at Gellifaelog. The youth side play at Caeracca, Pantyscallog.

PENYFAN UNITED FC

see LLANELLI (Carmarthenshire)

PEN-Y-FFORDD (Flintshire) SJ3061

Pen-y-ffordd FC of the Welsh National League (Wrexham Area), Division 1 play at Abbot's Lane Infants School, Pen-y-ffordd.

PEN-Y-GRAIG (Rhondda Cynon Taf) SS9991

Pen-y-graig RFC, formed in 1877, play in the WRU National

Division 5 South East at Graig Park, Pen-y-graig. Early games were played on the Ynys Field, before moving to Belle Vue Park. W D Jones also records that the club played on a field at the top of Dinas Mountain, Llestwyn Ground, Penrhiwfer, and finally at the Welfare Ground, Penygraig where they remained until Graig Park was officially opened on 1 September 1970.

Pen-y-graig BGC play in the Rhondda and District Football League at Ely Field, Pen-y-graig.

PEN-Y-GROES (Carmarthenshire) SN5813

Pen-y-groes RFC play in the WRU National Division 5 West at Pen-y-groes Park.

PEN-Y-GROES (Gwynedd) SH4653

Maes Dulyn is the home of Nantlle Vale FC, promoted to the Welsh Alliance League in 2008. This famous ground was revamped in 2007. The club enjoyed considerable success in the late 1950s and were crowned Welsh League (North) Champions in 1960. Some of their players, such as Idris 'Tarw Nefyn' Evans, Robin Ken (Thomas) and Orig Williams, reached legendary status and were feared opponents renowned for their uncompromising tackling.

PENYRHEOL (Caerphilly) ST1488

Penyrheol FC and Penrhos FC of the Taff Ely and Rhymney Valley Football Alliance League, Premier Division play at Aneurin Park, Penyrheol, Caerphilly. Aneurin Park is located near Heol Aneurin, Penyrheol, a street named in honour of Aneurin Bevan (1897-1960), the Labour Party deputy leader and architect of the National Health Service.

PENYWAUN (Rhondda Cynon Taf) SN9704

Penywaun FC play in the Aberdare Valley Football League Premier Division using their own pitch in conjunction with the Penywaun Welfare Social Club.

PERTHCELYN UNITED FC

see MOUNTAIN ASH (Rhondda Cynon Taf)

PFS ATHLETIC FC

see NANT-Y-GLO (Blaenau Gwent)

PHOENIX: FC

see LLANBADARN FAWR (Ceredigion)

PILCS FC

see GRIFFITHSTOWN (Torfaen)

PILLGWENLLY (Newport) ST3187

Pill Harriers RFC, originally founded in 1882 but re-formed in 1978, play in the WRU National Division 3 East at Court-y-Bella Terrace. The Pill Harriers Sports Club also runs a football side, Pill FC.

Pill FC, Pill Hibernians FC, and Ship and Pilot FC, based at the public house of that name in Church Street, all play in the Newport and District Football League, Premier Division X using the Pill Leisure Centre. Pill FC were crowned league champions in 2008-09. Ship and Pilot also played some games at Coronation Park but regrettably the team folded during the season and failed to complete their fixtures. Ship and Pilot FC also fielded a very successful side in the Newport and District Football League, Division 1, a team crowned champions of that division in 2008-09.

PIT STOP FC
see BARRY (Vale of Glamorgan)

PLOUGH COLTS FC
see PENLAN (Swansea)

PLOUGH INN FC
see ABERDARE (Rhondda Cynon Taf)

POINT OF AYR FC
see FFYNNONGROYW (Flintshire)

PONCIAU (Wrexham) SJ2946
Cae Jack 'Pwnch' at the bottom of Ffennant Road, Ponciau, was the home of Ponciau Dragons, who played in a local league during the 1930s.

see also RHOSLLANNERCHRUGOG (Wrexham)

PONTARDAWE (Neath Port Talbot) SN7204
Pontardawe Town, founded in 1947, of the Welsh League, Division 1, play at the Recreation Ground, Pontardawe, now

owned by the local authority but previously the property of the local steelworks, and originally established in the 1920s under the miners' welfare scheme. Plans to move to a new field on land at the nearby leisure centre are under consideration.

AFC Pontardawe of the Neath Football League, Division 1 and Pontardawe RFC, founded in 1896, of the WRU National Division 5 South West, also play at the Recreation Ground. It is probable that the game was played locally prior to this date, and it has been recorded that William Gilbertson's employees at his tin works played some games on a field near Glyndolau Farm, below the village of Gelli-nudd. From 1892 Pontardawe played on the Athletic Ground, a field that belonged to the Gilbertson family, which boasted a small wooden stand and became an important venue for cycling and athletics.

FC Clydach play in Neath Football League, Premier Division at the Pontardawe Leisure Centre.

PONTARDDULAIS (Swansea) SN5803

Pontarddulais RFC, formed in 1881, play in the WRU National Division 4 West at Parc Coedbach/Coedbach Park, Gwynfryn Road, Pontarddulais. Early games were played at Tynybonau.

Pontarddulais Town FC of the Carmarthenshire League, Division 1 also play at Parc Coedbach.

PONTCANNA (Cardiff) ST1677

Clwb Rygbi Cymry Caerdydd, formed in 1967, play in the WRU National Division 6 Central at Pontcanna Fields.

Clwb Cymric Caerdydd FC of the Cardiff and District Football League, Premier Division, and Canton Libs FC of Division 2, based at Canton Liberal Club, Cowbridge Road, also play at Pontcanna Fields. The fields are also used by many teams in the Cardiff Combination Football League such as AC Central FC, Cardiff Hibernians FC and Cathays United FC who all play in the Premier Division, and Cathays Conservatives who play in Division 1.

Pontcanna Fields hosted the 2008 National Eisteddfod of Wales, during which many of these teams had to play at alternative venues.

PONTERWYD (Ceredigion) SN7480

Ponterwyd enjoyed a brief period in the Aberystwyth and District League from 1948 until 1952. Friendly games had been played during previous seasons on the field where local primary school Ysgol Syr John Rhys now stands. However, it appears that the league matches were played on a field at Erwbarfe Farm, now a caravan site. Among the team's leading stars was the late Lord Geraint Howells (1925-2004), Liberal MP and peer, who lived and farmed in the village.

PONTHENRI (Carmarthenshire) SN4709

Ponthenri FC of the Carmarthenshire League, Division 1 play at Ponthenri Park.

PONTHIR (Torfaen) ST3292

Pont-hir FC play in the Newport and District Football League,

Division 2. Their pitch is situated in the village off Caerleon Road.

PONT-IETS

see PONTYATES (Carmarthenshire)

PONTLLAN-FRAITH (Caerphilly) ST1896

Pontllan-fraith FC has an illustrious history, and the team were Welsh League champions as recently as 1973. In 1964 the team merged with Fields Park FC to form Fields Park Pontllan-fraith FC, but sadly the team folded in 2005. Games were played at Islwyn Park, a ground named after the Revd William Thomas ('Islwyn'; 1832–78), renowned poet and preacher who took his bardic name from the local mountain, Mynyddislwyn.

Pontllanfraith RFC play in the WRU National Division 5 East at the Welfare Ground.

PONT-LLIW (Swansea) SN6101

Pont-lliw FC of the Carmarthenshire League, Division 1 play at Pont-lliw Park.

PONTLOTTYN (Caerphilly) SO1105

Pontlottyn Blast Furnace FC, who played in the Welsh League until 2003, were based at the Welfare Ground, Pontlottyn.

PONTNEDDFECHAN (Powys) SN9007

The Angel Field at Pontneddfechan is recorded as an early venue used by Glyn-neath RFC. The field was presumably located near the Angel Inn.

PONTNEWYDD (Torfaen) ST2996

Cwmffrwdoer Sports FC play in the Gwent County League, Division 1 at Cwmffrwdoer Sports Ground, Pontnewydd.

West Pontnewydd FC play in the Gwent County League, Division 3 at the Birches.

Pontnewydd United play in the Newport and District Football League, Premier Division X at Pontyrhydyrun Playing Fields. They also once played at the Clarkville Recreation Ground, Pontnewydd.

PONTNEWYNYDD (Torfaen) SO2701

Trevethin FC play in the Gwent Central League, Premier Division and were crowned champions in 2008-09 after achieving a remarkable 100 per cent winning record. They play at the Ruffetts, Folly Lane, Pontnewynydd, south of Trevethin.

PONTPRENNAU (Cardiff) ST2148

Glyncoed Corries FC of the Cardiff and District Football League, Division 1, together with Dui Dragons FC and Pontprennau Pumas of the Cardiff Combination Football League, Division 1 all play at Pontprennau Community Playing Fields.

PONTRHYDFENDIGAID (Ceredigion) SN7366

Parc Pantyfedwen, the home of Bont (Pontrhydfendigaid) FC, who play in the Aberystwyth and District League, Division 1, was originally two fields, purchased and adapted for community use through the generosity of Sir David John James (1887-1967), businessman and philanthropist, who was born in London but raised at the family farm of Pantyfedwen on the outskirts of the village, and who amassed a huge fortune as a London cinema magnate. He established the Pantyfedwen Trust in 1952 aimed at fostering religious, educational and charitable causes in Wales. Prior to moving to Parc Pantyfedwen games were played on Cae Dôl-fawr. One of the most successful village sides in Ceredigion, Bont FC celebrated its sixtieth anniversary in 2007. There is, however, a record of a team from Bont playing an away match as early as 1895 against neighbouring Ystrad Meurig Grammar School.

PONT-RHYD-Y-FEN (Neath Port Talbot) SS7994

Pont-rhyd-y-fen RFC play in the WRU National Division 6 Central at Pwll-y-glaw.

PONT-RHYD-Y-GROES (Ceredigion) SN7372

Pont-rhyd-y-groes FC played in the Aberystwyth and District League in season 1949-50, but folded only two games short of completing their fixtures in the following season. Home games were played on Y Ddôl Fach, near Ystwyth Villa, although several league fixtures were also played at Traws-goed.

PONTYATES (Carmarthenshire) SN4608

Pontyates RFC play in the WRU National Division 5 West at Cae Rygbi Pont-iets.

PONTYBEREM (Carmarthenshire) SN5011

Pontyberem RFC, formed in 1896, champions of the WRU National Division 3 West in 2008-09, and Bancffosfelen FC of the Carmarthenshire League, Division 3, founded in 1957, both play at Pontyberem Park which was opened in 1955. The rugby club previously played on a field known as Y Weun.

PONT-Y-CLUN (Rhondda Cynon Taf) ST0381

Pont-y-clun RFC, founded in 1887, play in the WRU National Division 4 South East at Windsor Park. Rugby was probably played in the village before that date, possibly on the Swlgu Field near the Ivor Arms. The club first played on a field which is now the site of a local school, Ysgol y Pant, until they moved to the Mill Fields, or Maesyfelin Field. Pontyclun were crowned champions of the WRU National Division 5 South East in 2008-09.

Pont-y-clun FC, founded in 1896, of the Welsh League, Division 3, play at the Ivor Park, Cowbridge Road, Pont-y-clun.

PONTYCYMER (Bridgend) SS9091

Blandy Park, Pontycymer, the home of Garw Athletic FC, who play in Division 3 of the Welsh League, is situated on land that was owned by the Blandy Jenkins family of Llanharran House, an estate that in 1873 measured 6,084 acres and carried an annual rental of £3,023. Originally the home of the Powell family, the estate eventually passed to Colonel John Blandy-Jenkins (1839-1915) of Kingston Bagpuize, Oxfordshire.

In 1925, Mrs Elizabeth Nora Blandy-Jenkins (d.1953), the

Blandy Park, Pontycymer: home of Garw Athletic FC. Photograph: the author.

colonel's second wife, decreed that Garw Stars FC could use the land for recreational purposes.

After the Stars disbanded, the local authority took responsibility for the land and they remain landlords to this day, renting the land to Garw Athletic FC, who were formed in August 1945 from an amalgamation of local clubs.

Blandy Park probably provides the best elevated view of any ground in Wales, apart, perhaps, from the Millennium Stadium!

Junior games are played at Carn Park, Pontycymmer.

Pontycym(m)er RFC play in the WRU National Division 4 South West at Lawrence Park. Opened in 1970, when Bridgend Ravens RFC provided the opposition, it is named in honour of a local councillor, Joseph Lawrence of Meadow Street, Pontycymer, who campaigned for the creation of this facility. Earlier matches were played on a field known locally as the Cow's Back.

PONTYMISTER (Caerphilly)

Risca United FC was formed in 1946 from an amalgam of clubs which operated in the area following the Great War. The new club joined the Monmouthshire Senior League and played home games on the Miners Welfare in Pontymister (later to be known as Tŷ-Isaf Park). The pitch had been utilized during the war years as an allotment but was quickly re-established and became the home of the club, which now plays in the Welsh League, Division 3.

AC Pontymister FC, 2008-09 champions of the Gwent Central League, Division 3, play at the Bowling Green, Pontymister. They once played at the Longbridge Field, Risca.

PONTYPOOL (Torfaen) SO2800

Pontypool RFC, one of the most famous clubs in Wales and a founding member of the WRU in 1881, play in the WRU National Premier Division at Pontypool Park. The birth of rugby at Pontypool can be dated from 1868, and the earliest games were played on Pontymoile Cricket Field. The club itself was formed in 1876 and its first fixture was played in that year on the Shepherd's Field at Park Road. In 1877, Henry Griffiths, the man who gave his name to Griffithstown, donated the use of the Canal Junction Field, Pontymoile, where rugby was played until 1882. Some games were also played at Knipe's Field, also at Pontymoile. The Knipe family were local landowners who lived at Kemys Bach Farm. In 1887 the Polo Grounds at New Inn were hired on a regular basis by the club, and these were re-named the Recreation Ground in 1891. In 1893 a new Recreation Ground was opened at Conway Road, at which the touring South African Springboks played in 1912. However, the Recreation Ground was requisitioned for military use during the Second World War and proved unsuitable for rugby when sport resumed in peacetime. Pontypool RFC, with the support of the local council, were permitted to play at Pontypool Park from that date. The park, which extends to 158 acres, was gifted to the town by John Capel Hanbury in 1918. The Hanbury family, originally from Worcestershire, settled in Monmouthshire in the sixteenth century, becoming significant ironmasters and landowners.

Pontypool United RFC, formed in 1946, play in the WRU National Division 3 East at the Memorial Ground, Conway Road, Pontypool.

Pontypool Town FC, established 1988, of the Gwent Central League, Division 1, play at Albion Road.

Race FC of the Gwent County League, Division 3 play at Coleg Gwent Pontypool playing fields. They played previously at the Race Welfare Ground.

PONTYPRIDD (Rhondda Cynon Taf) ST0789

Sardis Road is the relatively modern ground of Pontypridd RFC, who compete in the WRU National Premier Division. The club, founded in 1876, has played at a number of grounds during its illustrious history. These include Trallwng Field and Taff Vale

'The Rugby Match', from the original acrylic painting of Pontypridd RFC's Sardis Road ground, by Ronald H J Lawrence, Pontypridd. Reproduced by kind permission of the artist and the National Library of Wales, which holds the original work.

Park in Treforest, before they moved to the People's Park on the banks of the Afon Rhondda near Mill Street School. The club then played at Ynysangharad Park from 1908 until 1973. Sardis Road was built as a new ground for Pontypridd RFC in 1976 and became famously dubbed the 'house of pain'. Sardis Road takes its name from Sardis Welsh Congregational Chapel, built in 1834.

Ynysangharad Park, a memorial to the fallen of the Great War, was opened in 1923. As noted above, the venue was also home to Pontypridd RFC. Glamorgan County Cricket Club also played regularly at the ground until the mid 1990s. The ground is now used by Pontypridd Town, founded in 1895, who play in the Welsh League, Division 3, and Graig FC, who play in the South Wales Amateur Football League, Division 2. Ynysangharad Park houses the well-known sculpture by Sir W Goscombe John (1860-1952) of Evan James (1809-78) and his son James James (1833-1902), authors of *Hen Wlad fy Nhadau*, the Welsh national anthem.

Ynys-y-bwl FC play in the Taff Ely and Rhymney Valley League, Premier Division at Pontypridd Park. As a Welsh League club they played at the Recreation Ground, Ynys-y-bwl until they merged with Pontypridd in 1990.

Cilfynydd FC and Graigwen Juniors FC both play in the Taff Ely and Rhymney Valley Football Alliance, Premier Division at Ynysangharad Park.

PORT TALBOT (Neath Port Talbot) SS7589

Blue Stars FC play in the Port Talbot Football League, Division 1 at Talbot Park which was opened in 1925. The commemorative character of the park is emphasised by the impressive main gate which is dedicated to Second Lieutenant Rupert Price Hallowes VC, MC (1881-1915), who was killed in battle at Hooge, Flanders.

Grove Park FC played in the Port Talbot Football League, Premier Division at Vivian Park, until they disbanded at the end of the 2007-08 season. The park is associated with the Vivian family of Truro, who introduced copper smelting to the Swansea area in the early nineteenth century. Real Bay View CF FC of the league's Premier Division also play at Vivian Park.

Newton Wanderers FC, Port Talbot Royal Mail, Port Talbot Town Exiles and Port Talbot Tigers of the Port Talbot Football League, Division 1 all play at Western Avenue Playing Fields, Seaway Parade, Port Talbot.

Trefelin BGC FC play in the South Wales Amateur Football League, Division 1 at Ynys Park, Cwmavon Road, Port Talbot.

see also ABERAVON (Neath Port Talbot)

PORT TENNANT (Swansea) SS6893

Port Tennant Colts play in the Swansea Senior Football League, Division 1 at Maestag Park, St Leger Crescent, Port Tennant, Swansea.

PORTH (Rhondda Cynon Taf) ST0291

AFC Porth, founded in 1950, play in the Welsh League, Division 2 at Dinas Park, Porth. The club enjoyed a lengthy and successful period in the Welsh League until they were relegated in 2007. After one season in the South Wales Amateur Football League, they returned to the Welsh League in 2008.

Porth Harlequins RFC play in the WRU National Division 4 South East, and have played at the Welfare Ground for the last fifty years. Earlier games were played on Cae Nythbran. The name is associated with Nythbran Farm on the outskirts of Porth, the family home of the celebrated long-distance runner Griffith Morgan (1700-37; 'Guto Nyth Brân').

PORTH-CAWL (Bridgend) SS8277

Porth-cawl Town FC, founded in 1947, play in the Welsh League, Division 2 at Lock's Lane. Porthcawl Athletic of the Port Talbot Football League, Division 1 also play at Lock's Lane. The ground has recently been used as a temporary home by Bridgend Town FC.

Porth-cawl RFC play in the WRU National Division 4 South West at South Place.

PORTHMADOG (Gwynedd) SH5638

Clwb Pêl-droed Porthmadog of the Welsh Premiership play at Y Traeth. The club was formed in 1884 and is one of the oldest in Wales. They were particularly successful in the 1950s, winning the Welsh Amateur Cup on two occasions. In 1992 they became inaugural members of the League of Wales, but endured temporary relegation and Cymru Alliance membership from 1998 until regaining their premiership status in 2003. Y Traeth was also used as a groundshare facility by one of the most talented teams ever to grace football in Wales, Tonfannau 55th Royal Artillery FC, who boasted many professional footballers who were temporarily based in Wales as they undertook their national service.

Clwb Rygbi Porthmadog, a Welsh Districts Club, also play on an adjacent pitch located to the west of Y Traeth.

PORTH-Y-RHYD (Carmarthenshire) SN5115

Porthyrhyd FC were once a major force in Carmarthenshire League football and the club lifted the prestigious Mond Cup on more than one occasion. Their neat ground is located in the centre of the village and is still used regularly for junior football.

PORTSKEWETT (Monmouthshire) ST4988

Portskewett and Sudbrook FC play in the East Gwent Football League, Division 1 at the Recreation Field, Portskewett.

PRENDERGAST VILLA FC

see HAVERFORDWEST (Pembrokeshire)

PRESCOED (Monmouthshire) ST3499

Prescoed FC were crowned champions of the Gwent Central League, Division 2 in 2008-09. The team is based at Prescoed Open Prison, and all games are played within the confines of the prison.

PRESTATYN (Flintshire) SJ0682

The club's website notes that football has been played in the town since the early 1890s with games being played on an undeveloped field on Marine Road. Other pitches around the town were also utilised, but the present club came into being in the 1930s when it settled on the old Bastion Road ground behind what is now the Central Beach Club. In the late 1960s the old Bastion Road ground was developed for housing, and after considering using a pitch in the middle of the old Prestatyn Raceway, now the site of Pontin's Holiday Village, the club moved to their present headquarters at Bastion Road, off Bastion Gardens in 1970. Since this date the team has progressed steadily, and in 2006 was admitted to the Cymru Alliance League, winning the title in 2008 and promotion to the top tier of the Welsh pyramid. They have enjoyed relative success since their promotion to the Welsh Premiership.

Prestatyn Victoria, once of the Clwyd League, played at the Meadows Ground, Prestatyn.

PRESTEIGNE (Powys) S03164

Presteigne St Andrews FC, formed in 1897, play in the Mid Wales League at Llanandras Park. Llanandras (the church of Andreas) is the Welsh name for Presteigne and dates from at least the thirteenth century.

PWLL (Carmarthenshire) SN4801

Pwll Athletic FC of the Carmarthenshire League, Premier Division play at Pwll Park.

PWLLHELI (Gwynedd) SH3735

Pwllheli FC play in the Welsh Alliance League at the Leisure Centre, Recreation Road. Football in Pwllheli dates from 1879 when a local head teacher organised a game against neighbouring Porthmadog. Early games were played on a field between the railway station and Glan-y-don. The town's recreation facilities, built in 1898 and opened in 1899, were provided by the entrepreneur Solomon Andrews (1835-1908) who was largely responsible for developing the west end of the resort.

PWLLHELI RFC

see EFAILNEWYDD (Gwynedd)

PYLE (Neath Port Talbot) SS8282

Pyle RFC, champions of the WRU National Division 5 South
Central in 2008-09, play at Brynglas Field.

QUAR PARK RANGERS FC

see MERTHYR TYDFIL

QUEENSWAY (Wrexham) SJ3450

GAP Queen's Park played in the Cymru Alliance League
from 2005 until their resignation in 2008. They played at the
Queensway Athletics Stadium, Wrexham. The club's owners
have recently agreed a merger with Borras Park Albion FC and
have agreed a sponsorship deal with Connah's Quay Nomads.
The club can trace its origins to a Sunday League team formed
in 1988; the name Queen's Park, reflecting the team's origins on
one of Wrexham's largest housing estates, was adopted in 1994.

Venture Community FC, founded in 1994 as a community
base club, play in the Welsh National League (Wrexham Area),
Premier Division at the Dunks, Queensway, Wrexham. Dunks,
or Y Wern Dunk, is an ancient parcel of land cited in eighteenth-
century documents.

RACE FC

see PONTYPOOL (Torfaen)

RACING CLUB NEWPORT FC

see NEWPORT

RADNOR VALLEY FC

see NEW RADNOR (Powys)

RADYR (Cardiff) ST1280

The famous Cardiff Corinthians FC, established in 1897, five times winners of the Welsh Amateur Cup and Welsh League Premier Division Champions in 1985, play at the Riverside Ground, Station Road, Radyr, Cardiff. They currently compete in the Welsh League, Division 1. For the first six years of their existence they played at Sophia Gardens, but they led a rather nomadic life for the ensuing seventy years. After the Great War they played at Pengam Farm, Tremorfa, before moving to Llandaff Road in Canton after the Second World War. They also played briefly at Pontcanna Fields, Maindy Stadium and Fidlas Avenue, Llanishen before settling at the Riverside Ground in 1974.

RAFA BOYS FC

see ELY (Cardiff)

RAGGED SCHOOL FC

see SKETTY (Swansea)

RASSAU RANGERS FC

see CARMELTOWN (Blaenau Gwent)

REAL BAY VIEW CF FC

see PORT TALBOT (Neath Port Talbot)

REAL LLANDUDNO FC

see LLANDUDNO (Conwy)

RED LION FC

see TREDEGAR (Blaenau Gwent)

RESOLVEN (Neath Port Talbot) SN8202

Resolven RFC, formed in 1885, play in the WRU National Division 4 South West at Vaughan Field. According to John R Davies, rugby was probably first played at Resolven by visiting colliery engineers who were also members of Newport RFC and who enjoyed a kick-about on Cae'r Berllan. However, Resolven as a club first played at Tan-y-Rhiw, and after a few seasons moved to the Brick Field. In 1898 Sardis Field was used as a playing base before moving again, this time to the Farmer's Field. The club also took its first sabbatical in 1904-06 owing to the religious revival of that time. The Drehir ground was used between the wars. This had a dressing room and grandstand which were the club's greatest assets – the culmination of a half-century of hard work. The Second World War posed a threat to the very existence of the rugby club since a munitions factory (now known as TRW Steering Systems) was built at Drehir. In 1945 Resolven faced the unique position of being a member club of the Welsh Rugby Union without a ground.

However, owing to the hard work of officials and committee

members, the club moved to a new ground at Tan-y-Rhiw Field (the present home) which opened on 31 October 1946. The club was much indebted to Captain J N Vaughan who had granted the use of the field. On 14 October 1954 the Vaughan family of Rheola kindly donated the freehold of the property to Resolven Rugby Football Club and Tan-y-rhiw Field was re-named the Vaughan Rugby Ground and Pavilion in recognition of the family's generosity.

Football has been played in the Resolven area for over eighty years. The present side, Resolven FC, was formerly known as Cam Gears FC, a works team that competed at Welsh League level. The present team play at the Welfare Ground in the Neath Football League, Division 2.

CMB FC (formerly Metal Box) play in the Neath Football League, Premier Division at the Metal Box Ground, Resolven.

RHAYADER (Powys) SN9768

Rhayader Town FC play in the Mid Wales League at Y Weirglodd. Football has been played in the town since 1884, and the team enjoyed five years in the top flight of Welsh football until they were relegated in 2002. Rhayader Town folded in July 2006 and resigned from the Mid Wales League. A re-formed club, they now play in the third tier of the Mid Wales League having gained promotion in 2008.

Rhayader RFC, formed in 1976, play in the WRU National Division 5 North on an adjacent pitch at Y Weirglodd.

RHIGOS (Rhondda Cynon Taf) SN9205

Rhigos RFC, formed in the 1930s, play in the WRU National Division 5 South Central. The club's website provides a lot of information on the various fields used over the years. At first they played on Gwrangon Field, a name that refers to Nant Gwrangon and two farms of that name, located behind the present clubhouse. This proved rather wet, and the club moved to play at Cefn Rhigos on the top of Mountain Road hill. As this was rather a long way to walk, the club moved again to Newth's Field, which is opposite the present clubhouse. The Newth family are recorded in the Neath valley in the mid nineteenth century having migrated from Gloucestershire. Their descendants still live in Rhigos.

RHIWBINA (Cardiff) ST1581

Rhiwbina RFC play in the WRU National Division 4 South East at the Rhiwbina Recreation Ground, Lôn-y-Dail, Rhiwbina, Cardiff.

Whitchurch Blues FC of the Cardiff and District League, Division 1, Cardiff Cosmos Athletic FC of Division 2 and Gower Sports FC of Division 3, together with Park Lawn FC (relegated from the Cardiff Combination Football League, Premier Division in 2009), all play at Caedelyn Park, Rhiwbina.

RHIWLAS FC

see HIRAEL (Gwynedd)

RHOOSE (Vale of Glamorgan) ST0666

Rhoose FC of the South Wales Amateur Football League, Division 1 play at Ceri Road, Rhoose.

Cardiff Airport FC of the Vale of Glamorgan Football League, Premier Division also play at Rhoose.

RHOS (Neath Port Talbot) SN7303

Rhos FC play in the Neath League, Division 1 at Rhos Park, March Hywel.

RHOS UNITED FC

see RHOS-ON-SEA (Conwy)

RHOSGADFAN (Gwynedd) SH5155

Mountain Rangers FC, whose senior team disbanded a few years ago but who successfully re-formed for the 2008-09 season, play in the Caernarfon and District League, Division 2, where they were crowned champions. The team is based on land which was once part of Cae'r Gors, Rhostryfan. The name is synonymous with the birthplace of Dr Kate Roberts (1891-1985), the eminent Welsh novelist. Cae'r Gors itself has recently been restored and is now a successful heritage centre. Eight acres of land were once part of Cae'r Gors, which encompassed three fields. Cae Bach is now occupied by the Mountain Rangers Social Club, Cae Cefn Tŷ serves as its car park and the actual football field occupies land once known as Y Weirglodd. It is worth noting that the committee scenes in the successful Welsh-language comedy *C'Mon Midffild*, based on an imaginary village football team, were filmed at the village hall in Rhosgadfan. Mountain Rangers once played their home games on a field behind the Newborough Arms in Bontnewydd, a public house whose exterior was also featured in *C'Mon Midffild*.

RHOS-GOCH (Powys) SO1847

Rhosgoch FC play in the Mid Wales League (South) at Rhos-goch Primary School, Rhos-goch, near Painscastle, Powys. Cae Dresser has been recorded as an earlier home venue.

RHOSLLANNERCHRUGOG (Wrexham) SJ2946

Football has been played at Rhosllannerchrugog since 1877. When the Welsh League was first established in 1890, Rhos were one of its founder members. The earliest games were played on a field adjoining Llannerchrugog Hall. John Matthews, in his excellent pictorial history of football at Rhos, has cited several other fields in the village where football was played during the late nineteenth and early twentieth centuries. These include a field near Stryd Las which was home to Rhos Eagles, winners of the Welsh Amateur Cup in 1898, and Rhos Church, who played before the Great War. Cae Einion, Hall Lane, Rhos was used as a football ground from the early 1890s until 1910, and Huxley's Field (probably named after Edward Huxley, a local farmer) and Cae Dŵr (later renamed the Recreation Ground) are other important venues mentioned in his work.

Rhos Aelwyd, one of many clubs formed in the village, was founded in 1943 at Capel Mawr, the Welsh Presbyterian chapel, and has enjoyed considerable success over the last fifty years. The team currently play in the Welsh National League (Wrexham Area), Premier Division, but have played at a higher level in the Cymru Alliance League from 1992 until 1997. Rhos Aelwyd's home is at Ponciau Park, Clarke Street, Ponciau, where the pitch was laid in 1935 after three years of hard work. Matthews notes that Ponciau Park (known locally as Ponciau Banks) was created from old spoil heaps after the area had been purchased by the Rhos Recreation Scheme. In 1934 Edward, Prince of Wales, visited Ponciau Banks to view the scheme's progress. The field was originally known as Clarke's Field. Ponciau Park has recently been refurbished following a successful partnership between the local authority and the Heritage Lottery Fund.

Rhosllannerchrugog RFC of the WRU National Division 2 North also play at Ponciau Banks.

RHOS-ON-SEA (Conwy) SH8381

Colwyn Bay RFC play in the WRU National Division 4 North at Brookfield Drive, Rhos-on-Sea, where they have impressive facilities including three playing pitches. The club's excellent website records that the first rugby match in the area was held in 1923 when a team from Chester played a local XV at the Rhos Preparatory School Field. However, the foundations of the present club were not laid until 1953, and it was not until 1965 that its first permanent home was established at Glan-y-Don Home Farm, Old Colwyn, where cowsheds were utilised as changing rooms! Unfortunately, this field was required in the late 1960s for road improvements and a new police headquarters, but the club was compensated by the council with excellent new facilities that it had acquired at Brookfield Drive as a bequest from Victor C Wilde (1918-1966), a freeman of the borough of Colwyn Bay and a generous benefactor.

Rhos United FC of the Clwyd League, Division 2 also play on an adjacent pitch at Brookfield Drive.

RHOSYMEDRE (Wrexham) SJ2842

Cefn United FC, formed in 1999, run several teams including a senior side that played in the Welsh National League (Wrexham Area), Premier Division, and are based at the Church Field, Rhosymedre. The senior side disbanded in 2008 but intend to reform for 2009-10. NEWI Cefn Druids, who currently play at Cefn-mawr, plan to move to a new 3,000-capacity stadium at the Rock, Rhosymedre, which is due for completion in 2010. The team will be known as Elements Europe Cefn Druids from the 2009-10 season following a change of sponsor.

RHUDDLAN (Flintshire) SJ0278

Rhuddlan Town FC play in the Clwyd League, Premier Division at Pengwyn College. They also played at the Admiral's Playing Field, Rhyl Road, Rhuddlan.

Abbey Life FC, once of the Clwyd League, played at Fairlands Park, Rhuddlan.

Rhyl and District RFC play in the WRU National Division 2 North at the Waen, Rhuddlan.

RHYDYFELIN (Ceredigion) SN5979

Cae'r Felin, Rhydyfelin, was used as the home venue of Llanfarian Rovers FC of the Aberystwyth and District League when the club re-formed in 1962.

RHYDYFELIN (Rhondda Cynon Taf) ST0988

Rhydyfelin RFC, founded in 1905, play at the Hawthorn Recreation Ground in the WRU National League Division 2 East.

Rhydyfelin Labour FC play in the Taff Ely and Rhymney Valley Football League, Premier Division at Upper Boat and Ynysangharad Park, Pontypridd.

RHYDYFELIN AFC

see UPPER BOAT (Rhondda Cynon Taf)

RHYD-Y-MWYN (Flintshire) SJ2066

Rhyd-y-mwyn FC play in the Welsh Alliance League at Vicarage Road, Rhydymwyn.

RHYL (Denbighshire) SJ0181

Rhyl FC, founded in 1870, play in the Welsh Premiership at Belle Vue, Grange Road. Rhyl have always been considered as one of the leading clubs in Wales. On three occasions they have won the Welsh Cup, and in 2004 they were crowned champions of the Welsh Premiership and represented Wales in the UEFA Champions League but without success. However, in 2005-06, Rhyl recorded their first-ever win in European competitions when they defeated FK Atlantis from Lithuania 2-1 and, although they lost the return leg 2-3, they progressed to the second round on the away goals rule. They eventually lost 1-3 on aggregate to the Norwegian side Viking FC. The famous Serbian side FK Partizan Belgrade were visitors to the Belle Vue on 14 July 2009 in the second qualifying round of the UEFA Champions League, comfortably winning the tie by 0-4. Belle Vue has a ground capacity of 3,800 with seating for approximately 1,800. The club originally played at the Winter Gardens, which was situated near the promenade. In 1900 it acquired a piece of land at the Botanical Gardens, Grange Road. This became known as the Belle Vue and has been home to the club ever since.

Rhyl Nomads once played in the Clwyd League, Premier Division at the Coronation Gardens, Rhyl. This venue has been used by several teams who have competed in the Clwyd League and remains the venue for Sunday League matches. The Nomads folded at the end of the 2008 season.

Aztec Sports FC of the Clwyd League, Division 1 played at Rhydwen Drive, Rhyl. This club also folded in 2008.

RHYL and DISTRICT RFC

see RHUDDLAN (Flintshire)

RHYMNEY (Caerphilly) SO1107

Rugby has been played at Rhymney since the nineteenth century, and the present team play in the WRU National Division 3 East. In 1959 the club moved to a new ground at the War Memorial Park. During the early years of the twentieth century, games were played on the Eisteddfod Field where several important eisteddfodau were held during the nineteenth century.

Rhymney FC play in the North Gwent League, Premier Division at the Eisteddfod Field, Rhymney.

RISCA (Caerphilly) ST2490

The club's website records that Risca RFC was founded in 1875 and that early games were played on the Church House Field, situated opposite the Church House Hotel (since rebuilt as the Darren Hotel). Risca RFC re-emerged in 1906 and settled down permanently at the Stores Field. The team currently play in the WRU National Division 4 East.

Darren Inn FC, which disbanded in 2008, played in the Newport and District League, Division 3 at Fernlea Park, Risca.

AC Pontymister FC of the Gwent Central League, Division 3 once played at the Longbridge Field, Risca. The field takes its name from the 32-arch bridge, built in 1805 to carry a tram road and demolished a century later in 1905.

RISCA UNITED FC

see PONTYMISTER (Caerphilly)

RIVERSIDE FC

see CANTON (Cardiff)

RIVERVIEW HIBERNIANS FC

see LLISWERRY (Newport)

ROATH (Cardiff) ST1977

Roath is home to St Peter's RFC, a team founded in 1886 to provide recreation for Cardiff's growing Catholic population. The name is taken from the Roman Catholic parish of St Peter's, Roath. St Peter's play in the WRU National Division 3 South East at the Harlequins Ground, a famous Cardiff sporting venue that was home to Cardiff Harlequins (who disbanded in the 1890s) and also used by Cardiff City prior to their acquiring Ninian Park. Des Childs, in his centenary booklet, has outlined in detail how the club acquired the ground in the late 1970s. They had previously played at Roath Park, the Glider Field at Llanishen (where pilots were once taught to fly gliders) and the Maindy Barracks Field, now the site of Companies House.

Cardiff Cosmos FC of the Cardiff and District Senior League, Division 1 also play some games on an adjacent pitch to the Harlequins Ground.

Roath Park Royals of the Cardiff Combination Football League, Division 1 play at Roath Park.

ROATH LABOUR ROVERS

see LLANDAFF (Cardiff)

ROCKFIELD (Monmouthshire) SO4814

Rockfield Rovers FC play in the Gwent County League, Division 3 at the Rockfield Community Centre, Cornwallis Close, Monmouth.

Wyesham Wanderers FC, founded in 2007, who play in the

East Gwent Football League, Division 2 are also based at the Rockfield Community Centre.

ROCKSPUR FC

see PENLAN (Swansea)

ROGERSTONE (Newport) ST2787

Rogerstone FC play in the Gwent County League, Division 2 at the Welfare Ground. Iron workers from Shropshire first brought the game to the town in the nineteenth century, and Rogerstone enjoyed considerable early successes. For example, a team from Rogerstone won the South Wales Cup final in front of 3,000 spectators at Cardiff Arms Park in 1887.

ROGIET (Monmouthshire) ST4687

Rogiet FC play in the East Gwent Football League, Division 3 at Rogiet Football Field, near Chepstow.

RTB (EBBW VALE) RFC

see EBBW VALE (Blaenau Gwent)

RTB PANTEG FC

see GRIFFITHSTOWN (Torfaen)

RTL CHEMICALS FC

see CAERPHILLY

RUABON (Wrexham) SJ3043

The 1894 Welsh Cup final which Chirk won 2-0 against Westminster Rovers was played at Wynnstay Park, Ruabon in front of an estimated crowd of 3,000. The legendary Billy Meredith (1874-1958) played on that historic day for Chirk, winning his first important medal during a career which bestowed on him the accolade of being soccer's first superstar. Druids FC, possibly the oldest club in Wales, played at Plas Madoc in Ruabon.

RUMNEY RFC

see LLANRUMNEY (Cardiff)

RUTHIN (Denbighshire) SJ1258

Ruthin RFC play in the WRU National Division 1 North at Cae Ddôl in the shadow of the town's famous castle.

Ruthin Town FC, founded in 1951, of the Cymru Alliance League play at the Memorial Playing Fields, Parc y Dre. The team has played in the Alliance since 1992-93. Football in Ruthin, however, dates from 1880 when the local side lost in the final of the Welsh Cup to the all-conquering Druids.

ST ALBAN'S FC and RFC

see TREMORFA (Cardiff)

ST ASAPH (Denbighshire) SJ0374

St Asaph FC of the Clwyd League, Division 2 play at Roe Plas Meadows, St Asaph.

CPD Y Glannau of the Clwyd League, Division 1 are based at St Asaph Sports Centre.

ST ATHAN (Vale of Glamorgan) ST0168

St Athan FC play in the South Wales Senior League, Division 1 at the St Athan Community Centre Field, Glyndwr Road, St Athan.

ST CLEARS (Carmarthenshire) SN2716

St Clears FC play in the Pembrokeshire League, Division 2 at the St Clears and District Leisure Centre, Station Road.

St Clears RFC, who play in the WRU National Division 5 West, are also based at the Leisure Centre.

ST DAVIDS (Pembrokeshire) SM7525

St Davids RFC, formed in 1953, play in the WRU National Division 5 West. Their present field was purchased in 1955 for £350. Early games were played at St Non's Retreat. St Non was the mother of St David.

ST DIALS FC

see CWMBRÂN (Torfaen)

ST DOGMAEL'S (Pembrokeshire) SN1646

St Dogmael's FC of the Ceredigion League, Division 1 play at the School Field.

ST FLORENCE (Pembrokeshire) SN0801

St Florence FC play in the Pembrokeshire League, Division 3 at St Florence Village Playing Fields.

ST HARMON'S (Powys) SN9872

St Harmon's and District FC, founded in 2000, play in the Mid Wales League (South) at the Lingen, St Harmon's.

ST ISHMAEL'S (Pembrokeshire) SM8307

St Ishmael's FC of the Pembrokeshire League, Division 1 play at St Ishmael's Sports Field.

ST JOSEPH'S FC

see HAFOD (Swansea); HEATH (Cardiff)

ST JOSEPH'S OB FC

see ELY (Cardiff)

ST JOSEPH'S RFC

see HEATH (Cardiff)

ST JULIAN'S HSOB RFC

see NEWPORT

ST JULIAN'S YOUTH FC

see NEWPORT

ST MELLON'S SPORTS FC

see STM SPORTS FC

ST PATRICK'S FC

see GRANGETOWN (Cardiff)

ST PETER'S RFC

see ROATH (Cardiff)

ST THOMAS (Swansea) SS6693

Swansea Dockers FC (of the Swansea Senior Football League, Division 1), Seren Goch FC and Union Rangers FC (both of the Swansea Senior District League, Division 4) all play at Ashlands, Wern Fawr Road, St Thomas, Swansea. Ashlands was opened in 1990 on the site of the old Carbon Black works.

Naval and Military FC of the Swansea Senior District League, Division 4 play at Banfield, Tir John, St Thomas, Swansea.

SARON (Carmarthenshire) SN3738

Saron, near Llangeler, fielded a team in the Cardiganshire League until they withdrew at the end of the 2001-02 season. Their neat little ground at Cae Chwarae Saron is still well maintained and will again host Ceredigion League football in 2009-10.

SAUNDERSFOOT (Pembrokeshire) SN1304

Saundersfoot Sports FC play in the Pembrokeshire League, Division 2 at the King George V Playing Fields.

SCURLAGE (Swansea) SS4687

Fall Bay RFC of the WRU National Division 6 West play at the South Gower Sports Club, Monkland Road, Scurlage.

South Gower FC, founded in 1945, who were runners up in the Swansea Senior Football League, Division 1 in 2008-09, also play on an adjoining field in the same complex. The club will play in the Welsh League, Division 3 from 2009-10.

SEASIDE FC

see LLANELLI (Carmarthenshire)

SEBASTOPOL FC

see CWMBRÂN (Torfaen)

SENGHENNYDD (Caerphilly) ST1190

Senghennydd RFC, officially formed in 1898, play in the WRU National Division 5 South East at the Welfare Ground. Early games were played at the Gelli Fields until the new ground, immediately above the Gelli Fields, was opened in April 1914. The new ground was constructed by the Colliery Company to compensate for the shale tipping undertaken by the Windsor Collieries, which would have eventually encroached and engulfed the Gelli Fields.

SENNYBRIDGE (Powys) SN9228

Sennybridge FC play in the Mid Wales League (South) at the Riverside Field, sometimes called Riverside Park.

SEREN GOCH FC

see ST THOMAS (Swansea)

SEVEN SISTERS (Neath Port Talbot) SN8109

Seven Sisters RFC of the WRU National Division 3 South West play at Maes Dafydd, a ground renamed in 1979 in honour of DJ Davies, a former secretary and treasurer of the club who died in 1978. The club has been fortunate to have had such an eminent historian and academic as Dr Hywel Francis MP to chronicle its history in a centenary booklet published in 1997. The author notes that it is possible that rugby was introduced to the area as early as 1881, and that a game against neighbouring Creunant was played in that year on one of the Blaendulais Farm fields. The first organised game apparently took place in 1887 on land known as the Sports Ground on which Bryndulais Avenue was subsequently built in 1911. This development forced a further move to a field near the old signal box, before the club later settled at a notoriously wet field on Tŷ'n y Garreg Farm. In the 1920s and 1930s many industrial villages took advantage of the Miners' Welfare Fund to enhance sporting facilities, and by 1934 Seven Sisters had a decent playing field and changing rooms which both the rugby and football clubs shared amicably for many years, before the rugby club moved to a new ground in 1973.

Association Football was not played in the village until after the Great War, when a team known as the 'Old Blues' played on land to the west side of the river at Blaendulais Farm. The Blues disbanded in 1924, and another team known as the 'Stars' was formed, playing on a field opposite Mary Street at Hillside Park.

268

In 1929 the 'Black and Tans' were formed, joining the Aberdare League in 1930. Seven Sisters FC now play in the Welsh League, Division 3 and are still based at the Welfare Ground, Dulais Road, Seven Sisters.

SHAFTESBURY YOUTH FC
see NEWPORT

SHIP and PILOT FC
see PILLGWENLLY (Newport)

SHIRENEWTON (Monmouthshire) ST4793
Devauden Green FC play in the East Gwent Football League, Division 1 at the Shirenewton Playing Fields, known locally as the Shirenewton Rec.

SHOTTON (Flintshire) SJ3068
Shotton Steel FC of the Clwyd League, Division 1 play at Rowley's Drive, Shotton, the playing fields associated with the steelworks. The street is named after Harry Rowley, a nineteenth-century industrialist and owner of the Shotton Lane Brickwork Company. Shotton RFC, a Welsh Districts side, also play on the same fields.

Aston Park Rangers of the Clwyd League, Premier Division play at Shotton Lane, Shotton, Deeside.

SIX BELLS (Blaenau Gwent) SO2203

Abertillery Bluebirds FC operate three teams in the Gwent County League. The first team, who play in the Gwent County League, Division 1, and their reserves play their home games at Cwm-Nant-y-Groes Field, located in the village of Six Bells, while the third team play at the Duffryn Sports Fields, located in Blaina. Abertillery Bluebirds, champions of the Gwent County League in 2009, have gained promotion to the Welsh League, Division 3 from 2009-10.

SKETTY (Swansea) SS6292

Ragged School FC of the Swansea Senior Football League, Division 1 play at the University Fields, Singleton Park, Swansea, at the junction of Mumbles Road and Sketty Lane. The team has played at many different park venues in Swansea, and was for many years based at the Dillwyn Llewelyn Centre at Cockett. The origins of this club can be traced to the early nineteenth century ragged school movement for destitute children. The Swansea school was opened in the 1840s, but the football team was not formalised until 1948. Ragged were champions of Division 1 in 2009.

Brunswick United FC of the Swansea Senior Football League, Division 1, and Hafod Brotherhood FC and Hafod Rangers of Division 4, all play at the King George V Playing Fields, generally known as Ashleigh Road, Mumbles Road, Sketty, where several pitches are available.

SKEWEN (Neath Port Talbot) SS7297

Tennant Park, Skewen, is the home of Skewen RFC and was also the home of Skewen Athletic FC until its merger with Neath AFC in 2005. The ground is named after the Tennant family who were instrumental in building a canal, opened in 1824, which ran from Swansea to Aberdulais, linking the rivers Tawe and Nedd and providing a much-improved infrastructure for the family's major industrial interests in the region. Established in 1883, Skewen RFC is one of the oldest clubs in the region. Early games were played on several locations including a field at Cwrt-y-Clafdy Farm. In 1904 the club secured a playing ground on Burrows Road called Cae Lynch, and at the end of 1906 it moved again to a new venue known as Cae Wathen. In 1935-36, Skewen moved to its present home at Tennant Park, and now compete in the WRU National League Division 3 South West.

Harp Rovers FC and Lôn-las Youth FC, for whom John Hartson played as a youngster, play in the Neath Football League, Division 1 at Tennant Park.

Park Travellers FC, founded in 2002, play in the Neath Football League, Premier Division at Skewen Park.

Skewen Greyhound Stadium was used in the 1960s by the Swansea Town A team who competed in the Swansea Senior League and, for one season (1968-69), by Skewen Athletic.

SOLVA (Pembrokeshire) SM8024

Solva FC play in the Pembrokeshire League, Division 1 at Maes-y-môr.

SOUTH GOWER FC

see SCURLAGE (Swansea)

SOUTH GOWER RFC

see BISHOPSTON (Swansea)

SOUTH PARK ATHLETIC FC

see BUTETOWN (Cardiff)

SOUTH WALES POLICE RFC

see BRIDGEND

SOUTHEND ATHLETIC FC

see TREDEGAR (Blaenau Gwent)

SOUTHSEA (Wrexham) SJ3051

Brynteg Village FC of the Welsh National League (Wrexham Area), Division 1 play at Solway Banks, Southsea, Wrexham.

SP CONSTRUCTION FC

see BARRY (Vale of Glamorgan)

SPENCER OLD BOYS FC

see LLISWERRY (Newport); NEWPORT

SPENCER YOUTH and BOYS FC

see NEWPORT

SPLOTT (Cardiff) ST1976

Bridgend Street FC, founded in 1899 and based in Splott, play in the South Wales Senior League, Division 1. Their home has been the University Playing Fields, Llanrumney, but they have recently returned to Splott Park in Muirton Road, an amenity opened in 1901 on land donated by Lord Tredegar, where the pitch has now been railed to meet the league's criteria. Their reserve side, who play in the Cardiff and District League, and Adamstown FC of the Cardiff and District Football League, Division 3, are also based at Splott Park. Adamstown Athletic FC, 2009 champions of the Cardiff Combination Football League, Premier Division and Little Blue United FC of Division 1 also play at the park. During their early years, Splott Albion FC, founded in 1968 at the Great Eastern Hotel, also played at Splott Park. The football field is known to locals as 'God's Little Acre'.

Moorlands Park in the Splott area of Cardiff is also used for local football.

SPLOTT ALBION FC
see LLANRUMNEY (Cardiff)

SPORTING LLANDAFF
see ELY (Cardiff)

STANLEYTOWN FC
see TYLORSTOWN (Rhondda Cynon Taf)

STM SPORTS FC

see LLANRUMNEY (Cardiff)

SUDBROOK (Monmouthshire) ST5087

Sudbrook Cricket Club FC play in the Gwent County League, Division 2 at the Sudbrook Cricket Club, Hill Lane, Sudbrook.

SULLY (Vale of Glamorgan) ST1568

Sully Sports FC play in the South Wales Senior League, Division 1 at South Road, Swanbridge, Sully.

Sully Sports Sharks RFC, formed in 1967, play in the WRU National Division 6 Central, also at Swanbridge.

SUNNYBANK WMC FC

see CLYDACH (Swansea)

SW FLOORING FC

see WENVOE (Vale of Glamorgan)

SWANSEA SS6494

Dr Andrew Hignell has chronicled the history of St Helen's in considerable detail, noting that the ground takes its name from a convent dedicated to Saint Helen that was built by an order of Augustinian nuns on the foreshore of Swansea Bay during the medieval period. Rugby was first played in the Uplands area of Swansea on Bryn-y-môr Field, opposite the Uplands Hotel (now a part of Uplands Crescent), and on Primrose Field where Chaddersley Terrace and Cromwell Street now stand. St Helen's was first opened as a cricket ground in 1873 and developed as a venue for international rugby matches between 1882 and 1954. Swansea were represented at the inaugural meeting of the WRU in 1881. St Helen's also hosted the very first soccer international match to be staged in South Wales when Ireland were defeated 4-1 on 24 February 1894. From 1921 it became a ground for first-class cricket matches as Glamorgan entered the County League. It has witnessed many historic moments during its long history. It was at St Helen's that Swansea RFC became the first club side to defeat the touring All Blacks, on 28 September 1935, winning 11-3. The touring Australians were also defeated 21-6 by Swansea in November 1992. However, the event that is always associated

Stadiwm Liberty / Liberty Stadium, Swansea. Photograph reproduced by kind permission of www.swanseacity.net

with St Helen's is Sir Garfield Sobers' remarkable feat in 1968 of hitting the first ever six sixes in one over in first-class cricket during a match between Nottinghamshire and Glamorgan. Today the ground is used mainly by Swansea RFC, who play in the WRU National League, Premier Division. The famous grandstand that backed onto the Mumbles Road was demolished in 2005 and replaced with a far less impressive structure.

Cae'r Vetch/Vetch Field (formerly known as Fleming's Meadow) in the Sandfields area of Swansea has been the home of professional football in the city since 1912. The field takes its name from vetch, a cabbage-like plant that was grown on the land. Although there are references to the Vetch Field being used for recreational purposes as early as 1879, it was not until 1912 that a formal lease was obtained from the Swansea Gas Company to use the land as a football pitch. For 93 years it provided a home for Swansea Town/City football club and during the 1980s staged First Division football for two seasons following Swansea's remarkable rise through four divisions under the management of John Toshack. The record attendance of 32,786 was achieved during an FA Cup fifth round tie against Arsenal on 17 February 1968. Swansea played their last game at the Vetch Field on 30 April 2005 before moving to the new Liberty Stadium, which they share with Neath-Swansea Ospreys RFC. After protracted legal problems it appears that the site can now be finally sold and developed for 120 housing units, with completion expected in 2010 or 2011.

Stadiwm Liberty/Liberty Stadium was built on the site of the former Morfa Athletics Stadium in the White Rock area of Landore on the banks of the river Tawe on the eastern side of the city. The area was famous for copper smelting, and the Bristol-born industrialist Thomas Coster apparently traded some of his products for slaves. The Liberty Stadium was built at a cost of £27m, is council owned, and has a capacity of 20,532. The first match played at the stadium was a friendly between Swansea City and Fulham held on 23 July 2005. The stadium takes its name from a sponsorship deal signed with Liberty Property PLC, commercial property developers based in London, Chester and Swansea. It is an impressive facility and since its opening it has staged many memorable matches in both codes.

SWANSEA DOCKERS FC

see ST THOMAS (Swansea)

SWANSEA UPLANDS RFC

see KILLAY (Swansea)

SWISS VALLEY (Carmarthenshire) SN5202

Tafarn United FC, founded in 2007 and based at Tafarn y Felin, Swiss Valley, Llanelli, play in the Carmarthenshire League, Division 3 at Coedcae School, Trostre Road, Llanelli.

SYCHDYN (Flintshire) SJ2466

Sychdyn FC was established in 1946 as Sychdyn Villa. During the 1960s and 1970s the club was known as Sychdyn United and played their home matches on Banks Park in the village, before the club moved to its present home at the Sychdyn Sports

Centre, Wat's Dyke Drive. The side later adopted the name CPD Sychdyn and now play in the Clwyd League, Premier Division.

TADROSS: AFC

see BARRY (Vale of Glamorgan)

TAFARN UNITED FC

see SWISS VALLEY (Carmarthenshire)

TAFF'S WELL (Rhondda Cynon Taf) ST1283

Taff's Well FC, founded in 1947, of the Welsh League, Division 1, play at Rhiw'r Dda, Parish Road, Taff's Well.

Taff's Well RFC, founded in 1887, play in the WRU National Division 4 South East at Maes Gwyn, Glanllyn Square, Taff's Well. Early games were played at the Castle Grounds, a pitch located behind the Castle Hotel, where part of King Street now stands. Subsequently, the team played at Rhiw'r Dda, Tŷ Rhiw and Cae Glas before Cae'r Afon was acquired in 1959 and officially opened in April 1963. In 2002 Taff's Well RFC moved again to a new field in the middle of the village which is named Maes Gwyn in honour of the club's president, Gwyn Davies. Taff's Well RFC has hosted the Six Nations home fixtures of the Wales Women's team, winners of the Triple Crown in 2009.

TAI-BACH (Neath Port Talbot) SS7788

Tai-bach RFC play in the WRU National Division 4 South West at the Talbot Memorial Park (Plough Field).

TALBOT GREEN (Rhondda Cynon Taf) ST0482

AFC Talbot Green of the Taff Ely and Rhymney Valley Alliance Football League, Premier Division play at Talbot Park. The village and the playing field derive their names from the Talbot Arms tavern, named in turn after the Talbot family of Hensol Castle.

TALGARTH (Powys) SN9690

Gwernyfed RFC, established in 1965, of the WRU National Division 3 East play at Trefecca Road. The club previously played at Gwernyfed High School, Three Cocks, Powys.

Gwernyfed FC play in the Mid Wales League (South) at the King George V Playing Fields.

TALIESIN FC

see TRE TALIESIN (Ceredigion)

TAL-Y-BONT (Ceredigion) SH6070

Tal-y-bont FC were founder members of the Aberystwyth and District League in 1934, but were subsequently absent from the league for lengthy periods. Since being re-formed in 1973, the team have played at a number of grounds including Plas-crug at Aberystwyth, and locally at Cae Erglodd, Taliesin, Cae Llety-Llwyd, Tal-y-bont and Cae Dôl Clettwr, Tre'r ddôl, their present home. They compete in Division 2 of the Aberystwyth and District League.

TAL-Y-SARN (Gwynedd) SH4853

Tal-y-sarn Celts, who compete in the Caernarfon and District League, Division 1, have played at Gloddfa'r Glai for the last decade where they have installed good facilities for both players and officials. Prior to moving to Gloddfa'r Glai, they played at various venues including Cae Tŷ Mawr West and Dôl Pebin, known colloquially as Dôl Beb. Dôl Pebin (the field of Pebin) appears in the *Mabinogion*, and a council estate, Bro Silyn, was built on the field in the mid twentieth century. It has been suggested that Edward I may have held a jousting tournament on Dôl Pebin.

TALYWAIN (Torfaen) SO2604

Talywain RFC, founded in 1898, play in the WRU National Division 4 East at Emlyn Park, Talywain. The park was opened in 1973.

Fairfield United FC play in the Gwent County League, Division 2 at Garndiffaith Ravine Football Pitch.

TANYGRISIAU (Gwynedd) SH6845

Bro Ffestiniog RFC, established in 1973, champions of the WRU National League Division 1 North in 2008-09, play at Y Ddôl, Tanygrisiau. The first games organised by the club were played at Cae Pont-y-Pant, Dolwyddelan. Y Ddôl at Tanygrisiau was acquired in 1976, following a land-reclamation scheme, although the land was initially earmarked for industrial development. However, rugby was not played on the new field until 1980 and the official opening was delayed until 1981.

TEGRYN (Pembrokeshire) SN2332

Boncath FC, who competed in the Ceredigion League in 2006-07, withdrawing the following season, played their games in the neighbouring village of Tegryn. The pitch has recently been used by Maesglas FC as a temporary home.

TENBY (Pembrokeshire) SN1300

Tenby United RFC play in the WRU National Division 4 West at Heywood Lane.

Tenby United FC, 2008-09 champions of the Pembrokeshire League, Division 2, play at the Clickets. B G Charles dates this name to 1549, suggesting that *clicket* is a dialect word for the latch of a door or gate.

THORNHILL (Cardiff) ST1782

Thornhill Athletic of the Cardiff Combination Football League, Division 1 play at Thornhill Park.

THORNTON (Pembrokeshire) SM9007

Hubberston FC play in the Pembrokeshire League, Division 3 at Milford Haven Comprehensive School, Thornton.

THORNWELL RED and WHITE FC

see BULWARK (Monmouthshire)

TINTERN (Monmouthshire) SO5200

Tintern Abbey FC play in the East Gwent Football League, Division 1 at Tintern Playing Field, which is also known as Leyton's Field.

TIPPLING PHILOSOPHER FC

see CALDICOT (Monmouthshire)

TIRYBERTH (Caerphilly) ST1496

AFC Tiryberth play in the Taff Ely and Rhymney Valley Football League, Premier Division at the Welfare Ground, Tiryberth.

TON PENTRE (Rhondda Cynon Taf) SS9695

Football in this area of the Rhondda Valley dates from at least 1896, and a successful club existed at Ton Pentre from 1905 playing in the South Wales, Western and Southern Leagues. In 1922 Ton Pentre were Welsh Cup finalists, but amid the economic depression the club folded in 1923. It was re-formed in 1935, and played continuously in the Welsh League with considerable success. In 1993-94 they were promoted to the League of Wales and in 1995 they became Wales' first representatives in the UEFA Inter-Toto Cup. However, their European exploits exposed their frail financial position, and in 1997 they were forced, reluctantly, to withdraw from the League of Wales. Since opting to play in the Welsh League, Ton Pentre have remained a highly successful club, winning five consecutive championships, and still harbour ambitions of returning to the top flight of Welsh football. Their traditional home, Ynys Park, is, however, in need of considerable refurbishment. They play in the Welsh League, Division 1.

Ynys Park is also the home of Ton and Gelli Boys' Club, who play in the South Wales Amateur Football League, Division 2.

TONDU RFC
see ABERKENFIG (Bridgend)

TONFANNAU 55TH ROYAL ARTILLERY FC
see PORTHMADOG (Gwynedd)

TONGWYNLAIS (Cardiff) ST1382
Tongwynlais FC play in the South Wales Senior League, Division 2 at Ironbridge Road, Tongwynlais.

TONMAWR (Neath Port Talbot) SS8096
Tonmawr RFC of the WRU National Division 1 West play at the Whitworth Field/Memorial Ground, Dan-y-coed, Tonmawr, Port Talbot. The Whitworth family were Northampton gentry and were involved in the exploitation of the South Wales coalfield. They acquired land in a number of parishes east and south of Neath. Early matches were possibly played on land belonging to Tŷ'n-Ton Farm and on a field known as the Isle of White, located behind John's Terrace on a farm of the same name. It was a field which was used again in the 1950s when the Whitworth Field was being levelled.

TONNA (Neath Port Talbot) SS7799

Tonna RFC, founded in 1887, play in the WRU National Division 3 South West at the Memorial Ground at Mount Pleasant. The club traces its origins to 1888, and early games were played on the adjacent Henfaes Field, or the Flat as it was also known, where part of Tonna's present clubhouse now stands. The club also played on fields known locally as the Ynys. After the Second World War, Tonna's home pitch was at Ynysygerwn Cricket Club during the period when Mount Pleasant was being levelled and improved for rugby.

TONNA (DENTICARE TONNA) FC

see NEATH ABBEY (Neath Port Talbot)

TONYPANDY (Rhondda Cynon Taf) SS9992

The Mid-Rhondda Athletic Ground at Tonypandy hosted many important games in the early twentieth century, including a rugby league match against the touring Australians on 3 October 1906. The ground also served as the home of Mid-Rhondda Rugby League Club from 1908-09. More famously, it hosted a Welsh Cup final replay in 1913, and was the home of Mid-Rhondda FC, formed in 1912, who played in the Southern League until their demise in 1928. The ground remains very much intact to this day.

TONYPANDY ALBIONS FC

see CLYDACH VALE (Rhondda Cynon Taf)

TONYREFAIL (Rhondda Cynon Taf) ST0188

Tonyrefail RFC play in the WRU National Division 4 South East at Parklands.

Tonyrefail Welfare, who once competed in the Welsh League, played at the Welfare Park. The ground still exists but is now derelict.

Tonyrefail Welfare FC now play in the Rhondda and District League at Penrhiwfer Park.

Tonyrefail BGC of the South Wales Senior League, Division 1 play at Tŷ'n-y-bryn Park.

TOTAL NETWORK SOLUTIONS (TNS) FC

see LLANSAN(T)FFRAID-YM-MECHAIN (Powys)

TOWNHILL (Swansea) SS6494

Gors FC, based at the Gors Inn, Townhill, play in the Swansea Senior League, Division 1 at Gors Avenue.

TOWY VALLEY FC

see LLANDOVERY (Carmarthenshire)

TRADESMAN'S ARMS FC

see MACHEN (Caerphilly)

TRALLWM FC

see LLANELLI (Carmarthenshire)

TRALLWN (Swansea) SS6996

Carreg Wen FC of the Swansea Senior Football League, Division 2, and Birchgrove Colts FC of the Swansea Senior District League, Division 4 both play at Bethel Road, Trallwn, Swansea. The playing fields are located in close proximity to Bethel Congregational Chapel.

TRANCH (Torfaen) SO2700

Tranch FC play in the Gwent County League, Division 2 at the Welfare Ground.

TRAWS-GOED FC

see ABERMAGWR (Ceredigion)

TRE TALIESIN (Ceredigion) SN6591

Taliesin FC were founder members of the Aberystwyth and District League but were dogged by problems in obtaining a playing field and were forced to play many games at Aberystwyth. However, some games were played locally at Cae'r Romans (the name is associated with early mining activity) and at Cae Dôlclettwr, Tre'r-ddôl.

TREARDDUR BAY (Anglesey) SH2579

The recently re-formed Trearddur Bay United FC play in the Anglesey League. Their ground does not have a name.

TREBANOG (Rhondda Cynon Taf) ST0190

Trebanog Rangers FC play in the Rhondda and District Football League, Premier Division at Trebanog Field.

TREBANOS (Neath Port Talbot) SN7002

Trebanos RFC, founded in 1897, play in the WRU National Division 5 South West at a ground owned and leased from Pontardawe Town Council and known locally as the Park. Early matches were played on Gwrach-y-llwynau Field, now a housing estate. Trebanos moved across Swansea Road to their present ground in 1946.

TREBOETH UNITED FC

see PENLAN (Swansea)

TREDEGAR (Blaenau Gwent) SO1409

Tredegar RFC, founded in 1893, play in the WRU National League Division 1 East at the Recreation Ground.

Tredegar Ironsides RFC, formed in 1946, of the WRU National Division 3 East also play at the Recreation Ground.

Tredegar Town FC, founded in 1968, of the Welsh League, Division 2, play at the Tredegar Leisure Complex, Stable Lane, Tredegar. Southend Athletic FC and Glamorgan TAP FC of the North Gwent League, Premier Division also play at the same venue.

Tredegar Athletic FC play in the North Gwent League, Division 1 at the same location.

Several teams in the North Gwent League play at Tŷ Trist – playing fields created on the site of the former Tŷ Trist Colliery where Aneurin Bevan (1897-1960) once worked. These teams include Coach and Horses FC and Tredegar Athletic of the North Gwent Football League, Premier Division and Red Lion FC of the North Gwent League, Division 1.

TREDEGAR ARMS FC

see NEW TREDEGAR (Caerphilly)

TREDOMEN ATHLETIC FC

see YSTRADMYNACH (Caerphilly)

TREFECHAN FC

see ABERYSTWYTH (Ceredigion)

TREFELIN BGC FC

see PORT TALBOT (Neath Port Talbot)

TREFEURIG AND DISTRICT UNITED FC

see BANC-Y-DARREN (Ceredigion)

TREFIL (Blaenau Gwent) SO1212

Trefil RFC played in the WRU National League Division 6 East in 2007-08 at the Trefil Rugby Field, but despite finishing fourth they were 'relegated' to the Gwent District League as they had not fulfilled three fixtures. They have now been reinstated.

TREFNANT (Denbighshire) SJ0570

Trefnant Village FC played in the Clwyd League, Premier Division in 2007-08, but folded at the end of the season. Their ground at Trefnant Recreation Field was located near the village hall.

TREFONEN (Shropshire) SJ2526

Trefonen play in the Montgomeryshire Amateur Football League, Division 2 at the Recreation Ground, School Lane, Trefonen.

TREFOR (Gwynedd) SH3746

Trefor FC of the Caernarfon and District League, Division 1 play at Parc Trefor. The park is named after Trevor Jones who managed the village's famous quarry in the 1850s and who gave his name to the village.

TREFOREST (Rhondda Cynon Taf) ST0888

Taff Vale Park at Treforest has a rich history which has been carefully documented in great detail by Gareth Harris. Opened in 1890, and used initially for rugby union by Pontypridd RFC, it soon developed into one of the premier stadiums in the South Wales valleys, hosting a variety of sports. It once boasted a cycle track, a cinder athletics track and a large wooden grandstand, and it often accommodated crowds in excess of 20,000. Today the park continues as a public amenity and is used by the Pontypridd RFC mini-section and serves also as a popular venue for local carnivals and fêtes.

Treforest FC play in the South Wales Amateur Football

League, Division 1 at the White Tips Stadium, Dan-y-bryn Road, Treforest, Pontypridd.

Bridgend Town FC of the Welsh League, Division 1 have recently found a temporary home at the University of Glamorgan's Tŷ'n y Wern Playing Fields.

TREFRIW (Conwy) SH7863

Clwb Rygbi Nant Conwy, established in 1980, play at Parc Carw (deer park), Trefriw. The name indicates that wild deer, still prevalent in parts of Snowdonia, were associated with the Vale of Conwy. The club, who play in the WRU National Division 1 North, has two playing fields, a spacious floodlit training area and modern changing facilities which include a gymnasium.

TREGARON (Ceredigion) SN6759

Tregaron Turfs FC of the Aberystwyth and District League, Division 1, and Clwb Rygbi Tregaron, founded in 1975, of the WRU National Division 6 West, both play on the fields of Ysgol Uwchradd Tregaron.

The first football match recorded at Tregaron was played in 1882 on a field in front of the vicarage and, at the beginning of the twentieth century, games were also played on Sunny Hill Farm. The term *turfs* was first coined for the re-formed team that emerged after the Great War in 1919 as they played on land adjacent to Tregaron Bog, between the Railway Cottage and Pont Einion, where turf cutting for peat was a prevalent activity at the time.

Post-war, they played on a field near Ystrad Caron, where

Maesamlwg Estate now stands, before moving to a field on Penlan Farm, next to the Railway Cottage, where they played until the team folded in 1960. Since being re-formed in 1969, the team has played at Ysgol Uwchradd Tregaron.

TREHAFOD (Rhondda Cynon Taf) ST0491

Lewis Merthyr FC play in the Rhondda District League at Trehafod Park.

TREHARRIS (Merthyr Tydfil) ST0997

Treharris Athletic Western FC, founded in 1889, of the Welsh League, Division 2, play at the Athletic Ground, Spencer Place, Treharris. Treharris Athletic claims to be the oldest football club in South Wales. Lile and Farmer have also recorded that a team from Treharris entertained a team from Cardiff on 30 January 1893, the game being played at Graig Berthlwyd before 'a large number of spectators'.

Western Hotel FC of the Merthyr Tydfil League, Premier Division play at Treharris Park and also sponsor Treharris Athletic.

TREHERBERT (Rhondda Cymon Taf) SS9498

Treherbert fielded a rugby league team from 1908-10 playing at the Athletic Ground, Treherbert.

TREHERBERT RFC

see TYNEWYDD (Rhondda Cynon Taf)

TRELAI FC

see ELY (Cardiff)

TRELEWIS (Merthyr Tydfil) ST1097

Trelewis Welfare FC, who play in the South Wales Amateur Football League, Division 2, play at the Welfare Ground, Brondeg, Trelewis.

TREMORFA (Cardiff) ST2087

St Alban's RFC of the WRU National Division 5 South East, and St Alban's FC, newly promoted to the South Wales Senior League, both play at Tremorfa Park.

Bridgend Street FC, based at Splott, once played their home games at Willows High School, Tremorfa.

TREORCHY (Rhondda Cynon Taf) SS9596

Treorchy RFC, formed in 1886, play at the Oval in the WRU National Division 2 East. The Oval was opened in January 1924 with a prestigious fixture against Cardiff RFC. Prior to establishing themselves at the Oval, Treorchy RFC played at a number of locations, beginning life at the Ystradfechan Fields before moving in 1896 to the Fair Field, behind Dumfries Street. When that land was required for housing to meet the growing demands of a vibrant mining town, Treorchy RFC was forced to move temporarily to neighbouring Pentre, where they played at Griffin Park from 1905–07 before moving once again to the New Athletic Grounds on the western fringes of the town, near the Abergorky Colliery. In 1922 the club again relocated to Cae

Mawr, adjacent to the Ystrafechan Fields, where they remained until their final move to the Oval.

Cwmparc Legion FC and Treorchy BGC FC both play in the Rhondda and District Football League, Premier Division at Cae Mawr.

Clive Thomas, the well-known former FIFA football referee and a native of Treorchy, makes several references to many of these fields in his autobiography, published in 1984.

TREOWEN STARS FC

see NEWBRIDGE (Torfaen)

TRE'R-DDÔL (Ceredigion) SN6692

Cae Dôlclettwr, Tre-ddôl, is home to Tal-y-bont FC, who play in the Aberystwyth and District League, Division 2. Taliesin FC, once of the Aberystwyth and District League but now defunct, also played at Cae Dôlclettwr.

TRETHOMAS (Caerphilly) ST1888

Trethomas Bluebirds play in the Gwent County League, Division 2 at Llanfabon Drive.

TREVETHIN FC

see PONTNEWYNYDD (Torfaen)

TREWERN (Powys) SJ2811

Trewern United FC of the Montgomeryshire Amateur League, Division 2 play at the School Field.

TRIMSARAN (Carmarthenshire) SN4504

Rugby has been played at Trimsaran since 1910. Trimsaran United RFC of the WRU National Division 4 West play at Cae Ffair.

Trimsaran FC of the Carmarthenshire League, Division 2 play at Trimsaran Park.

TRINANT (Caerphilly) ST2099

Trinant RFC was founded in 1956, although rugby was certainly played in the village at the turn of the twentieth century at the Pentwyn Field. The club currently play in the WRU National Division 5 East. Its ground was required for a new school in 1962 and the club purchased an alternative ground that required much levelling work.

Trinant FC play in the Gwent County League, Division 2 at the Recreation Ground, Trinant.

TROED-Y-RHIW (Merthyr Tydfil) SO0702

Troed-y-rhiw FC of the Welsh League, Division 3, whose predecessors Troed-y-rhiw Stars were a major force in Welsh football during the early years of the twentieth century, play at the Willows Community Centre, Troed-y-rhiw, Merthyr Tydfil.

Anchor FC, based at the Anchor Inn, Pontmorlais, of the Merthyr Tydfil Football League, Division 1, and Brunswick FC, founded in 2007, of Division 2, play at the Sekisui Ground, Troed-y-rhiw. Sekisui is a Japanese chemical company which opened a factory in Merthyr in 1978.

TROSTRE SPORTS FC

see LLANELLI (Carmarthenshire)

TUMBLE (Carmarthenshire) SN5412

Tumble RFC of the WRU National Division 4 West and Tumble United FC of the Carmarthenshire League, Division 1 both play at Tumble Park.

TURBERVILLE ARMS FC

see WILLIAMSTOWN (Rhondda Cynon Taf)

TŶ-CROES (Carmarthenshire) SH3472

Tŷ-croes RFC, founded in 1910, play in the WRU National League Division 4 West at Cae Gelli.

TYLORSTOWN (Rhondda Cynon Taf) ST0195

Tylorstown RFC of the WRU National Division 3 South East have an illustrious history which is well documented on the club's website. Rugby was probably played at this mining village in the Rhondda Fach as early as 1895, but documentary evidence dates the club's foundation to 1903. Early games were played on Cae Tŷ Gwyn on the valley floor but the land was soon required for industrial purposes, forcing the club to relocate to a field near Cefn Llechau Isaf Farm, known as the Stanleytown Tump, in 1907. In the early 1930s, Rhondda Urban District Council provided work for unemployed miners on the side of the mountain, creating the club's present ground at Penrhys

Park. The field was officially opened in the 1934–35 season with a game against Pontypridd.

Stanleytown FC of the South Wales Senior League, Division 2 were founded in 1976. Until 1991 they played in the Rhondda and District Football League at Darran Park, Ferndale, when they were invited to join the new South Wales Senior League. They have since played their matches at the Recreation Field, Tylorstown.

TYNEWYDD (Rhondda Cynon Taf) SS9399

Treherbert RFC, formed in 1875, play at Tynewydd RM (Rhondda Merthyr) Park in the WRU National Division 3 South East, a pitch located on reclaimed land which was opened in the early 1960s. The club has also played at the Hay Field and at Blaenrhondda Park.

The Baglan, a team associated with the Baglan Hotel, Tynewydd, play in the Rhondda and District Football League at the Baglan Field, a relatively new pitch that stands on the site of the Ynysfeio Colliery, a pit that operated from 1854 until its closure in the 1930s.

Wyndham FC, a team based at the Wyndham Hotel, Tynewydd, play in the Rhondda and District Football League, Premier Division at Pentre Park (Astroturf), Pentre.

TYNEWYDD FC

see BARRY (Vale of Glamorgan)

TYNTE ROVERS FC

see PENRHIW-CEIBR (Rhondda Cynon Taf)

TYWYN (Gwynedd) SH5850

Tywyn has a rich football tradition. A team called Towyn St Cadfan's played Aberystwyth in 1885 at the Corbett Arms Field, a venue that was used for football until Towyn FC amalgamated with neighbouring Bryn-crug in 1989. Towyn FC were champions of the Cambrian Coast League in 1946. The Corbett Arms Field is located behind the Corbett Arms Hotel, and is now used as an open-air market venue. Football was also played at Sandilands Park, Tywyn. The field is now a caravan park.

TYWYN-BRYN-CRUG FC

see BRYN-CRUG (Gwynedd)

UNDERWOOD (Monmouthshire) ST3888

Underwood FC play in the East Gwent Football League, Division 2.

UNDERWOOD SOCIAL CLUB FC

see LLANMARTIN (Newport)

UNDY (Monmouthshire) ST4386

Undy Athletic FC play in the Gwent County League, Division 1 at the Undy Playing Fields, The Causeway.

UNION RANGERS FC

see ST THOMAS (Swansea)

UPPER BOAT (Rhondda Cynon Taf) ST1087

Rhydyfelin AFC of the South Wales Amatuer League, Division 1 play at the Upper Boat Playing Fields.

USK (Monmouthshire) SO3700

Usk RFC play in the WRU National Division 5 East. The club's website notes that their ground at Red Shed Meadow was originally held on a lease from a local landowner, but in October 1952 an advertisement appeared in the *Western Mail* noting that the ground was to be offered for sale at a local auction. Without the knowledge of club members a Cardiff solicitor saw the advertisement, contacted the club secretary and asked him to attend the auction and bid for the ground on his behalf. On 28 October 1952 the rugby club committee were informed that a Mr Ewan Davies, a former Welsh rugby international, had purchased the ground and wished to donate it to Usk Rugby Club. David Evans George Davies (1887-1979), generally known as Ewan, was also owner of the Plaza Cinema in Swansea, a Liberal Party parliamentary candidate and a breeder of Herefordshire cattle on his Pembrokeshire farm.

Usk Town FC play in the Premier Division of the Gwent Central League at the Island, a park named after a small island located in the middle of the River Usk, which flows through the parkland. It is recorded that an Usk rugby team played a local derby against Chepstow at the Island in November 1887.

UWIC FC

see CYNCOED (Cardiff)

VALE OF ARROW FC

see GLADESTRY (Powys)

VALLEY (Anglesey) SH2979

Valley FC, formed in 2005, play in the Anglesey League at the community council owned Parc Mwd. It is called Parc Mwd as the soil originally came from Cae Mwd, the home of Holyhead Hotspur. Their pitch was dug up to make way for a new dry dock and the soil was subsequently dumped at Valley to create a new pitch named in honour of Cae Mwd.

Clwb Rygbi Dyffryn, a Welsh Districts Club, play at RAF Valley, Station Playing Fields, Anglesey.

Holyhead RFC, a Welsh Districts side, play at Bryn-y-Mor, Four Mile Bridge, Valley.

VARDRE (Swansea) SN6901

Vardre RFC, founded in 1926, of the WRU National Division 4 South West, play at Maes-y-Bioden (field of the magpie), reflecting the club colours of black and white hoops. Early games were played on a field opposite Gellionnen Road (now the school ground) and on the Sewerage Field. They also once played at the INCO Recreational Fields, Clydach.

VENTURE COMMUNITY FC

see QUEENSWAY (Wrexham)

VILLA FC

see LLANDAFF (Cardiff)

VILLA DINO/CHRISTCHURCH FC

see NEWPORT

WALES TARTAN FC

see YNYSTAWE (Swansea)

WATERLOO ROVERS FC

see WELSHPOOL (Powys)

WATTSTOWN (Rhondda Cynon Taf) ST0193

Wattstown RFC, champions of the WRU National Division 6 Central in 2008-09, now play in National Division 5 South Central at the Memorial Ground, Wattstown.

WAUNARLWYDD (Swansea) SS6095

Waunarlwydd RFC, formed in 1900, have played since 1912 at the Waunarlwydd Recreation Ground, Roseland Road, Waunarlwydd, Swansea in the WRU National Division 2 West. Early games were played at a variety of locations including the Common at Mynydd Bach y Glo and Marie Hicks, a field in the Bishwell area of neighbouring Gowerton.

Waunarlwydd FC of the Swansea Senior District League, Division 3 also play at the Roseland Road complex.

WAUNFAWR (Gwynedd) SH5359

Waunfawr FC of the Caernarfon and District League, Division 2 play at Cae Gosod Waunfawr.

WELLFIELD ATHLETIC FC

see LLANELLI (Carmarthenshire)

WELSHPOOL (Powys) SJ2207

Football has been played in Welshpool since 1878 and early games were played on the Foundry Field. The extensive Maes-y-dre Recreation Fields have provided a home since 1895 for Welshpool's teams and, from 2001, Welshpool Town FC have enjoyed Welsh Premiership status. The Maes-y-dre complex also includes separate fields used by Waterloo Rovers FC, who play in the Mid Wales League and whose origins date back over a century to a pub team based in the Waterloo area of the town, and Welshpool RFC, originally founded in 1923, but re-formed in 1967, who currently play in the WRU National Division 2 North. The facilities for premiership football at Welshpool compare rather unfavourably with other clubs. The pitch actually forms a part of the field used by Welshpool Cricket Club, making it difficult to improve the ground. There is a strong possibility that Welshpool will exchange pitches with Waterloo Rovers in order to meet the required ground criteria and to preserve Welsh Premiership football in the town. Welshpool changed its name to Technogroup Welshpool Town following a deal with its main sponsor in August 2008, but the club has now abandonded its ambitions to continue in the restructured Welsh Premiership season after 2010–11.

WENVOE (Cardiff) ST1272

Ely Rangers FC, founded in 1965, who play in the Welsh League, Division 2, are based at Station Road, Wenvoe.

SW Flooring FC of the Vale of Glamorgan Football League, Premier Division, and Wenvoe Exiles FC, who play in Division 1, play some games in the village. The Exiles also play at the Barry Sports Centre and Pencoedtre Park, Barry.

WEPRE RANGERS FC

see CONNAH'S QUAY (Flintshire)

WERN FC

see BRYNHYFRYD (Swansea)

WEST DRAGONS FC

see CRUNDALE (Pembrokeshire)

WEST END FC

see MAYHILL (Swansea)

WEST END UNITED FC

see LLANELLI (Carmarthenshire)

WEST PONTNEWYDD FC

see PONTNEWYDD (Torfaen)

WESTERN HOTEL FC

see TREHARRIS (Merthyr Tydfil)

WHITCHURCH (Cardiff) ST1580

Cardiff HSOB (High School Old Boys) RFC, originally conceived in 1923, of the WRU National Division 4 South East, play at the Diamond Ground, Forest Farm Road, Whitchurch, Cardiff. They played their first full season in 1923-24 using a field on which Rhydypenau Primary School in Cyncoed now stands. The club, however, appears to have folded after its first season. It was revived in 1929, and a field adjoining the Butcher's Arms, Rhiwbina was used for home fixtures. After four seasons at Rhiwbina, the club moved again to the Glider Field, Llanishen which remained its home until the outbreak of war in 1939. The club was re-convened in 1947 and played at the famous Harlequins Field at Roath. In 1961 the club gained a lease on the Elyn Ground in Whitchurch, and in August 1963 it was renamed the Diamond Ground in honour of the school's long-serving headmaster, George Clifford Diamond (1902-85). He was a former pupil of Cardiff High who graduated from Queen's College, Cambridge, and who was appointed headmaster of the school in 1934 at the tender age of 32 years.

AFC Whitchurch play in the South Wales Senior League, Division 2 at Whitchurch Hospital, Park Road, Whitchurch.

WHITCHURCH BLUES FC

see RHIWBINA (Cardiff)

WHITE HORSE FC

see GURNOS (Merthyr Tydfil)

WHITEHEADS FC

see BASSALEG (Newport)

WHITLAND (Carmarthenshire) SN2016

Whitland RFC, formed around 1910, of the WRU National League Division 1 West, play at Parc Llwyn Tŷ Gwyn.

Whitland FC of the Carmarthenshire League, Division 3 play at Parc Dr Owen. The park is named after Dr William David Owen (1888-1937), a local general practitioner. Dr Owen's sister, Mrs Mildred Morris of White Hall, Pembroke, gave the land to the town in 1960 for recreational use to perpetuate his memory.

WILLIAMSTOWN (Rhondda Cynon Taf) ST0090

Turberville Arms FC play in the South Wales Amateur Football League, Division 1 at Ely Field, Williamstown.

WINCH WEN (Swansea) SS6896

Winch Wen FC of the Swansea Senior Football League, Division 1, formed in 1933, and Brynawel FC of the Swansea Senior Football League, Division 2, both play at Halfway Park, Carmel

Road, Winch Wen, Swansea. Jack Kelsey (1929-92) and Gary Sprake, two local boys who are amongst Wales' best-known goalkeepers, both started their careers playing on the Halfway Park.

WINDSOR FC

see BARRY (Vale of Glamorgan)

WREXHAM SJ3350

Y Cae Ras/The Racecourse, home of Wrexham FC and the premier stadium serving North Wales, occupies land originally developed for horse-racing by Sir Watkin Williams Wynn of Wynnstay (1772-1840), involving the Wrexham Yeomanry Cavalry. The first race was held on 29 September 1807 and they continued on an annual basis until 1858. Wrexham Cricket Club used the Racecourse for its matches during the latter part of the nineteenth century, and it was its members that formed Wrexham Football Club in 1872. The first football match at the Racecourse was played on 5 October 1872. Since that date, Wrexham FC have played continuously at this venue, with the exception of the period 1883-87 when they played at the Recreation Ground, Rhosddu due to an unacceptable increase in their rent charges. The ground has witnessed many stirring matches and has been an important venue for international football. It is now recognised as the world's oldest international football ground. It has also hosted rugby union and rugby league international matches. With Wrexham's relegation from the English Football League, it has hosted Conference Football since 2008-09.

The Pryce Griffiths stand at the Racecourse, Wrexham, which in 1992 replaced the two old Mold Road stands, demolished in 1985. Reproduced by kind permission of the photographer, Les Evans, and Geraint Parry, secretary of Wrexham FC.

Acton Park, Wrexham was the venue for the first ever Welsh Cup Final held in 1878. The park was originally laid out in 1785 by the landowner Sir Foster Cunliffe (1755-1834) who lived in Aston Hall. In 1947 the then owner, alderman William Aston, presented the council with the hall and parklands. Between 1930 and 1970 about half of the park was developed as an area for housing. The remaining 55 acres of the original estate forms the majority of the present day park.

Owen's Field, Chester Road, was the venue for the 1887 Welsh Cup Final, won 5-0 by Chirk against Newtown.

Stansty Park is the home of Lex XI FC, who play in the Cymru Alliance League. In 1965 a group of Wrexham solicitors began playing friendly fixtures, largely for social purposes, opting to call themselves LEX, which is Latin for law. The team eventually moved into competitive football and enjoyed considerable success in the Welsh League during the 1980s. In 1990 the club was received into the newly formed Cymru Alliance League. Lex led a nomadic existence for many years before settling at Stansty Park training ground, close to the Mold Road roundabout. Stansty was one of the thirteen townships of Wrexham; Stansty Park was a sizeable house built for the ironmaster and colliery owner Richard Thompson (1799-1866). The house was demolished around 1920.

Borras Park Albion FC, formed in 1980, of the Welsh National League (Wrexham Area), Premier Division, play at Dean Road, Wrexham. They are one of the largest and most successful community-based teams in Wales, and in 2008 they ran no less than thirteen teams. In 2008 they agreed to a merger with GAP Queen's Park FC, formerly of the Cymru Alliance League, but still field a team in the Welsh National League (Wrexham Area), Premier Division.

Brickfield Rangers FC of the Welsh National League (Wrexham Area), Premier Division play at Court Road, Wrexham.

Wrexham Rugby Club of the WRU National League Division 5 North play at Bryn Estyn Road where they have two pitches. NEWI, a Welsh Districts side, also play at the same venue.

WYESHAM WANDERERS FC

see ROCKFIELD (Monmouthshire)

WYNDHAM FC

see PENTRE (Rhondda Cynon Taf)

YNYS-DDU (Newport) ST1792

Ynys-ddu RFC, who can trace their history to a local derby
against Aber-carn on the Church Field, Mynyddislwyn, in 1894,
now play in the WRU National Division 5 East at the Welfare
Ground, High Street, Ynys-ddu.

Ynys-ddu Welfare Crusaders FC, formed in 1947, who play
in the South Wales Amateur Football League, Division 1, also
play at an adjacent pitch at the Welfare Ground.

YNYS-HIR (Rhondda Cynon Taf) ST0292

Ynys-hir Oval is the home of Ynys-hir Albions FC, of the South
Wales Senior League, Division 2, and Ynys-hir/Wattstown BYC
FC, champions of the Rhondda and District Football League,
Premier Division in 2009.

YNYSMEUDWY (Neath Port Talbot) SN7305

Ynysmeudwy Athletic play in the Neath District League,
Division 1 at Cae Corbwll. *Corbwll* is Welsh for whirlpool. Ynys
y Corbwll is a farm name in the parish of Llan-giwg, which
includes Ynysmeudwy. The team was quite a formidable force
in the 1950s, winning the West Wales Amateur Cup in 1959

at Richmond Park, Carmarthen, defeating Pembrokeshire navy side HMS Goldcrest 3-1.

YNYSOWEN RFC

see ABERFAN (Merthyr Tydfil)

YNYSTAWE (Swansea) SN6800

Ynystawe Athletic FC of the Swansea Senior District League, Division 3, and Wales Tartan FC of the Swansea Senior District League, Division 4, both play at Ynystawe Park, Park Road West, Ynystawe, Swansea.

YNYS-Y-BWL (Rhondda Cynon Taf) ST0594

Ynys-y-bwl RFC, founded in 1898, play in the WRU National League Division 2 East at the Recreation Ground.

YNYS-Y-BWL FC

see PONTYPRIDD (Rhondda Cynon Taf)

YNYSYGERWN FC

see ABERDULAIS (Neath Port Talbot)

YSTALYFERA (Neath Port Talbot) SN7608

Ystalyfera RFC, founded in 1880, play in the WRU National Division 3 South West at the Ynysydarren Ground, Ffordd Glandŵr, Ystalyfera. The field was offered to the community by local landowner R D Gough of Ynyscedwyn House in 1922, provided that it was used for recreational purposes. Until 1921, games were played on the Alder Field.

YSTRAD (Rhondda Cynon Taf) SS9895

Ystrad Rhondda RFC of the WRU National Division 1 East play at Gelligaled Park, Ystrad Rhondda.

YSTRADGYNLAIS (Powys) SN7810

Ystradgynlais RFC, founded in 1890, play in the WRU National Division 4 South West at the Recreation Ground, a field given, like neighbouring Ystalyfera, by the Gough family of Ynyscedwyn House. The club's centenary history suggests that some other fields may have been used during the nineteenth century, but the evidence to support this is somewhat tenuous. These include the Brecon Road Field, Tirwaun and Muzzey (or Buzzy's) Field.

Ystradgynlais FC, founded 1910, and relegated from the Welsh League to the Neath Football League in 2009, also play at the Recreation Ground.

YSTRADMYNACH (Caerphilly) ST1494

Penallta RFC, founded by a group of miners from Penallta Colliery in 1952, play in National Division 1 East at Ystrad Fawr in Ystradmynach. Although the colliery closed in November 1991, the rugby club continue to play under its name. Penallta played their last game at Ystrad Fawr in February 2008 as the ground is being redeveloped to provide a new district hospital. Penallta RFC played temporarily at Islwyn Park, Pontllanfraith for the remaining games of the season, and will play at a new venue, Trinity Fields, in 2008-09.

The Valley Greyhound Stadium at Ystrad Mynach was the home of Tredomen Athletic FC.

YSTWYTH ROVERS FC

see LLANILAR (Ceredigion)

INDEX

The arrangement adopted for this volume is alphabetical by place-name. The following index of place-names, arranged within local authorities, may prove helpful.

Bridgend

Aberkenfig
Bettws
Blaengarw
Bryncethin
Bryntirion
Caerau
Cefn Cribwr
Cornelly
Coychurch
Glyncorrwg
Heol-y-cyw
Lewistown
Llangeinor
Llangynwyd
Llanharry
Maesteg
Nantyffyllon
Nantymoel
Ogmore Vale
Pencoed
Pontycymmer
Porth-cawl

Caerphilly

Aberbargoed
Aber-carn
Abertridwr
Abertysswg

Bargoed
Bedwas
Blackwood
Cefn Hengoed
Cross Keys
Crumlin
Cwmfelinfach
Deri
Fleur De Lys
Fochriw
Graig-y-rhacca
Llanbradach
Llanhilleth
Machen
Markham
Nelson
New Tredegar
Oakdale
Pantside
Pen-y-bryn
Penyrheol
Pontllan-fraith
Pontlottyn
Pontymister
Rhymney
Risca
Senghennydd
Tiryberth
Trethomas

Trinant

Ystrad Mynach

Tremorfa

Wenvoe

Whitchurch

Cardiff

Butetown

Canton

Creigiau

Cyncoed

Ely

Fairwater

Gabalfa

Grangetown

Gwaelod-y-garth

Heath

Leckwith

Lisvane

Llandaff

Llanishen

Llanrumney

Pentwyn

Pentyrch

Pontcanna

Pontprennau

Radyr

Rhiwbina

Roath

Splott

Thornhill

Tongwynlais

Carmarthenshire

Abergwili

Alltwalis

Ammanford

Betws

Brynaman

Burry Port

Bynea

Cae'r-bryn

Carmarthen

Carway

Cefneithin

Cross Hands

Dafen

Drefach Felindre

Felin-foel

Ffair-fach

Furnace

Glanaman

Hendy

Johnstown

Kidwelly

Laugharne

Llanboidy

Llandeilo

Llandovery
Llandybïe
Llanelli
Llangadog
Llangennech
Llanmiloe
Llanpumsaint
Llansteffan
Llanybydder
Meinciau
Mynydd-y-garreg
Nantgaredig
Newcastle Emlyn
Pantyffynnon
Pembrey
Pencader
Peniel
Pen-y-banc
Pen-y-groes
Ponthenri
Pontyates
Pontyberem
Porthyrhyd
Pwll
St Clears
Saron
Swiss Valley
Trimsaran
Tumble

Tŷ-croes
Whitland

Ceredigion
Aberaeron
Aber-arth
Abermagwr
Aber-porth
Aberystwyth
Alltyblaca
Banc-y-darren
Borth
Bow Street
Cardigan
Cilcennin
Felin-fach
Ffostrasol
Goginan
Lampeter
Llanbadarn Fawr
Llanddewibrefi
Llandysul
Llanfarian
Llangrannog
Llanilar
Llan-non
Llanrhystud
Newquay
Penrhyn-coch

Ponterwyd
Pontrhydfendigaid
Pont-rhyd-y-groes
Rhydyfelin
Tal-y-bont
Tre Taliesin
Tregaron
Tre'r-ddôl

Conwy

Abergele
Betws-yn-rhos
Cerrigydrudion
Glan Conwy
Llandudno
Llandudno Junction
Llanefydd
Llanfairfechan
Llanrwst
Llansannan
Mochdre
Old Colwyn
Penmachno
Penmaenmawr
Rhos-on-sea
Trefriw

Denbighshire

Corwen

Denbigh
Holt
Llandyrnog
Llangernyw
Llangollen
Rhyl
Ruthin
St Asaph
Trefnant

Flintshire

Broughton
Brynford
Buckley
Caerwys
Connah's Quay
Ffynnongroyw
Flint
Greenfield
Halkyn
Hawarden
Holywell
Hope
Meliden
Mold
Mostyn
Mynyddisa
Overton
Penley

Pen-y-ffordd
Prestatyn
Rhuddlan
Shotton
Sychdyn

Gwynedd

Aberdyfi
Bala
Bangor
Barmouth
Bethel
Bethesda
Blaenau Ffestiniog
Bontnewydd
Bryn-crug
Caernarfon
Corris
Deiniolen
Dolgellau
Dolwyddelan
Efailnewydd
Felinheli
Harlech
Hirael
Llanberis
Llandygái
Llanllyfni
Llanrug

Llanuwchllyn
Llanystumdwy
Nefyn
Penrhyndeudraeth
Pen-y-groes
Porthmadog
Pwllheli
Rhosgadfan
Tal-y-sarn
Tanygrisiau
Trefor
Tywyn
Waun-fawr

Merthyr Tydfil

Abercannaid
Aberfan
Bedlinog
Cefncoedycymer
Dowlais
Gellideg
Gurnos
Heolgerrig
Pentrebach
Penydarren
Treharris
Trelewis
Troedyrhiw

Monmouthshire

Abergavenny
Bulwark
Caldicot
Chepstow
Clydach
Govilon
Llan-arth
Llanfoist
Mardy
Mathern
Monmouth
Pandy
Penpelleni
Portskewett
Prescoed
Rockfield
Rogiet
Shirenewton
Sudbrook
Tintern
Underwood
Undy
Usk

Neath Port Talbot

Aberavon
Aberdulais
Allt-wen
Baglan
Banwen
Blaen-gwrach
Blaengwynfi
Briton Ferry
Bryn-coch
Cilfrew
Cimla
Croeserw
Crynant
Cwmavon
Cwmllynfell
Cwm-twrch
Cymmer
Glyn-neath
Godre'r-graig
Goytre
Gwauncaegurwen
Kenfig Hill
Llandarcy
Margam
Neath
Neath Abbey
Onllwyn
Pontardawe
Pontrhydyfen
Port Talbot
Pyle
Resolven

Rhos
Seven Sisters
Skewen
Tai-bach
Tonmawr
Tonna
Trebanos
Ynysmeudwy
Ystalyfera

Newport

Bassaleg
Bettws
Caerleon
Duffryn
Llanmartin
Llan-wern
Lliswerry
Malpas
Marshfield
Newport
Pillgwenlly
Rogerstone
Ynysddu

Pembrokeshire

Angle
Boncath
Broad Haven

Camrose
Carew
Clarbeston Road
Crundale
Crymych
Fishguard
Goodwick
Hakin
Haverfordwest
Herbranston
Hundleton
Johnston
Kilgetty
Lamphey
Lawrenny
Letterston
Llangwm
Manorbier
Merlin's Bridge
Milford Haven
Monkton
Narberth
Newport
Neyland
Pembroke
Pembroke Dock
St David's
St Dogmael's
St Florence

St Ishmael's
Saundersfoot
Solva
Tegryn
Tenby
Thornton

Powys

Abercrave
Abermule
Abertridwr
Berriew
Brecon
Builth Wells
Caersws
Carno
Churchstoke
Coelbren
Crickhowell
Four Crosses
Gilwern
Gladestry
Glangrwyney
Guilsfield
Hay-on-wye
Kerry
Knighton
Llandrindod Wells
Llandrinio

Llanfair Caereinion
Llanfechain
Llanfyllin
Llangadfan
Llangedwyn
Llanidloes
Llanrhaeadr-ym-Mochnant
Llansan(t)ffraid-ym-Mechain
Machynlleth
Meifod
Montgomery
New Radnor
Newtown
Pen-y-bont
Pontneddfechan
Presteigne
Rhayader
Rhos-goch
St Harmon's
Sennybridge
Talgarth
Trewern
Welshpool
Ystradgynlais

Rhondda Cynon Taf

Aberaman
Abercwmboi

Aberdare
Beddau
Blaenrhondda
Bryncae
Brynna
Carnetown
Cilfynydd
Clydach Vale
Cwmaman
Cwm-bach
Evanstown
Ferndale
Gilfach-goch
Glyncoch
Hirwaun
Hopkinstown
Llanharan
Llantrisant
Llantwit Faerdre
Llwydcoed
Llwynypia
Maerdy
Mountain Ash
Penrhiw-ceibr
Penrhiwfer
Pentre
Pen-y-graig
Pen-y-waun
Pont-y-clun

Pontypridd
Porth
Rhigos
Rhydyfelin
Taff's Well
Talbot Green
Ton Pentre
Tonypandy
Tonyrefail
Trebanog
Treforest
Trehafod
Treherbert
Treorchy
Tylorstown
Tynewydd
Upper Boat
Wattstown
Williamstown
Ynys-hir
Ynys-y-bwl
Ystrad

Shropshire

Bishops Castle
Newcastle-on Clun
Oswestry
Trefonen

Swansea

Birchgrove
Bishopston
Bôn-y-maen
Brynhyfryd
Clydach
Cwmbwrla
Dunvant
Fairwood
Glais
Gorseinon
Gowerton
Grovesend
Hafod
Killay
Landore
Loughor
Mayhill
Morriston
Mumbles
Murton
Penclawdd
Penlan
Penlle'r-gaer
Pontarddulais
Pont-lliw
Port Tennant
St Thomas
Scurlage

Sketty
Townhill
Trallwn
Vardre
Waunarlwydd
Winch Wen
Ynystawe

Torfaen

Blaenavon
Cefn Fforest
Coed Eva
Croesyceiliog
Cwmbrân
Garndiffaith
Griffithstown
New Inn
Newbridge
Pont-hir
Pontnewydd
Pontnewynydd
Pontypool
Talywain
Tranch

Vale of Glamorgan

Barry
Cadoxton
Cowbridge

Dinas Powys

Llandough

Llantwit Major

Penarth

Rhoose

St Athan

Sully

Wrexham

Acre-fair

Bradley

Brymbo

Cefn-mawr

Chirk

Coed-poeth

Glynceiriog

Gresford

Johnstown

Llay

New Brighton

Pen-y-cae

Ponciau

Queensway

Rhosllannerchrugog

Rhosymedre

Ruabon

Southsea

Bibliography

100 Years of Rugby and Village Life at Llandybïe: 1901-2001 (Llandybïe RFC, 2001).

Aberaman Rugby Union Football Club: Centenary 1890-1990 (1990).

Aberystwyth RFC, 1947-1997: 50th Anniversary (1997).

Alexander, David, *Stars on a Saturday Afternoon: The Story of Crynant Rugby Football Club* (1991).

Ambrosen, A, *Amber in the Blood: A History of Newport County* (1993).

Arber-Cooke, A T, *Pages from the History of Llandovery* (1994).

Barrett, Clive, *100 Years of Spa Football, 1883-1983* (Llandrindod Wells, published by the club, 1983).

Bevan, Kenny, *Bois y Llan: Llangennech RFC (1885-1985)* (1987).

Boulton, William G, *Senghenydd: The Village and its Rugby Club* (1982).

Bowen, E G, *A History of Llanbadarn Fawr* (1979).

Cadwalladr, T Graham, *Record: History of Rugby Clubs in the Amman, Dulais and Swansea Valleys* (1966).

Carmarthen Rugby Football Club: Centenary Year, 1874-1974 (1974).

The Centenary History of Amman United Rugby Football Club, 1903-2003 (2003).

Charles, Alwyn C, *History of Llangennech* (1997).

Charles, B G, *The Place-names of Pembrokeshire* (1992).

Charles, John and Harris, Bob, *King John: the autobiography* (2003).

Childs, Des, *One Hundred Years of the 'Rocks'* [St Peter's RFC] (1986).

Clwb Rygbi Bethesda, 1974-1984 (1984).

Clwb Rygbi Bro Ffestiniog: 1973-1994 (1994).

Clwb Rygbi Caernarfon: y deng mlynedd ar hugain cyntaf (2003).

Collins, Dave, 'Football Clubs of Caerphilly', *Welsh Football*, 52 (1999), 11-13.

The Colourful History of the Lillywhites [Rhyl AFC] (1989).

Crooks, John, *Cardiff City Football Club: the official history of the Bluebirds* (1992).

David, John, *Hard Kicks but Good Touches: A Celebration of 100 years of Rugby at Pontyclun* (1987).

Davies, Daniel E, *Cardiff Rugby Club: History and Statistics 1876-1975* (1976).

Davies, David Wyn, *The Maglonians: One Hundred Years of Football in Machynlleth (1885-1985)* (1985).

Davies, Elwyn (ed.), *Rhestr o enwau lleoedd / A gazetteer of Welsh place-names* (1967).

Davies, Gareth M, *A Coast of Soccer Memories, 1894-1994: The Centenary Book of the North Wales Coast Football Association* (1994).

Davies, Gareth M and Garland, Ian: *Who's Who of Welsh International Soccer Players* (1991).

Davies, John R, *Resolven Rugby Football Club: 100 years of Rugby, 1885-1985* (1985).

Davies, Keith, *125 years of rugby, 1875-2000: Abergavenny Rugby Football Club* (2001).

Davies, T E, *Tycroes Rugby Football Club* (1979).

Davies, Tony, 'Narberth RFC – 120 years of rugby', *Pembrokeshire Life*, Dec. 1998-Jan. 1999, 23-5.

Davies, Vernon, *Treorchy Rugby Football Club, 1886-1986* (1986).

Davies, W Oswald, *Sardis, Eglwys yr Annibynwyr, Pontypridd: hanes canmlwyddiant yr eglwys, 1834-1934* (1934).

Davis, Haydn, *A history of the borough of Newport* (1998).

Dodd, A H, *A History of Wrexham* (1990).

Edwards, R Wendell, *100 Years of Rugby Football in Bangor* (1981).

Ein Canrif / Our Century (Ceulanmaesmawr) (2000).

Evans, Barbara M, *Blaina Rugby Football Club, 1875-1976: Memories of Mutton Tump* (1976).

Evans, Ceiriog G, *Once Upon a Time in Goginan* (2009).

Evans, Chris, *The Industrial and Social History of Seven Sisters* (1964).

Fairs, G L, *A History of the Hay: The Story of Hay-on-Wye* (1972).

Farmer, David, *Ivor Allchurch, MBE: The Authorized Biography of the Legendary Golden Boy* (1998).

Farmer, David, *The Life and Times of Swansea RFC* (1995).

Fisher, Paul, *100 Years of Port Talbot Football Club: Celebrating 1901-2001* (2001).

Fowler, Brian, *Ammanford RFC Centenary, 1887-1987* (1987).

Francis, Hywel, *Magnificent Seven, 1897-1997: The Centenary History of Seven Sisters Rugby Club* (1997).

Francis, Sheila, *I Remember Loughor* (2004).

Garland, Ian, *The History of the Welsh Cup, 1877-1993* (1994).

Garland, Ian and Gray Thomas, Wyn, *The Canaries Sing Again: A History of Caernarfon Town Football Club* (1986).

Grandin, Terry, *Red Dragons in Europe: A Complete Record* (1999).

Gray-Jones, Arthur, *A History of Ebbw Vale* (1992).

Griffiths, David F, *A History of Llanelli Borough Council* (1996).

Harding, John, *Football Wizard: The Billy Meredith Story* (1998).

Harragan, Bob, *Llanelli Rugby Club* (1998).

Harries, W John, *Glynneath Rugby Football Club* (1990).

Harris, Gareth, *Taff Vale Park: Memories Lost in Time* (2000).

Harris, Gareth and Alan Evans, *The Butchers Arms Boys* [Pontypridd RFC] (1997).

Harris, John, 'Association football in Breconshire, 1900-1929'. *Brycheiniog*, 29 (1996/97), 105-11.

Hartson, John, *The Autobiography* (2006).

Heatley, Michael and Ford, Daniel, *Football Grounds Then and Now* (1994).

Hignell, Andrew, *Cricket Grounds of Glamorgan* (1985).

Hopkins, Bleddyn, *Swansea RFC* (2002).

Howley, Rob and Clutton, Graham, *Number Nine Dream: An Autobiography* (1999).

Hughes, Chris, *John Toshack* (2002).

Hughes, D G Lloyd, *Hanes tref Pwllheli* (1986).

Hughes, Gareth, *The Scarlets: A History of Llanelli Rugby Football Club* (1986).

Hughes, Hugh Derfel, *Hynafiaethau Llandegai a Llanllechid* (1866).

Hussell, Alan, *A Concise History of Aberavon RFC* (1990).

James, Brian L and Francis, David J, *Cowbridge and Llanblethian Past and Present* (1979).

Jarvis, Bernard, *The Origins of Chepstow Rugby Football Club* (1978).

Jefferies, Horace, *100 Years in Black and White* [Cross Keys RFC] (1985).

Jenkins, David, *Bro Dafydd ap Gwilym* (1992).

Jenkins, David R and Lloyd, David, *Magic, Sheer Bloody Magic: Nantyffyllon RFC* (2002).

Jenkins, Gwyn, *The History of the Aberystwyth and District League, 1934-1984* (1984).

Jenkins, John; Pierce, Duncan and Auty, Timothy, *Who's Who of Welsh International Rugby Players* (1991).

Johnes, Martin, 'Mushrooms, scandal and bankruptcy: the curious case of Mid-Rhondda FC'. *Welsh Football*, 71-72 (2001), 12-13, 12-15.

Johnes, Martin, *Soccer and Society: South Wales, 1900-1939* (2002).

Jones, Aled E, 'Pêl-droed yn Llanrhystud'. *Y Ddolen*, 142 (1991), 4.

Jones, Andrew S, *Tonna Rugby Football Club: Centenary Year* (1987).

Jones, Arwel, *Y Darans: clwb pêl-droed Llanberis* (1991).

Jones, Arwel Lloyd, 'Clwb pêl-droed Llanuwchllyn'. *Llên y Llannau*, 50 (1987), 20-26.

Jones, Beti, *Etholiadau'r ganrif / Welsh elections, 1885-1997* (1999).

Jones, Cledwyn, *Fy Nhalysam i* (2009).

Jones, Colin, *Swansea Town/City FC: The First Comprehensive Player A-Y* (2005, 2007).

Jones, Francis, *Historic Carmarthenshire Homes and their Families* (1997).

Jones, Howard M, *Yr Hendy: The Village and Rugby Club* (1993).

Jones, J R, *The History of Pontardawe RFC* (1985).

Jones, Jenkin, 'Dewi Stars'. *Yr Ancr*, 3 (1975), 4.

Jones, Joey, *Oh Joey, Joey!: My Life in Football* (2005).

Jones, Ken, *Hanes hanner can mlynedd Clwb Pêl Droed y Bont* (1997).

Jones, Mansel D, *Canmlwyddiant Ystradgynlais RFC* (1992).

Jones, Vernon A, *The Turfs: A Brief History of Tregaron Football Club* (1994).

Jones, W D, *Penygraig RFC: 100 Years of Valley Rugby* (1977).

Kelland, John, *Five Golden Keys: Llantwit Fardre Centenary Season, 1999-2000* (1999).

Kelly, Vivian, 'Llantwit Major Rugby Football Club'. *Llantwit Major: Aspects of its History*, Vol. 6 (2006), 8-27.

Lawrie, W A D, *The History of Bridgend Rugby Football Club: the first 100 years* (1980).

Lewis, E T, *Local Heritage from Efailwen to Whitland* (1975).

Lewis, Gerrard, *Between the Lines* (2007).

Lewis, Steve, *Newport Rugby Football Club, 1974-1950* (1999).

Lewis, Tony, *A History of Kenfig Hill RFC* (1973).

Lewis, W J, *Born on a Perilous Rock: Aberystwyth Past and Present* (1980).

Lile, Brian and David Farmer, 'The early development of association football in south Wales, 1890-1906'. *Transactions of the Honourable Society of Cymmrodorion*, (1984), 193-215.

Llewellyn, Arthur and Don, *Pentyrch RFC: A Club for all Reasons, 1883-1983* (1983).

Lodwick, Joyce and Lodwick, Victor, *The Story of Carmarthen* (1994).

Peter Lush and Dave Farrar (eds), *Tries in the Valleys: A History of Rugby League in Wales* (1998).

Macdonald, Tom, *Y Tincer Tlawd* (1971).

McInnery, Jeff, *The Linnets – An Illustrated, Narrative History of Barry Town AFC, 1888-1993* (1994).

Matthews, John E, *From Pit to Pitch: A Pictorial History of Football in Rhos* (1991).

Mole, Robert, *Whatever Happened to the Tugboatonians: A History of the Newport and District Football League* (2002).

Moses, Anthony J, *A History of Dinas Powys Rugby Football Club* (1982).

Owen, Andrew, *Come on the Bay: Colwyn Bay Football Club 125th Anniversary* (2005).

Owen, Gwyn Pierce, *C'mon Reff!* (1999).

Owen, Hywel Wyn and Richard Morgan, *Dictionary of the Place-names of Wales (2007)*.

Parry, Peter; Lile, Brian and Griffiths, Donald, *The Old Black and Green: Aberystwyth Town Football Club 1884-1984* (1987).

Pierce, Gareth, *Nabod Cwm Rhymni* (1990).

Pierce, Gwynedd O, *Place Names in Glamorgan* (2002).

Powell, Terry, *An Illustrated History of Newbridge RFC* (1988).

Preece, Tony and Huskings, Charles, *Abercarn Rugby Football Club: Centenary Souvenir Book* (1995).

Prescott, Gwyn, *'The best and happiest team': a history of Cardiff High School Old Boys rugby football club, 1929-1978* (1978).

Price, Mike, *Neath Athletic: 50 Years of Rugby* (1997).

Rees, Ben D, *'Dechreuadau Dewi Stars – y pumdegau'. Yr Ancr*, 3 (1975), 4.

Rees, Ben D, *Hanes plwyf Llanddewi Brefi* (1984).

Rees, Eiluned (ed.), *Carmarthenshire Memories of the Twentieth Century* (2002).

Rees, Hywel J, *The Gowerton Rugby Football Club, 1884-1984: One Hundred Years On* (1984).

Richards, Brinley, *History of the Llynfi Valley* (1982).

Richards, H P, *A Short History of Caerphilly* (1975).

Risoli, Mario, *John Charles: Gentle Giant* (2001).

Roberts, Ann, *Estuary People: Penclawdd 1900 to 1970* (2001).

Roberts, Nigel, *The History of Chirk Football Club, 1876-2002* (2003).

Robinson, John, *The Supporters' Guide to Welsh Football Grounds* (2004).

Ruddick, Ray, *Pontypool Rugby Football Club* (2002).

Samuel, Michael (ed.), *Pembroke Dock Harlequins Rugby Football Club: 1880-1980* (1981).

Shepherd, Richard, *Cardiff City Football Club, 1899-1947* (1996).

Skrine, John Huntley, *Uppingham by the Sea* (1878).

Smith, David and Williams, Gareth, *Fields of Praise: The Official History of the Welsh Rugby Union* (1980).

Sprake, Stuart and Tim Johnston, *Careless Hands; The Forgotten Truth of Gary Sprake* (2006).

Spurrell, William, *Carmarthen and its Neighbourhood* (1879).

Stenton, M and Lees, S, *Who's Who of British Members of Parliament,* Vol. III (1979).

Tapscott, Derek and Grandin, Terry, *Tappy: From Barry Town to Arsenal, Cardiff City and Beyond* (2004).

Thau, Chris, *Tonmawr RFC, 1887-1997: A Century of Passion* (1997).

Thomas, Arwyn, *Hanes Llanpumsaint* (2004).

Thomas, Clive, *By the Book* (1984).

Thomas, Cyril D, *Swansea Senior Football League: 1901-2001, 100 Years of Local Soccer* (2002).

Thomas, David Peter, *A View from the Garth: One Hundred Years of Taff's Well Rugby, 1887-1987* (1987).

Thomas, Eric, *Canmlwyddiant Clwb Rygbi Brynaman* (1998).

Thomas, Keith, *Faces and Places of Ebbw Vale*, Vol. 1 (1987).

Tremlett, George, *Laugharne RFC 1893-1993: Centenary Booklet* (1993).

Twydell, Dave, 'Aberdare Athletic'. *Rejected FC: Comprehensive Histories of Ex-Football League Clubs,* Vol. 1 (1988), 7-28.

Twydell, Dave, 'Lovell's Athletic'. *More-defunct FC* (1990), 30-69.

Twydell, Dave, 'Merthyr Town'. *Rejected FC: Comprehensive Histories of Ex-Football League Clubs,* Vol. 2 (1989), 255-93.

Walters, Philip M, 'Rugby Football at Aberdare'. *Old Aberdare*, 3 (1984), 29-55.

Watkins, David, *Merthyr Tydfil Football Club; Memories of Penydarren Park* (2006).

Westcott, Gordon, *A Century on the Rugby Beat: A History of 100 Years of Police Rugby Football in the South Wales Constabulary Area* (1992).

Williams, Alan, *100 Years of Mumbles Rugby, 1887-1987* (1987).

Williams, Alister W, *The Encyclopaedia of Wrexham* (2001).

Williams, J P R, *Given the Break: My Life in Rugby* (2006).

Williams, Terry, *The History of Forgeside JFRC, 1880-2000* (2001).

Wmffre, Iwan, *Language and Place-names in Wales* (2003).

Also available from Y Lolfa:

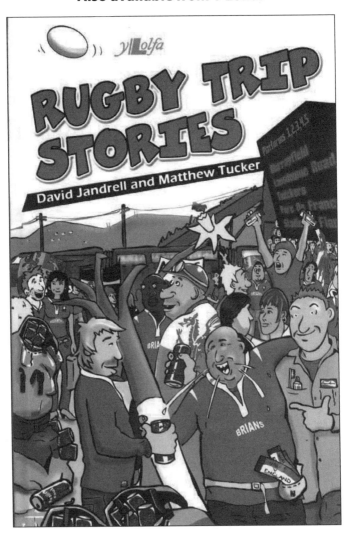

£3.95

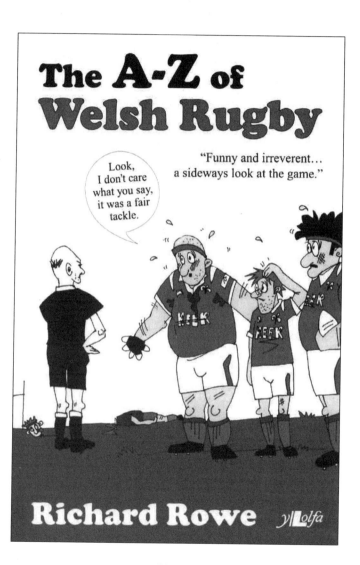

£3.95

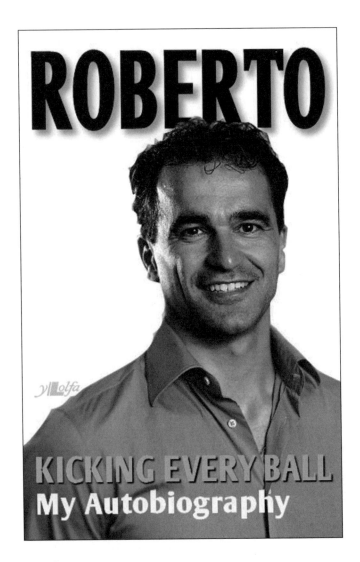

ROBERTO

KICKING EVERY BALL
My Autobiography

£12.95

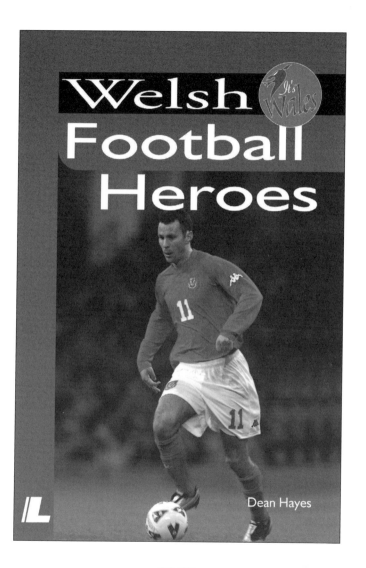

Welsh Football Heroes

Dean Hayes

£3.95

The Football and Rugby Playing Fields of Wales
is just one of a whole range of publications
from Y Lolfa. For a full list of books currently
in print, send now for your free copy of our
new full-colour catalogue. Or simply surf into
our website

www.ylolfa.com

for secure on-line ordering.

TALYBONT CEREDIGION CYMRU SY24 5HE
e-mail ylolfa@ylolfa.com
website www.ylolfa.com
phone (01970) 832 304
fax 832 782